"YOUR LIFE WILL NEVER BE THE SAME."

Thus came the first chilling words to Captain David Morehouse as he sat facing the program director of Stargate, the U.S. government's top-secret, psychic espionage program.

"What we do here is train selected personnel to transcend time and space, to view persons, places, or things remote in time and space . . . and to gather intelligence information on the same. We want you to become one of us."

The young army officer's heart nearly stopped.

—from *Psychic Warrior*

PSYCHIC WARRIOR

DAVID MOREHOUSE

St. Martin's Paperbacks

PSYCHIC WARRIOR. INSIDE THE CIA'S STARGATE PROGRAM: THE TRUE STORY OF A SOLDIER'S ESPIONAGE AND AWAKENING

Copyright © 1996 by David Allen Morehouse.

Cover photography by Glen Gyssler.

Library of Congress Catalog Card Number: 96-3085

ISBN: 0-312-96413-7
EAN: 80312-96413-9

Printed in the United States of America

St. Martin's Press hardcover edition published 1996
St. Martin's Paperbacks edition / January 1998

15 14 13 12 11 10 9 8

To my darling wife, Debbie, whose love has nourished and sustained me for longer than I can remember. We are together, eternally.

AUTHOR'S NOTE

*What is the greatest experience you can have? It is
the hour of the great contempt. The hour in which
your happiness, too, arouses your disgust, and even
your reasons and virtue.*

FRIEDRICH NIETZSCHE

Psychic Warrior is a journey through time and space. It
is a private witness of one man's rise, awakening, fall, and
rebirth. It is a testimony to life outside the physical dimension, to the gift of remote viewing, to hope for all humanity,
and to the reality of those who would preclude you from
ever hearing the message.

This book tries to explain, with some degree of simplicity, a very convoluted and intricate story of espionage and
spiritual awakening. I have labored carefully, striving in
every regard to abstain from any act or reference that might
be construed as less than honorable. Right, wrong, unjust,
or fair, it is not my intent to pass judgment on my nation
or my comrades. I tell this story as I saw it and lived it.
You may draw your own conclusions.

Even the most seemingly sinister of those in the intelligence community do what they do because of their unfaltering belief in the "Mission." The mission is to protect
our nation against all enemies, foreign and domestic. It is

this passion that often drives them beyond the moral and ethical expectations of duty. It is the passion that prompts them to put aside all rationale, answer the call to duty, and quickly turn a former colleague into a hated target. I understand that; you should as well.

Out of regard for my former associates in and around the intelligence community, I've chosen fictitious names and, when necessary, disguised their physical characteristics. It is my desire to keep them clear of any unwanted attention. I have used the real names and identities of only three former remote viewers, my colleagues Mel Riley and Lyn Buchanan, and Joe McMoneagle who preceded me. They are included in the story, but this is my version of the story, not theirs. Any three people witnessing an event will provide an interrogator with three different versions of the same event. This is certainly true of descriptions of events spanning years of evolution and interpretation. For the sake of clarity and continuity, several meetings described in this book as a single event, in a single place, actually consisted of multiple meetings, in multiple locations, with multiple attendees. There is no intent to deceive by doing this; it is necessitated by space requirements. I beg your indulgence.

PROLOGUE

I lay there staring at the ceiling, listening to my wife's breathing as I conjured shapes in the darkness. No amount of effort could force the excitement from my mind; it was as if a fluorescent light burned just behind my eyes each time I closed them. My mind reeled at the idea of what I was becoming.

Three months had passed since I had been recruited; I could hardly bear, let alone comprehend, the physical and emotional transformation taking place. Grinning in the darkness I mumbled, "I'm becoming a time traveler." Even *I* struggled to believe it. Everything I was destined to become was changing before my eyes. I didn't know who or what I was anymore; my very essence had been torn apart and pieced together again by modern-day seers, travelers in time and space. But they were only ordinary men, I kept telling myself. How could they know these things? How could they be sure that what they were doing was right? What if we weren't supposed to do this . . . this thing we do?

The alarm shocked me into the world of consciousness and I slapped groggily at it until it fell off the nightstand, ringing and clanking the room awake. Patting Debbie back to sleep, I dragged myself into the morning's routine and continued my deliberations during the drive to the office. It was strange going to work in civilian clothing and with long hair. For the past twelve years I had been an infantry officer, short hair and all. Now I looked and felt like a civilian, so as not to attract attention to the unit.

I pulled into the parking lot of the ramshackle buildings, the highly classified special-access program where I was now undergoing my metamorphosis. I was to spend over two years here, and every day I chuckled at the worn-out structures that had seen better days as a bakers' school during World War II. Now, the two wooden buildings sheltered a group of soldiers and Defense Department employees.

This was the home of an espionage program that skirted the limits of imagination and spirituality. It was the haunt of a clan of spies, hand-picked from the tens of thousands who filled the ranks of the army and Department of Defense. A well-kept secret, the unit's existence and location were known only by a few members of the Defense Intelligence Agency, of which it was a part. Ironically, some of the DIA's more conservative members came to think of the members of this unit as evil, even satanic, because of what we learned and practiced here. And now I was part of it . . . this aberrant crew of eight that the DIA code-named Sun Streak.

I was never first into the office—several of the others always managed to earn that honor—which was good, because that meant the much-needed coffee was always ready. Grabbing a cup, I made my way to the vault and withdrew my notes from yesterday's sessions. Well into my training by now, I had enjoyed strong successes on my early missions; in fact, the program manager, Bill Levy, had accelerated my indoctrination into this new world. It was this acceleration that had prompted yesterday's excursion into the unknown.

I swallowed the coffee while staring at the strange drawings and data I had scribbled the day before. Among my sketches, one mysterious figure stood out—faceless, cloaked, hooded, and pointing a gnarled hand toward someone or something unseen. The pages that followed contained descriptions of another world, perhaps another dimension . . . things that just now were incomprehensible. I pored over them, trying to grasp their significance, when *smack!* a firm hand clamped down hard on my shoulder. "Not bad for the new guy in town."

"Christ, Mel, you scared the hell out of me."

He grinned. "You shouldn't be so shaky. You haven't seen anything yet." He took a swig of his coffee and walked back to his cubicle. I followed.

Mel Riley was an army master sergeant; a thin, gray-haired man with pale eyes and the forgiving disposition of a grandfather. He smoked cigarettes like a madman and drank coffee strong enough to etch glass. He was my trainer and coach along my two-year journey of self-discovery. He was the first military remote viewer—the first man to transcend time and space for the purpose of viewing selected targets and collecting intelligence information. I learned early to rely on his counsel. What he said was always true: no lies, no exaggerations, no betrayal, and no ego.

"Mel, what in the world is this place you sent me to yesterday? I'm comfortable with the training targets I've worked so far, but I'm struggling with this one. This was . . . what did you call it?"

"An open search. We all do it from time to time—it keeps us humble."

"Humble? Ever since I walked in here I've been humbled daily. I don't think I need to float aimlessly into the ether, landing on God knows what, to be humble."

Riley looked at me with fatherly eyes and smiled. "Maybe you don't need humility now, but trust me, you will." He paused for another sip of coffee, but his eyes never left mine. "When you get your wings in a few more months, walk into that viewing room alone, and jump into the ether—when you've soared into time and space and returned—you'll start to think you're a god, a fucking *god*. But you're not. What you are is a very mortal tool . . . an instrument of the government. Staying humble and realizing how insignificant you are in the spectrum of things is critical to surviving as a remote viewer. Without that thread connecting you to reality, you'll forget who you are, and you won't last out there . . . or back here.''

''Out where?'' I asked.

He drew a large circle in the air with both hands. ''Out there . . . in the ether. Where we work.'' He smiled. ''But now, I think Bill wants to see you. Don't worry about that stuff.'' He pointed at the papers in my hand. ''That will all become clear soon enough.''

Bill briefly glanced at me over the tops of his glasses and then refocused on the papers in front of him. ''Sun Streak'' 's director, an olive-skinned man with dark hair and dark eyes, had an intensity about him that rarely broke. He was intolerant of many things, and I was careful not to get on his bad side. ''Mel said you wanted to see me.''

Bill continued to scratch away at the papers. ''Yes, I do. I have another target for you to work . . . a training target.'' He paused long enough to look up at me. ''Not an open search. This is a standard mission. I want to get you through Stage Four of training as soon as possible. We'll be losing a viewer in another week or so, and I want you to take his place. Operationally, that is.''

''Well, that's wonderful, I guess. I want to move along as fast as I can . . . I find this stuff fascinating.''

''Good! Do you have any questions so far?''

I assumed he was expecting some sort of intellectual query on the theory or practice of remote viewing, but I couldn't think of a damned thing. I sat there biting my lip like a third-grader. Suddenly, out of nowhere, a ghost from my past came into my thoughts. ''There is one thing,'' I began. ''I hate to bring this up because it's personal, but it's important to me.'' Levy said nothing, simply stared into the wall behind me as I talked. ''I've been wondering if I could work—or have some other viewers work—a special project.''

''What sort of project?''

''I had a friend some time ago, in Panama. A chopper

pilot. He was flying a classified mission with another pilot and a crew chief, monitoring the border wars between Ecuador and Colombia.''

''And?''

''They never returned from the mission. And they were never found.''

''And now you want to see if you can find this—''

''His name is Mike Foley. Chief Warrant Officer Foley. I know this is unusual, but he was like a brother . . . I mean, I loved this guy. We did everything together, our wives did everything together, and I never got to say good-bye. One day he was suddenly listed as missing in action, and the next thing I knew Debbie and I were helping Sharon Foley pack for the States. It still seems like a nightmare, and it happened eight years ago.''

Like radar, Levy keyed in on the word ''nightmare.'' He sat forward in the chair and laced his fingers under his chin. ''Does he come to see you, in nightmares?''

''Yeah. Sometimes he does.''

''How? Tell me about them.''

''Oh, I don't know. It's nothing morbid or horrifying. It's just that I see him, you know. . . . I don't talk to him; he doesn't talk to me.'' A knot began to swell in my throat, and I fought back tears. ''I'm sorry, I don't mean to be emotional. I thought by now I was over it.''

''You'll find that the more closely you embrace the art of viewing, the less you'll be able to escape all that makes us human. You'll eventually learn to live beyond sorrow and anguish, and countless other emotions. Of course you'll always feel them, but you'll understand them unconditionally, and that understanding will give you the wisdom you need to survive. So don't be ashamed of your emotions. Release them freely. We all do around here; it's healthy.'' He was briefly silent. ''Now tell me more about your friend Foley.''

''I don't know much. I was a general's aide at the time, and we were participating in a training exercise when it happened. The general had just gotten a briefing in the tactical operations center when the aviation battalion commander approached him quietly. Right away I sensed something was wrong with Mike—I just knew it. The battalion commander filled my boss in, and the general left for the office. I stayed behind and asked if Foley was okay.

"The battalion chief looked at me strangely; it was obvious he was wondering who might have told me. I said I didn't know anything particular, but I just sensed something was wrong with Mike. Reluctantly, he told me Mike's chopper had gone down somewhere in the mountains and hadn't been found. That's all he'd say."

"What about the nightmares? Tell me about Foley's visits to you."

"Well, like I said, it's not like he jumps out of the ground and grabs my ankles or anything. It's actually very tranquil, almost like he's trying to comfort me. Sharon says he's come to her as well."

"When did this occur? In 19—"

"He went down in 1980. The last words anyone heard from the chopper came from Mike. He said, 'Wait a minute . . . I have a problem.' And then there was nothing but static. They mounted several searches for the aircraft, but nothing was ever found."

"That's because it was never Americans looking for Americans."

"What?" I sat bolt upright. "What do you mean?"

Levy stood up, flipping his pencil onto the papers. "Wait here."

Five minutes later he returned with a stack of blue folders and dropped them in my lap. "I think you'll find these very interesting. Look them over carefully, and we'll talk after lunch."

He sat back down at the desk and picked up his work as though I'd never been there. I sat there stunned for a few seconds; finally, he looked at me again over the top of his glasses.

"Okay?"

"Okay." I replied awkwardly. "Okay . . . thanks."

I stepped out of the door and hurried back to my desk. There were about twenty-eight folders, each with the words "TOP SECRET—PROJECT: GRILL FLAME" in inch-high red letters front and back. I'd seen these markings before, when I was being recruited for the unit. Inside each folder was a copy of some teletype message traffic: "MISSING—Army helicopter (UH-1H) tail number November Seven Nine, with crew: CW4 David Suitter (Pilot in Command), CWO Michael Foley (Co-Pilot) and Sergeant First Class William Staub (Crew Chief)." The remainder of the message dealt with the area in which they were presumed to have gone down, along with reports from locals about seeing or hearing the copter before the crash. I tore through all the official message traffic, straining to read as fast as I could, but I couldn't move fast enough. I began flipping through the folders, until finally I stumbled on what Levy had wanted me to see.

I was looking at the results of eight-year-old remote viewing sessions that had begun hours after Mike and the rest of the crew were reported missing. Twenty-eight sessions had been conducted by five different remote viewers, each session describing the crash in detail. I read graphic accounts by remote viewers who were psychically clutching the tail of the chopper as it rolled off axis and plunged into the jungle. I could hardly believe it; the viewers described, as if seeing through the eyes of the crew members, what each one experienced in his final moments. I read two viewers' descriptions of how Mike watched CW4 Suitter die. Illustrations showed the chopper separated from its tail and resting on its left side. Mike was still strapped in, looking at Suitter, who had been thrown forward about twenty feet out of the aircraft. "Foley winced in pain," the viewers wrote, "while CW4 Suitter crawled along the jungle floor several feet away. Suitter died several minutes after impact with Foley watching. The crew chief died within seconds of making contact with the jungle canopy. Foley expired last, perhaps twenty-five or thirty minutes after going down."

I pressed my sleeve into my eyes to absorb the tears. For the next several hours I turned the pages detailing the final hour of Mike's life. The sketches were uncanny, almost photographic in quality. Reference points were given; the viewers described the surrounding terrain and landmarks. There were even sketches showing the aircraft's location in relation to the Ecuadorean search teams. In every sketch there was a phantom, a transparent body: sort of a self-portrait of the viewer in the target area. I could sense the frustration of the viewers in their written messages to the different agencies controlling the search. "They were so close," I mumbled. "Why couldn't they find them?"

"The weather was bad on that one!" The voice was Mel's.

"How long have you been here?" I asked without looking up.

"A while. Bill wanted me to check in on you."

"Which one were you?"

"Viewer Number 03, just like I am now." He smiled gently. "That was a bad one. Bill tells me you knew one of them."

"Yeah, I knew Chief Foley. We were sort of brothers for a few years."

"Well, if it's any consolation, I know for a fact that he wasn't in any pain toward the end. He was confused—they always are—but he wasn't suffering."

"Why couldn't they find them? Your sketches are outstanding! What was the problem?"

"Terrain, weather . . . Ecuadoreans . . . you name it. It's tough to get someone from another country to brave the elements to find somebody they don't know and didn't want there in the first place. We weren't really invited to that party. We kind of crashed their private border war, and when the chopper went down there was a less than enthusiastic response to our requests for a prolonged search."

"So why didn't we launch our own?"

"Because there was a war going on and we weren't players. We weren't permitted to put U.S. troops on the ground and swarm all over an already disputed terrain. It was a quagmire of politics and everything else bad. I'm sorry.''

"Ah, shit, Mel." I snorted. "I don't mean—"

"I know you don't.''

I sat there staring at the folders, shaking my head in disbelief and bewilderment. "I wish I could bring this to closure somehow. You know? I'd just like to have been able to say good-bye.''

Mel drained the last of his cold coffee and made a face. Then he touched my shoulder. "You want to say good-bye? Meet me in the other building in ten minutes, and you'll get to say good-bye.''

Ten minutes later I was standing in the viewing room facing Mel. "Adjust your environment and we'll get started,'' he said. I adjusted the rheostat on the control panel next to the bed and found the lighting I wanted. Just as I had been taught in the preceding weeks, I took my place on the viewing platform, a specially designed bed like something from a science fiction movie. "Okay, I think I'm ready. Where exactly are you sending me?''

Mel had seated himself in the monitor's chair overlooking my position. He used the control panel on the desk in front of him to turn on the video cameras and tape recorder. "I'm giving you the same coordinates we used during the final missions on the aircraft. With luck you can pick up right where we left off eight years ago.'' He looked down at his panel. "Ready?''

I took a deep breath and exhaled slowly. "Yeah.''

"Your coordinates are seven, five, seven, four . . . eight, three, three, six.'' Mel waited in the dim light for my first response.

As I had been trained to do, I cleared my mind and began the regimented procedure of entering an altered state. At first the sensation was relaxing, almost euphoric; but in minutes it began to accelerate. Vertigo overtook me and I felt drugged and confused. Seconds later, a tearing sound— it's like Velcro being torn open—ripped through my ears.

The separation had begun. Suddenly my phantom body rose out of its physical self and shot forward into space. The sensation of speed was overwhelming, and I kept my eyes closed, waiting for it to end.

Why and how all of this happened, nobody knew. The theories were complex and unclear. None of the viewers tried to understand the mechanics; they just braced for the ride and described what they saw when they arrived. And so I suddenly found myself suspended in the darkness of space, gazing down on the planet.

I began my descent into what was called the tunnel, falling faster and faster until the surrounding stars blurred into horizontal streaks of light and then a cylinder of energy. It was as if I were traveling through a tube of neon light at blinding speed. As I fell, the sides of the tunnel danced by hypnotically until my phantom body struck a membranelike substance: I'd arrived in the target area. I landed on all fours in a sticky haze, somewhere in time.

Mel was a skillful monitor who knew instinctively when the viewer had arrived at the target. "Tell me what you see, Dave."

"Um, I don't see anything yet. It's foggy here . . . and hot. . . . It's hard to breathe." I struggled to get my bearings and peer deeper into the haze. "It's very muggy here."

"I understand," Mel said. "But you need to move to where you can see. I'm going to give you a movement exercise. Pull back from the target to an elevation of five hundred feet. From there something should be visible."

I concentrated on moving through the ether to Mel's designated spot. The mist blurred as I pulled back from the earth's surface and hovered. There.

Mel's voice penetrated the ether again. "Describe your perceptions now."

"I see a white blanket of clouds covering the earth. There are points of jagged rock and foliage piercing the blanket. I can't see through the mist to the surface, though."

"Okay, listen carefully. You haven't done this type of

movement before. You'll be okay; just follow my instructions. I want you to travel in time to a point when the
surface is clear and visible."

"How the hell do I do that?"

"Concentrate on the movement. It's no different from
the others you've done. Concentrate on moving forward or
backward in time until you see the surface below you."

Straining, I tensed my neck, rolled my head backward,
and closed my eyes. I began to feel something moving
through me, like an energy fluid or an electrical charge. I
rocked my head forward and opened my eyes to see time
peeling off the earth day by day, the picture beneath me
changing with each passing moment.

"Christ, that's unbelievable!" I shouted.

"Concentrate. You have to stop quickly when you get
the picture you want."

I watched in amazement. The terrain below me remained
unchanged, but the cloud patterns flickered and strobed
their way through time, changing like a rapid-fire slide
show. I noticed the cloud cover beginning to dissipate,
slowly chiseled away at its outer perimeter. Focusing carefully, I waited for the exact moment. "Okay, I got it! It's
clear!"

I thought I heard Mel laughing at my novice enthusiasm,
but I couldn't help it. This was like my first solo flight in
an airplane—I was in control, but out of control.

"All right, start your movement to the surface. Go back
to the coordinate site and tell me what you see."

In an instant I was standing in a small clearing maybe
thirty feet in diameter, surrounded by triple-canopy jungle.
The trees towered around me in every direction, but
through the undergrowth I could see another mountain in
the distance. In the strange apparitional way one moves in
the ether, I moved to the break in the undergrowth. My
gaze fixed on the distant hills and rock formations; I lost
track of the ground beneath me. At a break in the dense
foliage, I paused to see what was around me. For some
reason I looked down at my feet, only to find that I was

floating in midair, hundreds of feet above the next level of the jagged rocks. With my eyes locked on the distance, I had walked out of the jungle and straight off a ledge into thin air. "Shit!" I exclaimed, startling Mel.

"What? What's wrong?"

"I'm okay. . . . I'm okay. I just scared the hell out of myself there for a second, but I've got it now."

"I want you to go to the crash site. Get control of yourself and concentrate; go to the crash site."

"I'm moving there now—at least, that's where I think I'm going. I'm beginning to move pretty quickly." The trees and undergrowth were flashing past me in an iridescent green blur. I began to experience vertigo again, that sickening feeling in my stomach boiling up until I thought for sure I would vomit.

Mel watched in amusement as my physical body grew pale and clammy. He had seen viewers bilocate to a target like this before. He had also seen them get sick before. "Concentrate on slowing down, Dave. You're moving too fast. . . . Slow down. . . . Keep your bearings."

I tried as hard as I could to slow my progress, but it was like trying to stop a train. I kept moving at the same speed. My phantom body passed through anything that got in its way. When I hit small stuff, nothing happened; but when I hit bigger stuff, like trees and rocks, I felt as if a flat puff of air was hitting my face. It was the oddest thing I'd ever experienced. Everything I was perceiving began to darken, as if the sun were setting, but there was no longer any color, only gray and black. "Something's wrong!" I shouted. "Something's really wrong!"

"What? Tell me what you see."

"Everything is turning dark. . . . Everything is . . ." I lost consciousness. My physical body lay there suspended between reality and the world I'd found in the ether. Mel left me to the silent world. He knew where I was; he'd been there.

I opened my eyes as the shroud of darkness slowly withdrew. It was an eerie feeling standing there in some other world at some other time. I couldn't tell if I was dreaming or not; the images before me were there, but not there. If I looked at them too hard, they turned into something else. I could see the ground beneath my feet, but I couldn't feel anything. A light mist surrounded the place where I stood, thickening as it snaked back into the surrounding jungle.

A roughly triangular object caught my attention and I approached it in the darkness. It was about a foot across and maybe two feet wide at the base, with jagged edges as though it had been ripped from where it belonged. I reached out to touch it, and gasped as my hand passed through to the other side. "Damn!" I looked at my hand to see if it was intact.

Mel asked, "Would you like to tell me what happened?"

"I'm sorry. I tried to touch something, a piece of something, but—"

"You can't touch anything. There's nothing physical there. Don't waste time trying, it only confuses you. Look for your target, but also search within yourself; focus on the event you came to witness. Think about—"

"Wait!" I said. "Something's moving. Over there, near the edge of the jungle, where the trees get thicker." I moved to where I thought the noise came from, where I saw something down low, glistening in the eerie light. It was an object much like the first one, only bigger. I stared at it, trying to make it out.

"That's all that's left," said a voice from the mist.

"Who's there? Who said that?"

"The Indians carried most of it away. It took them about a year. Anything useful to them is gone now. Just as well . . . it served its purpose."

A gaunt young man appeared in the mist some ten feet away from me. I could make out only his silhouette; nothing else was visible in the drifting haze. "Who are you?" I asked, squinting.

"Has it been that long for you, David?"

"What are you talking about? Been that long—?" And then it struck me. "Mike? Mike, is that you?"

"I wondered what it would be like again. . . . I've come to you so many times, but you just don't remember."

"I do remember—it's the dreams, right? You've come to me in the dreams, haven't you?" I moved closer to the figure. I stopped about three feet away from him, but he was no more clear than he had been at ten feet.

"It won't help you to get any closer. This is as perfect as we get to your eyes."

"I can't see your eyes or your face."

"That's because you haven't yet learned to see in this world. But you will. Those who came here before, they knew how to see. They watched us die. I felt them. I felt them in me and around me; they were very comforting. They helped me understand what had happened."

"What did happen?" Boy, I felt stupid asking that. I'd walked into it just as I always did when he was alive. I could almost feel him grinning.

"Well, I died, of course."

"Of course. But what happened—I mean, what happened to the chopper?"

"None of that is important anymore." There was a long pause. "What's important is for us to say good-bye . . . and I love you. And thank you for taking care of Sharon all these years."

"How—?"

"We see everything here. Forward, backward . . . everything. I watched you cry. I even watched your second daughter come into your world. I knew her before you did."

Eight years of emotion welled up inside me, and I felt tears streaming down my face. "Oh, Jesus." I wept openly, overcome by grief and happiness.

"It's okay, David. It's okay. Don't weep for me."

"I'm not crying for you, you big ass. I'm crying because I miss you. You were my brother, and I miss you." Mike stepped closer to me, and as he did I felt a warmth I cannot explain. He stood there close to me, watching me weep, and everything around me became lighter than before. It was as if there were an unseen light or energy around him, and his being close to me let me inside its protective glow somehow. I looked up at him, and I could see his face, his wonderful loving face, just as I had seen him eight years ago.

"How are you?" he asked.

I choked on my words, trying to be funny. "Well, better than you." I tried to smile.

Mike smiled back. "Oh, yeah? Who's getting old, and who's not?"

"Yeah, you're right about that." I paused, trying to sort out the ten thousand things I wanted to say. I wanted to catch up on the void that eight years had brought to my life. "You know, I never got over your leaving me. Neither did Debbie or Sharon. You just couldn't be explained, or accepted, or forgotten."

"Good—not being forgotten, that is. It's kind of a status thing here." He glanced around. "But acceptance—you need to feel that. You need to understand that I'm dead, but not gone. I've moved on to other things, things I can't explain to you. You don't have the eyes for it yet, but you will. That other guy with you now, what's his name?"

"Mel Riley."

"Yeah, that's him, Mel Riley." Mike sighed. "Well, he's got the eyes, and I've seen him before. He's a gentle man with an honest and giving heart. He wept when he found us. Listen to him and he'll get you through all this. He'll give you your eyes and the gift. I know you've seen others. They told me you were given a message in the desert. Listen to what you're told, David; it's important. Not just to you, but to all humanity."

I shook my head. "Now, wait a minute—"

Mike interrupted me. "It's time to say good-bye, Dave. I have to go; our business is over for now. You tell Debbie I miss her, and tell Sharon I'm happy for her as well. Tell her I said she should marry him."

I didn't know what he was talking about, and it must have showed.

"Just tell her that. She'll understand."

I knelt there looking up at him as if he were a god. The tears came again as the warmth in me intensified. Mike reached out for me with his hand, touched my shoulder, and moved to brush my cheek. I was grateful for what I'd seen. I was filled with something I'd never known existed, something I couldn't explain. I watched as Mike's image paled in the light. "Don't go," I pleaded. "Please, don't go." I reached for the place where he had been only an instant before . . . and there was nothing. As the darkness crept back around me, a voice pierced it from somewhere: "Get your eyes, Dave." And then there was nothing. I felt numb, kneeling there.

"Time to come back, Dave," said Mel's calming voice. "You're done for now. Break it off and come on back."

I did what I'd been taught, and the cycle began to reverse itself. Over the years, the process of accessing a target was to become easier for me. I eventually became one of the best viewers Mel had ever trained. But it wasn't really anything I did. Mel was the teacher; he was the Watcher and I was to learn from him as a son learns from his father.

I never forgot what Mike told me. Four years passed before I saw him again, there in the ether. But things were different that time; my life had changed and a new destiny was confronting me. This is the story of how I arrived at that destiny, and how I became the Watcher.

ONE

THE DAWN

I spent my childhood in the army; I was a young nomad, traveling from post to post with my family. I knew nothing of life except what a soldier and a soldier's wife taught me, and I never consciously expected to be anything but a soldier. When I was young I played games with soldiers' children, and we always imitated our fathers. We were very proud of them even though we seldom saw them. Photographs from my youth are filled with images of plastic weapons, with miniature vehicles painted olive green with the words "U.S. Army" emblazoned on them. Every aspect of my young life centered on the army, its way of life, its weapons and equipment. By the age of four I could name most of the major exterior components of the army's current tank.

It was a life where you respected the authority of your father even though he was only an occasional presence. You learned to love the fading mental picture rather than the physical existence. You could say I was raised in a era of patriotism and service to the nation, an era that would pass, as I grew older, into a generation where outward rebellion was in vogue.

My patriotic conviction drained from me under the steady pull of popular opinion, and what I had been taught to hold sacred gradually faded away into the fog of my teens. I finally succumbed to the tide of opprobrium against the war in Vietnam in 1970. During the conflict I opposed the traditions of my family, as I guess all children eventually do (at least that's holding true for my son). I grew my hair long, wore clothing that would have fit well in San Francisco's Haight-Ashbury district, and essentially did anything that I thought might annoy my parents. Frankly, I'm surprised that I survived those years.

In high school I spun from one focus to another, giving little thought to what the future held. My first year out of high school I spent doing pretty much nothing. I worked as a lifeguard and went rock climbing with my brother. I enrolled in a small community college, Mira Costa. Eventually I ran for and was elected president of the student body, which in turn led to a scholarship at a larger university. I also joined the Mormon church while I was there. Even though I was very much opposed to organized religion, the Mormon faith made sense to me, and I became a convert several months later. That was my first experience with institutional religion.

Since my future had basically been handed to me, I'd never really concentrated on what else I might do. However, one thing was clear at this point: I had to move on. I sensed there was more for me somewhere out there, and I had to go and find it. Perhaps that is why I never earnestly tried to become a doctor, or a lawyer, or anything other than a soldier. Despite the gap I'd engineered between myself and my family, I think I always knew deep in the recesses of my mind that I had a destiny. We all have a destiny, and one fall day in 1975 I recognized mine.

Planning on becoming a medical doctor, I attended Brigham Young University on a student leadership scholarship. I scheduled pre-med classes, told people of my plans, and so on. Fate confronted me high on a mountain overlooking Provo, Utah. Above the campus is a giant "Y," the collegiate symbol of Brigham Young University. This "Y" requires a coat of whitewash every year to keep it visible to the entire valley. Hundreds of students form an old-fashioned bucket brigade and pass the heavy containers of slopping whitewash up a winding narrow trail, while an unlucky few sling the messy goop onto the rocks that form the "Y." It was rumored among freshmen that this was a good place to "meet a mate." I had a hard time understanding this "mate" thing. At BYU the concept of "date" and "mate" were often confused, as far as I was concerned. However, it didn't take me long to figure out that things at this university tended to be looked at in "eternal" terms. After all, BYU was a church school. People got married, settled down, had children ... and still went to school. I was new to this way of life, and a date sounded much better than a mate. But I gathered my courage, convincing myself that I would not succumb to the "mate" philosophy, and cautiously accompanied several friends to join the festivity.

There were plenty of women there all right, but we were all so busy huffing and puffing and slinging those nasty buckets that few if any of us ever had the time or the breath to speak. By the time there was a moment for reflection, the day was nearly gone and I was covered head to toe with dirt and sweat and whitewash.

I had managed to work my way toward the top of the bucket line, and as the final buckets of wash were scattered onto the rocks I turned for the first time to look out at the beautiful valley behind me. It was a stunning and wondrous place. At that moment I realized what the first Mormon settlers must have felt when they cast their gaze on it so many decades ago, and I welled up with an unexplained peace.

Wiping the sweat from my brow with the back of a painted hand, I saw him—an army colonel standing there with the sun at his back, talking to a much younger man who was in fatigues as well. As ridiculous as it might sound, what I saw struck a chord. In all the confusion a nineteen-year-old man experiences, seeing this officer was like coming home again. I suddenly knew that my future was standing there in front of me. I joined the army ROTC program the next day.

I loved being a cadet. I'd never felt so much in the right

place. I learned more about myself in those few short years than I'd ever thought possible. I experienced the army, and the dedication and service it requires, from a new perspective. I was educated by good men, who saw my potential and mentored me from the beginning, picking up where my father had been forced, by my adolescent rebellion, to leave off.

My father taught me how to understand and be sensitive to others, which is probably the most critical aspect of leadership. Without it you are only a manager; that's the plight of many of today's military executives. These men taught me how to lead. They shared with me the intimate experiences of battle, often bringing tears to my eyes. All of this they did with a spirit I have never before or since witnessed. They taught me to be an officer.

There were others at this time in my life. I remember Wayne Rudy, a World War II veteran whom I worked for in the cadet supply room. Mr. Rudy was an intense but loving man who gave me daily lectures on everything under the sun, but mostly about leadership, courage, and the love of service. He often spoke of his son, who was a church missionary. As fate would have it, the son was killed in a car accident less than two months after returning from his mission. Mr. Rudy was devastated, but just when I expected to see everything in him fall apart, he rose up in defiance, understanding, and spirit to such a degree that he cast a positive glow across the entire episode. It was he who gave comfort to the grieving, it was he who explained the reason for the death, and it was he who helped everyone to understand the nature of tragedy and its place in life's pattern. He was a marvelous man, a man who helped set the stage for what I became.

Then there were my cadet friends, who have surely forgotten me over the years, but to whom I will forever be indebted for their lessons and examples. This was a good time in my life, a time where I felt proud and invincible, and closer to the truth than I'd ever been. These people seemed to bring out the best in me, and I loved being around them. So much was changing, and so quickly.

There was, however, one other inevitability; it was the issue of a mate. I'd bet my father two hundred dollars that I wouldn't get married until I was twenty-one. I absolutely wasn't in the market for anything steady.

One of my roommates, a guy by the name of Mike Seawright, owed a hometown girl a favor. She had previously arranged a date for him which had gone well, and now it was his turn to reciprocate. He set me up on a blind date with a woman by the name of Debbie Bosch. Reluctantly, I trudged to her dorm, not knowing what to expect. Standing in front of her dorm room, I sighed and knocked. The door opened just enough for a pretty face to peer through the small vertical crack, and smile.

I smiled back, elated that she didn't have a horn growing from her forehead.

"Debbie?" I asked.

"Debbie will be right out," the face announced. The pretty head disappeared as the door was quickly closed.

I shook my head. What the hell was I doing this for? I was certain that the scout was now informing an ugly duckling that I was an appropriate mate. I was half turned away when the door opened.

"Hi, I'm Debbie," said a soft voice.

I turned to see an outstretched hand welcoming me.

"You must be David. Mike told me a lot about you. Won't you come in? I'd like you to meet my roommates."

I couldn't speak. I just nodded like a fool and followed her in. I don't remember much about her roommates; in fact, I don't even recall speaking to them. All I saw was Debbie. She was a beautiful brunette, with dark, loving eyes that sparkled with purity. She hailed from rural Worland, Wyoming, where she was homecoming queen, valedictorian of her high school class, and winner of a presidential scholarship to BYU.

I'd never met anyone like her, and from that moment on I followed her like a puppy. I called her every chance I had, sent flowers, even showed up on her doorstep unannounced. I don't think I'd ever been in love before, so I wasn't exactly sure what was going on with me. I just knew that this was a very special and exciting woman, and I never wanted to let her out of my sight. I had to do something creative, something drastic—and fast, before I lost her.

One night, three months after meeting Debbie, I called and asked her for a date, a quiet, romantic dinner. I told her to dress nicely, because we were going to one of the finest restaurants Provo had to offer. With the help of four whiting friends, I dragged a cardboard box to her dorm and set it up in the lobby. I covered it with a red-and-white-checked tablecloth and lit two candles for atmosphere. I positioned two chairs on either side of the makeshift table and turned on the cassette player, which shrieked a not-so-good copy of some Neil Diamond ballad. My friends took up their posts to give us some privacy, and I knocked on the door to retrieve Debbie.

She looked radiant, and I was nervous as hell about what I was doing. Naturally she thought I was taking her out for dinner; when I seated her in the lobby and pushed her chair closer to the paper table that had been set for her, the look on her face was priceless. I seated myself as one of my friends appeared in a suit with a white terrycloth towel draped over his arm.

"Some sparkling cider for Madam?" he asked, not waiting for a response and slopping the beverage over the edge of the foam cup and onto the table.

Debbie was tight-lipped, her arms folded tightly across her chest.

"Is everything okay?"

She snapped, "Exactly what are you up to?"

I was off to a slow start and sinking fast. I knew it . . . so did my buddies. I could see it in their faces. One of them approached us with the menus, which were hand-drawn and listed the preselected bill of fare. Another delivered a dozen red roses while simultaneously turning up the volume on the cassette player. I was gaining ground again . . . Debbie was smiling.

She stared at the menu I had prepared. "What's this . . . spiced beef?"

"It's a specialty. I hope you like it." I bit my lip trying not to laugh. I snapped my fingers in the air, and the waiter returned with a folding TV tray and two boxes of C rations. He snapped the tray into position and immediately began wrenching open the cans of vile-smelling military rations. With a fork stolen from the cafeteria he pried out the contents, which fell onto the paper plate like dog food. He mashed it down and presented it to Debbie.

She stared at it for a moment and looked at me, hard. "Do you expect me to eat this?"

"Yes," I said as my meal was placed in front of me. "It's good—try it." She stared at it again, poked at it with her fork, and to my surprise, took a small bite. I knew then that I'd made the right choice in this woman. Anybody who would put up with this was very special indeed.

We "dined" for hours. C ration crackers for bread, canned lima beans for vegetables, and canned fruit cocktail poured over canned maple-nut cake for dessert. We listened to that Neil Diamond tape over and over again. My friends whisked away the paper plates and turned Neil over one last time . . . and then disappeared.

We held hands talking for a while. Then I took a deep breath and knelt beside her, trying to be composed and romantic. "Debbie," I said, my voice cracking, "I've never done this before. . . ."

"Of course you haven't." She smiled. "You're only twenty. Unless there's something I don't know about you."

"No, no, I've really never done this before. So I don't know if I'm doing it right . . . or what you expect."

It was obvious that I was struggling. "Somehow, David, I think you will always do what I least expect. . . . But I love you anyway."

I took a deep breath. "I love you, too. And I want to marry you—that is, if you'll have me. All I'll ever be is a soldier, and all I can promise you is that you'll move every three years, and live in crummy places, and . . ."

She put her fingers on my lips, ''Shhh, it's okay. Wherever it is, we'll make it a home.''

The feeling of peace was overwhelming. I was scared, but I was calm. I knew this was right; I just didn't know how I was going to do it. I'd not given much thought to being a husband before now, and I wasn't sure what I was supposed to do next. I didn't even have a ring. I couldn't afford a full tank of gas; how was I supposed to finance a ring? My mind was racing. I took a deep breath, we kissed, and went for a walk in the brisk night air. My friends remained to clean up the mess, grinning in victory. I'll never forget them.

Debbie and I were married April 22, 1975, in the temple at Manti, Utah. Exactly nine months later, Debbie bore us a beautiful baby boy whom we named Michael. Our lives changed forever on that day. My world was coming together fast. I was a father, and I cherished every second of it. I wasn't very good at diapers, but I was good at getting up at night, being blanketed with vomit, stuff like that. I loved being a dad, even if I was petrified. There we were, sophomores in college, married and parents. The sacrifices had only just begun.

Debbie was a wonderful army wife, even when I was just a cadet. She supported me in virtually every possible way, which was not the case with all spouses. In the years to come Debbie and I watched as many marriages of many of our friends fell by the wayside because of the stresses and trials of army life. Being a soldier isn't easy, but being a soldier's wife is more difficult still. It's a team effort if you are to succeed; both must believe in the profession and believe that it will always take care of you. You overlook the bad—the loneliness, the cramped quarters, the mediocre hospitals, and the lousy pay—because you believe in the greater good of what you are doing. You call yourselves patriots—and Debbie was as much a patriot as I ever was. You trust that your comrades will always be that, comrades, and that they will be there if and when you ever need them. That was the army my father told me about; that was the army Debbie and I believed in and sacrificed for.

In the first ten years of our marriage we moved seven times, living in everything from roach-infested apartments to incredibly cramped military quarters. I remember the two of us laughing on the front lawn of our quarters in Savannah, Georgia, when we had every inch of floor space covered with furniture and half of the house was still on the truck. Have you ever tried to put a family of five in less than a thousand square feet of living space? It's a challenge.

I was commissioned a second lieutenant of infantry on April 16, 1979, and immediately entered active duty. Debbie and my father pinned the lieutenant's bars on my epaulets. I wept at the pride in my father's eyes. Because of my success as a cadet I was granted a regular army commission and designated a Distinguished Military Graduate. I won the General George C. Marshall Award, given to the top graduating cadet of the university. I was also chosen by a national review board to be the recipient of the national Dr. Ralph D. Mershon Award, which is given to the number one cadet among the 2,500 officers who receive regular army commissions. In retrospect, none of that was worth the price of a soda, but it seemed to be setting the stage for me.

From the beginning it was clear that my father had trained me well. Maybe success comes from simply following one's destiny. I graduated from the Infantry Officer Basic Course at Fort Benning, Georgia, in 1979, and was the Honor Graduate of my class. While we awaited orders to our first duty station, I attended the army Pathfinder school, again becoming the Distinguished Honor Graduate. I finished my basic officer professional instruction with the Infantry Mortar Platoon Leaders Course, and then Debbie, little Michael, and I reported to my initial assignment in the Republic of Panama, in November 1979.

During our first tour of duty, I served in a myriad of leadership positions. I was a mortar platoon leader, a company executive officer, an airborne rifle platoon leader, and finally, aide-de-camp for two different commanding generals. I attended the army scuba school in 1980, and in 1981 the army jumpmaster school, where I was the Distinguished Honor Graduate of my class. As a first lieutenant, I was selected to command the army's only separate airborne rifle company—Alpha Company (Airborne), 3rd Battalion, 5th Infantry, located at Fort Kobbe, Panama—a position formerly held only by senior captains. I barely outranked those I was commanding.

We were young and the train moved fast. Debbie learned to counsel the wives of my subordinates in everything from finances to marriage. She was a natural. She worked as hard as I did, and harder. We raised our children to think of the army first.

One thing becomes clear after the newness of the army wears off: you are simply a number, and expendable. I guess I knew this, and it was certainly clear to Debbie. We just wouldn't let ourselves dwell on it. We kept busy with the business of being a soldier and a soldier's family. As the years wore on it became increasingly clear that sacrifices didn't matter, that your belief in the profession was expected, not appreciated. You were manipulated, and you were expected to manipulate; how else could you get over two hundred men to do what no normal human being would ever do? An idealist (which is what I was) will tell you that you accomplish that through leadership. A pragmatist will tell you honestly that leadership is a series of overt and covert manipulative acts arranged so as to entice another human being into marching forty miles with a ninety-pound rucksack, into sleeping in the mud at night only to awaken in battle, and into finishing the day by carrying dead friends to a medevac chopper in plastic body bags. Normal men and women are not inspired to act in such a manner, and they don't do it for love of country or fear of consequences. There is a psychology to it, a psychology I slowly began to be aware of over the years, a psychology that would ultimately be used against me.

Despite the pace of Panama, Debbie and I found time to have two more children, our daughters Mariah and Danielle, who, to their amusement, sport dual citizenship to this day. Finally, after four and a half arduous years, it was time to leave Panama. Good friends remained behind and fond memories came with us. The officers and their wives and children were all family to us. Debbie and the children miss Panama to this day.

After a six-month tour back at Fort Benning for the Infantry Officer Advanced Course, we were off to our next assignment, the prestigious 1st Battalion, 75th Ranger Regiment, at Hunter Army Airfield, in Savannah, Georgia, in 1984. Life with the Rangers was completely different from anything I'd experienced before. These are hardened and serious men, hell-bent on kicking someone's ass in battle. I served as a battalion training officer, battalion adjutant, and finally as a Ranger company commander, our second company command. I was better at it the second time around.

The best part of the Rangers was the noncommissioned officers. I stood in awe of these men. Men like Sergeant Major Leon Guerra, First Sergeant Sam Spears, and First Sergeant Peterson, to name only a few of many. They are dedicated, fit professionals who rarely crack a smile and view officers with a doubting and critical eye—that is, until you prove yourself to them. I'm not certain I ever did that—perhaps they were just forgiving in my case—but I counted them as friends. Every day they drew breath, they pushed their troops to the limit, never faltering, never wanting a break. Officers come and go quickly in the Rangers— most of them rarely spend more than a year in any one assignment—but the sergeants were always there, steady and solid. They were an impressive lot, and it was my honor to serve with them.

I'd been in command a little over a year when my company was selected by the regimental commander, Colonel Joseph Stringham, to go to the Kingdom of Jordan for a lengthy desert deployment. It would be the first time in history that the United States military would send a combat command into the kingdom. The situation was highly political and would be scrutinized from every possible angle during pre-deployment and deployment and, of course, upon our return back to home base.

Naturally, we were excited. The company endured long hours of extra training, learning some of the basic language skills, customs, and courtesies of the host country. We began shifting our sleep cycle to match the time change. We even spent time assimilating a handful of Arabic linguists into the company. They, to their chagrin, were on permanent loan from a military intelligence unit at Fort Stewart, Georgia. These guys hated being part of the Rangers. Being unaccustomed to the rigors of our life, they were miserable from about five minutes after they showed up until we released them back to their parent unit several months later. I should say that *most* of them were miserable. Several of them, including the warrant officer attached to my headquarters, proved to be real troopers.

After seemingly endless training and preparation, the day arrived for our deployment. The families of our troops had been well briefed on the activities of the company, but that never made it easy to say good-bye. We had the standard prayers from the chaplain, prayers to keep our families safe. But the faces of the children saying good-bye to their fathers never changed; they were always guarded and sad. Even though this was a peaceful mission, all was not safe. There had been peaceful missions before, when young men didn't come home again. In the Rangers death was always a possibility, and the families lived with that knowledge daily.

I knelt in front of my son, the oldest and most aware of what was happening. "I love you, Michael."

A single small tear dropped from his eye. "Be careful, Daddy. Don't get hurt." He squeezed my neck with his arms, his face pressed beside mine.

"Don't worry, I'll be fine. I'll bring you back some desert sand, how's that?"

His face beamed as he wiped away another tear. "And a big spider?"

I chuckled, giving Debbie a quick glance. "Yeah, and the biggest spider I can find."

I gave Mariah a tight hug and kissed little Danielle on the cheek before turning to my wife. "You know I'll miss you."

"We'll miss you, too. You do like your son said and stay safe, you hear me?"

"I hear you. I promise I won't ride any camels. I love you." I embraced her and turned toward the aircraft to load it. As I walked I could feel her eyes on me and I turned to give her one last glance before disappearing into the belly of the C-141 Starlifter.

TWO

THE BULLET

It seems like a hundred years ago. I slapped a platoon leader on the back, took my position in the order of movement, and crossed the line of departure under the cover of mortar and machine-gun fire. It was the spring of 1987.

I tried to keep my mind on what we were doing, but it kept wandering back home to Debbie and the children. I remember thinking that Debbie and I had had an unusual parting. I didn't quite understand why this time had been different, but she seemed to have held on a little tighter when we kissed good-bye. The look in her eyes when she let go of me still made me uneasy. I ordered myself not to think about it.

I glanced upward and saw two silent birds circling in the pale, arid sky; then I closed my eyes and thought again of my family back home. My eyes snapped open when one of my Rangers stumbled to the ground next to me and cried out. He picked himself up, dusted off his precious weapon, and continued to move forward with his platoon. I followed close behind. What happened in the hours that ensued has remained a blur, but the result began a metamorphosis that has redefined my life.

I was commanding Bravo Company of the 1st Ranger Battalion, 75th Ranger Regiment, and we were in Jordan training Jordanian Rangers—probably to kill Israelis. Of course nobody would ever admit to that, but who else would we be training Jordanians to fight?

I vividly remember the night before I started my transformation. I remember it as though I were supposed to remember it, as though it was the beginning of something that had been set aside for me since the beginning of time. I had marched for an hour or so with my company to a scorched spot on the floor of the valley called Baten el Ghoul, the Belly of the Beast. The Jordanians considered it a haunted valley, where the demons came out at night to murder people. It was not unusual to have one's sleep interrupted by the screams and howls of frightened Jordanian soldiers who swore in the light of day that they had seen a demon. My men and I nervously wrote it all off as superstition, much to the chagrin of our Jordanian counterparts, who repeatedly made every effort to convince us that this was a bad place. We joked about the hauntings at night as we sipped tea around the campfires, but we put no stock in them. From our perspective, if it couldn't be killed it didn't exist.

Baten el Ghoul was a desolate and jagged valley carved out of the desert that spilled over from Saudi Arabia. It looked like the surface of the moon. There was no life there, except for the wide variety of arachnids that crawled out of their hiding places onto the cooling sand at night. If I were God, and wanted to set aside a place where the souls of the living were taken from them as they made their way to Mecca, this would be it. The valley had a kind of energy that made your thoughts drift toward it unconsciously. After a few days of living in it you became comfortable, and as time passed you reluctantly saw some forbidden beauty in it. Still, it was an unclean place. There was something evil here, something I recognized the moment I set foot in it. I wasn't the only one to think so, and yet none of us could ever put a finger on it.

On this evening I was going to hear a Jordanian colonel, the commander of the Jordanian Ranger battalion, speak to my soldiers about the valley, his faith, and his hatred for the Israelis. The colonel was our host, and while I can't remember his name, I can remember everything else about him. He was a short, stout man, filled with pride for his country and even more contented to be its only Ranger battalion commander. He hated the Israelis and showed no compunction when it came to talk of killing them. His passion for soldiering was the equal of any of ours—and that is rare, to find someone who loves being a soldier as much as an army Ranger does.

We gathered, 260 men, on a barren piece of high ground, a natural amphitheater. The colonel's stage was a section of railroad track half buried in the sand, abandoned decades ago. It was the same track that Lawrence of Arabia's infamous bedouin guerrillas used to blow up, built by the Germans under contract by the Turks. This forgotten section of track surfaced just long enough to take a breath and intersect the ancient road to the holy city of Mecca—the *hajj* road.

As the sun passed beyond sight, a stunning red glow swallowed the valley and everyone in it. For several hours after sunset, the colonel lectured our group of dirty-faced and hardened men on the finer points of the Muslim faith. He spoke on the life of the prophet Muhammad, of the Quran, of the nature of the one true God he called Allah. He told us of the five pillars of Islam: the repetition of the creed, or *shahadah;* of daily prayer, or *salah;* of the sharing of possessions with the poor, or *zakah;* of fasting, or *swam;* and of pilgrimage, or *hajj.* The faces of my men remained phlegmatic as the colonel spoke of the variations of the Muslim faith, of its Sunnis and Shi'ites. He beamed as he spoke of the spread of Islam and grew angry again as he told why his people felt Palestine was their birthright. But his most expressive moment came when he spoke of Allah, how blessed he was to know Him and how certain he was that He watched over him and protected him in peace and in combat. That comment made some heads nod in the group, which was a standing ovation from a Ranger's perspective. And so it was at this historic but forbidding site that I spent my final hours in the world I had known.

The next morning, after the usual business gatherings of officers and noncommissioned officers had broken up, I had joined my battalion commander, Colonel Keith Nightingale, for a canteen cup of tea. Tea was not our usual drink but something we had picked up being with the Jordanians. For them it was a holdover from British colonial rule, something they hadn't rid themselves of since the last British flag left their soil decades ago. For us it was just good, much better than the instant coffee we had in our packaged rations. Tea, like everything else in this country, sort of grew on you.

Colonel Nightingale was a tall, gangly man with a brilliance I've yet to see matched. You might out-soldier him in some way but you damned sure weren't as ingenious. He was a Mensa man, proud of it and as resourceful as they come. He was an excellent teacher and never missed an opportunity to pass on a lesson in military history. Like most well-read military leaders, he had an anecdote for every possible tactical situation. There were plenty of opportunities for instruction, and if his Rangers were too busy to listen, he could always venture over to the Jordanians for a quick lecture or two.

We drank our tea and walked the mile and a half to the training site. The platoon leader, First Lieutenant Kevin Owens, and his men had just completed the finishing touches on the four enemy bunkers that made up the objective. In a few hours a Ranger platoon reinforced with two squads of Jordanian Rangers would attack it with every weapon in their arsenal. They would be evaluated on their tenacity, accuracy, and ability to systematically destroy the objective with indirect and direct fires. Specially designed targets representing enemy soldiers would fall if struck with a potentially lethal shot, or remain in position if only wounded or missed. The attacking leadership would have to orchestrate the entire operation unrehearsed, adapting to each tactical situation as it confronted them.

Colonel Nightingale and I stood there, our thumbs laced into our web belts.

"It looks good, Kevin." I grinned from under my helmet. "It looks real good." And it did. His platoon had built an objective consisting of five bunkers, complete with automatic weapons, trenches, concertina wire, and booby traps. It would be difficult to take down correctly and safely.

"Let's get up there to watch this mortar registration," Nightingale said, pointing toward a small rise about fifty meters away from the objective.

The mortar platoon was registering—that is, they were dropping rounds onto the target to make sure that they would hit it and not friendly troops as they maneuvered toward the bunkers. Suddenly, *thwack!* a mortar round landed well off its mark, sending buzzing shrapnel past our heads. Nightingale and I looked nervously at each other and shrugged. We felt strange, and very foolish. It had happened so fast there wasn't time to react, but shouldn't we have run for cover, or ducked, or something? Instead we just stood there trying not to look shaken. Perhaps it was an omen.

Several hours later a young Ranger platoon leader received the order to attack; he crossed the line of departure with sixty men, and I followed. The sun was high, baking the valley and everything in it. Heavy, salty sweat stung my eyes while small black flies pestered every orifice. Despite the weight of weapons, ammunition, and radios, it was almost a pleasure to move and try to outrun those goddamned flies.

The platoon leader moved cautiously, picking routes that covered and concealed his men from the enemy. Mortar shells slammed into the objective, sending smoke and shrapnel and pieces of the bunkers high into the air. As he drew closer, the platoon leader screamed into the radio for his support position to open fire. Six medium machine guns ripped the air with their fires, hammering with such volume that several bunkers' wooden beams collapsed under the pressure, crushing the "occupants." Tracers spun off rocks and bunkers in every direction, dissolving in the smoke that filled the sky around the objective. The air rang with the songs of the weapons and the smell of cordite. To a warrior's eye, it was great!

I moved behind the platoon leader, watching him closely as he made contact with the left flank of the objective. His intent was to take out the flank bunker and roll up the rest of them one by one, using his machine guns to cover his movement. It was a standard technique, one he had used many times before in the mountains of Washington State and the jungles of Central America. He gave the signal for the guns to shift their fires away from him, to leave the first bunker alone and concentrate on those remaining. This would allow his men to clear each bunker in turn, the fires shifting in front of them bunker to bunker until there were no more. He threw a yellow smoke canister behind him to signal a second time for the guns to shift, and they did— all but one.

A rogue Jordanian gun shifted in the wrong direction, into the assault element, kicking up rock and dust as the Rangers dove for cover and hugged the ground. Men scrambled for shelter. The last thing I saw was the platoon leader screaming into the radio for the guns to lift, and then the world turned black.

As if it were another day, another year, another place, this darkness slowly dissolved into a white mist. I distinctly recall not knowing what I had been doing up to that instant. It was as if a channel had been changed and suddenly there I was standing in this endless white mist. I couldn't feel my body or my arms or legs; I couldn't feel anything. But I sensed I was upright. I tried to walk, but nothing happened. I just stood there, paralyzed and confused.

In what seemed only seconds the mist around me began breaking up, slowly revealing my surroundings. I was standing at the base of a grass-covered hill, and I felt the warmth of the sun on my shoulders. I looked down at myself and saw that I was completely naked, but it didn't seem to matter. A gentle breeze brushed my face. At the top of the hill stood a small gathering of people, perhaps eight or twelve. They were dressed alike, in white, long, flowing clothing. I stood there unable to move, but watched as one of them turned to look down the hill at me. His face was kind, expressionless, and he almost immediately turned away. Then he turned to face me again, this time motioning for me to approach the gathering. For the first time I could feel my limbs as I moved in some strange way to the top of the hill. As I approached, the circle parted and I was ushered into it by the being who had beckoned me. As I entered, the circle closed behind me and I stood alone and naked in its center for what seemed an eternity. Finally, a kind but powerful voice came from behind me; turning, I saw that it was, again, the one who had beckoned.

"Welcome, David. We have been waiting for you."

"What's going on?" I said in a trembling voice. "Where am I?"

No one answered.

"Didn't you hear me?" I asked. "Why am I here?"

"We called you to give you instructions."

"Instructions? Instructions about what? Who the hell are you guys?"

"Who we are is unimportant. What we have called you here for is this: you are to know from this point forward that what you have chosen to do in the world is wrong."

- "Wrong? What's wrong?" I was confused and indignant—and scared to death. "What the fuck are you talking about?"

"Your choice is wrong. Pursue peace. Teach peace, and the path to it will be made known to you. You have tasted death . . . now bring life. We will be with you, always."

A piercing sound filled my head, a ringing that made me clasp my hands against my ears. My eyes stung and my knees buckled. Opening my eyes briefly, I was aware of the absence of the sun and the wind as the strange mist encircled me once again. The mist remained unaffected by the wind, yet encircled me and the hill, as if we were in the eye of a hurricane. The air was thick as death and heavy. I tried to speak, to cry out, but nothing came from my mouth. All I could do was lie there with the pain, alone and frightened beyond description. The mist crept back around me, masking the hill from my view, and in a few moments it was completely black.

When my eyes opened, they revealed the sweat-smeared face of Private First Class Sheridan, the platoon leader's radio operator.

"Jesus Christ, sir," he said, squinting at me from four inches away. "Are you all right? You have a bullet in your head."

"Shit!" I cried, instinctively reaching to search for the hole. I patted my head and face several times, expecting to see my hands wet with my blood. When there wasn't any, I melted into the ground as the tension drained from my body. Glancing into the sunlight I saw that there were several new faces inspecting me.

"What the hell do you mean, I have a bullet in my head?"

"Well, not in your head, in your helmet," he replied apologetically. "It hit you in the helmet, see?" The private handed my Kevlar helmet to me and grinned sheepishly, pointing to a large tear in the camouflage cover. I snatched it from him and stared into the hole. Sure enough, a bullet had struck an inch above my right eye, and it lay lodged deep in the helmet.

"Must have been a ricochet," said the platoon leader.

"Yeah," volunteered one of the others. "A direct hit would have gone clean through . . . wouldn't it?" He looked around for supporters, most of whom only shrugged.

In minutes, the rumor of a bullet in the head of the company commander had permeated the platoon. It seemed every man there was surprised to see I was still alive, and as usual with soldiers, Rangers in particular, the jokes soon followed. Not twenty minutes after I staggered to my feet, one of the sergeants chastised a sniper for missing a perfect head shot.

"Let's see if it was a direct hit or not," said Platoon Sergeant Ricketts, an amiable, grinning old country boy who had been in the Rangers forever. He politely took the helmet from me and gouged at the bullet with his bayonet until it fell into his palm. After carefully inspecting it in the sunlight, he held it up for all to see.

"This wasn't a ricochet. Look, it doesn't have a mark on it. This was a direct hit from one of those guns in the support position." He tossed the helmet back to me and passed the bullet around for the men to inspect. "You're fucking lucky to be here, sir," he said in as serious a tone as he could muster. "Real lucky!"

For the rest of the day we pummeled that objective with platoon after platoon until there was nothing left to attack. I grew a red knot on my head as big as a half grapefruit, and a headache that Motrin just wouldn't make go away. As darkness crept across the Belly of the Beast, the last platoon marched back to the bivouac site. I followed, lagging some distance behind, alone and reflecting on what had happened.

That evening we dined on lamb and rice, courtesy of our hosts. My officers and I stood with our counterparts in a lonely tent surrounding a table laden with the traditional *mansif*. In what had become a weekly custom and a welcome break from the bagged ready-to-eat rations we came to Jordan with, we conversed over a tray of rice laced with nuts and vegetables and adorned with the head of a goat boiled in yogurt. In the months that had passed we had learned to dine like natives, grabbing handfuls of rice and crushing the moisture from them, rolling the mixture between palm and fingers until it formed a bite-sized ball to be launched into the mouth with a flick of the thumb.

This time away from our traditional surroundings proved great therapy for us. To lose ourselves in the ways and stories of these men, so closely tied to two millennia of desert warriors, was enchanting. Even this gnarled and forbidden valley came to life in the evening hours, under the glow of brilliant stars and a welcome moon. It wasn't until the moon set and true darkness fell that the alleged demons came, and it was in this darkness that the Jordanians who believed in the spirits—in the *jinn*—would gather close and frightened in their tents.

We finished the meal and retired to our respective camps for tea and more conversation. My officers and I listened to the BBC on shortwave radio, trying to capture news of world events and maybe a story or two of home. At the end of the broadcast each man disappeared into the night, headed for his own platoon and tent. I gazed across the valley, contemplating my brush with death, laboring over my vision of the mist, and the hill, and the strange beings who stood atop it. Their message—what the hell could it have been? What did that mean, "Teach peace"? Had it been a dream, or some random image generated by my mind?

I gingerly touched the tender spot on my head and found that the knot had receded. With a last look across the valley I crawled into the command post tent and found the opening between bodies that would be my spot to sleep. It had been forty-seven days since we'd last bathed, and the tent reeked of bodies and methane. I laid my head on a rolled poncho, closed my eyes, and thought of home and Debbie and the children.

Sometime in the night my eyes opened to a surreal light outside the tent. I figured one of the cooks was lighting the gas stove for breakfast and morning tea. Rising, I crawled over the sleeping bodies of my soldiers and into the fresh air of the night. The light—it was like the light of an eclipsed sun—wasn't coming from any stove. It filled the night sky. The entire Baten el Ghoul and the hills beyond were painted in the strange bluish gray light; I walked to the edge of the bluff and stared into the valley. Dark figures moved effortlessly across its floor, like apparitions. They poured from the rocks in various heaps and shapes and moved about the clusters of tents. I could hear muffled cries from the Jordanian encampment, and momentarily I thought we were being overrun by thieves or maybe even Israelis.

Panicked, I turned to run for help. Colliding with one of the figures, I reflexively closed my eyes—except I didn't collide. I walked right through it. Turning around I watched the figure disappear over the edge of the bluff.

Gripped by fear, I thought I must be losing my mind again. I reached for the lump on my head, but it was gone. I dropped to my knees trembling and tried to speak or maybe to pray, but my voice would not come. I lapsed into unconsciousness.

A stab of sunlight opened my eyes and I quickly felt the goad of the lump on my head. *Christ, what a nightmare,* I thought as I crawled out of the tent and staggered toward the cook tent for some tea.

"How's your head?"

It was the battalion surgeon, Doc Mellin. Doc was an interesting fellow, a medical doctor who had volunteered for duty with the Rangers but always looked out of place anyway. He wasn't the physical specimen his predecessor had been, which motivated him all the more. He enjoyed his work, and that ever-present smile on his face made sure you knew it.

"I guess it's okay," I said, rubbing the spot.

"Come on, I'll buy you a cup of tea." We dipped our canteen cups into the caldron of tea the cooks had prepared and sat down.

"Let's take a look at this," he said, poking the lump mercilessly. Every time he jabbed it I flinched.

"Damn, do you have to poke at it like that? If you want to know if it hurts, the answer is yes," I said, pushing his hand away.

"Did you have any trouble sleeping last night? comfort, pain, stuff like that?"

I thought for a moment about divulging my st

periences. But if for a second Doc thought I might be hallucinating . . . well, that would have been the end of me. In the Ranger battalion, men are as expendable as ammunition, and when it comes to the bottom line you'll be gone and a suitable "healthy" replacement will fill your shoes before you're even missed.

"No, nothing unusual happening . . . a little pain, that's all. I'll be fine, just keep that Motrin coming."

"Morning!" came a voice from behind us. It was Nightingale grabbing himself a cup of tea. "We need to talk about yesterday," he said, sitting down next to me. "Do you want me to put a call in to Debbie or something? We can have the regiment notified and the regimental adjutant can call her and let her know what's going on."

I thought for a moment, looking at Doc. "Naw, it's too risky, sir. You know how it is. The message will get screwed up and twenty-four hours from now Debbie will think she's a widow." We all chuckled.

"You're right," Nightingale said. "I guess as long as you're alive, we'll just keep it quiet." He paused for a moment, staring at the dirt in the bottom of his cup. "Well, big day ahead. I guess I'll let you get back at it."

"Rangers lead the way, sir." Doc and I snapped to attention as Nightingale walked away.

"All the way!" he said, never looking back.

Several days after getting in the way of that bullet, we mounted trucks to make the long motor march to a new training site on the western edge of Jordan. We camped on a rocky ridgeline high above the mouth of a valley called Wadi Mussa, or the Valley of Moses. For the most part this was green farmland, flanked on three sides by mountains of smooth rounded boulders and sparse vegetation. It's said to be the place where Moses struck the rock to bring forth water. A small mosquelike building was constructed on the site to commemorate that event, and inside the monument you'll find a rock from beneath which water flows. It even looks as if lightning has struck it a few times over the centuries. I drank from it once and pulled a small stone from the water, placing it in my pocket for safekeeping. I grinned at myself for doing it but reasoned that in light of recent events . . . one never knew.

The wind blew hard and relentlessly across this ridge, making the living conditions at the bivouac site just slightly above bearable. To make matters worse, getting to the training site in the valley required a long truck ride down a steep, winding one-lane road with thirty-two switchbacks in it. What kept the twice-a-day trips interesting was the fact that Jordanian trucks were used to transport us. To say the least, they were not well maintained. Some of them really were held together with tape and wire where screws and bolts were supposed to be.

To keep morale and interest up, Colonel Nightingale and I planned a trip for the entire company to the ancient city of Petra, which rests at the foot of the stream that flows from Moses's rock. On a sunny day in March we trucked the company to the entrance of a narrow passage called the Seth which leads visitors into the city of Petra. We spent the day wandering among the ruins and thinking about what it must have been like to defend or attack such a fortress. It was magnificent, and I've seen nothing like it since.

I split from the rest of the group and made my way to a point well above the city, called the High Place. Everything I had read about Petra suggested that this was where humans and beasts were sacrificed to various gods over the centuries. A large obelisk marked the sacred place, and below this vantage point lay the domain of the City of the Dead, a myriad of cubbyholes, rooms, and dwellings carved into the sandstone canyon walls of Petra. This was an entire city constructed by Petra's inhabitants to be the exclusive resting place of their dead. Like so many places in Jordan, it was declared haunted by the locals, a place to steer away from when it got dark.

The wind blew small bits of rock and dust, pelting my face. It was then I had the perception I was being watched. There, next to the obelisk was the same being I had seen in the first vision, the one who had spoken to me from the hilltop. He stared at me from fifty feet away, his white robes blowing in the wind. I raised my head until I was looking him dead in the eye, and stayed that way for what seemed an eternity.

He smiled knowingly. "Seek peace . . . and become a teacher of it," said that enchanting voice. He then nodded slightly and turned to walk out of sight behind the obelisk. I ran so I could see behind the obelisk—but he wasn't there. I circled it, but found nothing. I didn't know whether to run for my life or cry out for the being to return. "Goddamn it, who are you?" There was no answer, only the rush of the wind and the wisping of sand across the flat rocks of the High Place.

As I walked down I tried to see around every corner and bend in the narrow trail before I reached it, but there were no more surprises. I didn't know what to do or what was happening. I must have asked myself a hundred times whether I was going insane. I kept touching the bruise on my head as I made the hour-long walk back to the main city.

Over the next week and a half we dedicated ourselves to training assault climbers in the jagged cliffs lining the bottom of the valley. Our time in Jordan grew short, and the pace picked up in anticipation of home. Eleven days later we were in a secret Jordanian airbase conducting airborne operations with their paratroopers. They were a wild bunch who did their duty without the luxury of having the best equipment available the way their American counterparts did. It wasn't unusual to see the Jordanian paratroops tying their jump helmets on with twine or wire, as they did with the rest of their equipment. Their parachutes were a memorable sight, frayed and even torn; it took a brave man to strap one of those raggedy things on and jump out of a plane. We continued training with them for another week or so before beginning final preparations for the trip home. It was here I decided to ask a man I trusted some guarded questions about the visions.

We bivouacked in a large hangar, all of us together in

one big swarming mass of humanity. When that many men get together and snore in an open hangar it's tragic. We slept on the floor, which at least was softer than most of the rocks I'd pulled from under me in recent months. To pass time we watched movies on an old projector someone had borrowed from our hosts. All in all it was a good time: the last of the mail was handed out, and the best of the remaining rations were consumed, and hot showers—well, sort of hot—were taken. But most important, we were going home.

The battalion chaplain was Captain George Duffy. Duff and I had always supported one another—that is, I encouraged my men to attend his services and he always gave me good advice and counseling when I needed them. I needed them now. We sat together behind the hangar watching the C-141 Starlifters that would take us home as they landed one after the other and taxied to their parking spots. We talked casually of home and wives and of our lonesome men, until well after dusk. I tried to find some place to throw in my questions, but as time wore on Duff started talking at a pretty good clip, and getting a word in became more difficult with each passing minute. Finally I jumped in with both feet.

"I know you believe in God, Duff, and I assume you believe in angels, but do you believe in ghosts and demons?"

Duff rambled on for a few seconds until the question sank in. He stopped talking for about five seconds and looked at me with the biggest grin I'd ever seen on his face. When he saw I wasn't kidding he burst out laughing and picked up the conversation right where he'd left off.

"What the hell's so funny about that?" I interrupted. "I know it's not the first time you've heard that question, so why all the chuckles?"

"I just never thought I'd hear it from you, that's all. I mean it's not what we've usually talked about, is it?"

"No, it's not. . . . But there have been some things . . ."

I stopped before I said anything I'd be sorry for. "It's just something I want your thoughts on."

He pulled his cap off and scratched the top of his head. "If I can believe in God and His domain, and in His angels, then I guess I'd have to believe in the other guy's team as well. Wouldn't I?"

"Probably," I answered. "But that means you believe only in good and evil as man defines them—you believe that there's God and his angels, and Satan and his angels, nothing more or less. Is that right?"

"Yeah, that's how I see it. I mean, they didn't give classes in seminary on any other options."

"Don't you think it's possible there's something else?"

"Like what?"

"Perhaps something in between, or maybe yet something parallel?"

Duff looked at me carefully and then laughed again. "You're really scaring me, you know that?" He shook his head in disbelief. "Since when did you become a philosopher?"

"Look, I'm not calling myself a philosopher. I simply believe there has to be something else out there besides what religion outlines for us. Why does everything have to be good or evil, black or white?"

"Because that's the nature of all things in this world. There is good, and because there is good there is evil. There must be opposition, or there can't be any good. There'd be no purpose in it, don't you see?"

"No, I don't. Are you telling me that good and evil exist for balance?"

"Not balance . . . choice," he said quietly. "They exist so that you have a choice. You're talking to a chaplain"— he smiled—"so I'm gonna tell you that salvation lies only with the pursuit of the good. But the other way is there to explore if you choose to. People do it every day."

"Well, I'm making a choice right now," I said, patting him on the back. "A choice to go watch the rest of that movie with the boys and then hit the sack. How's that for picking the good from the bad?''

"That's an excellent choice." Duff grinned. "But your question isn't answered, is it?"

"It is and it isn't. I guess I'm looking more for an explanation than an answer."

"An explanation of what?"

"Of something I saw." I hesitated. "Let me put it this way. Would one of these people, these beings, visit somebody? Say, somebody who wasn't dead?"

"Sure! I mean we hear about it all the time. Of course there are skeptics, and events are often disproved or explained away, but I believe it happens. Why not?"

"Okay, then, why would they visit this person?"

"Who knows? It could be anything. They might be trying to warn him of some impending catastrophe, or protect him, or maybe teach him."

"Teach him about what . . . God?" I said, more sarcastically than I meant to.

"That could be it. They might also teach him about himself, about his fellow man, about his calling and election or about life in general—hell, I don't know."

"Yeah, I guess that would make more sense. Thanks!" I shook his hand. "Thanks a lot. You always help, even when you don't mean to."

On our way back to the front of the hangar Duff stopped before we got within earshot of anyone. "Something tells me this won't be the last time we have this conversation," he said. "Why is that?"

I must have had a shocked look on my face, because he reached out and grabbed my arm just above the elbow and hung on. Finally I told him, "It probably won't be, but I can't talk about it right now. I need to think, okay?"

He released his grip, trading it for a touch on the shoulder. "You know where I am, and you damned sure know I'm available whenever you need me."

"I know, and I appreciate it. Come on, let's see if there's

any soda left." We disappeared into the hangar, closing the night behind us.

The next morning I joined my officers for tea outside the hangar. Several of the Jordanian officers were present, saying good-bye to their new friends and comrades. The Jordanian colonel glanced at me over his cup of tea and excused himself from his conversation with Duff. "Good morning, Captain Morehouse."

"*Salaam aleikum,* Colonel," I said, bowing my head slightly.

He smiled broadly. "*Aleikum salaam,* my friend. I trust you slept well, out of the desert for once."

"I slept like a child, sir. And you?"

"Well, thank you."

I took another sip of tea. He'd never approached me like this. There must be a reason.

He looked out at the desert, nodding his head slightly as if he'd answered a question for himself. "Ah . . . Captain Duff and I were talking about something that may interest you."

"What might that be, sir?" I asked, glaring at Duff.

"The *jinn,*" the colonel said.

"The who?"

"The *jinn,* evil spirits, ghosts and demons. Creatures that plague mankind. Ghouls who devour the bodies of the dead."

"Sir, wait. I apologize for anything Duff might have said about all this. I don't want you or anyone else to think—"

"Think what? That you are crazy? I assure you, Captain Morehouse, that is not the case. I will also assure you that Duff said nothing to me about you except that you had an interest in this sort of phenomenon. Do you?"

"Well, no . . . at least, not until a few weeks ago, in Baten el Ghoul."

"Ah." He seemed relieved. "So you saw something, did you?"

"Yes, sir, I saw something. At least I think I did. It may have just been a reaction. . . ."

"To the bullet."

"Perhaps."

"Yes, perhaps it was just that, a reaction to the bullet. Perhaps it was not. Perhaps you were given a message?"

His words sent a chill down my spine. How the hell did he know anything about a message? "What do you mean, a message, sir?"

"Many men receive messages here. They go into the hills to ponder their fate, much as Muhammad did in pondering the fate of his people. It is here that the angels speak to them. It is not odd."

"I'm sorry to disagree, sir, but I find it very odd. Speaking to angels, that is. And I'm obviously not Muhammad." We both laughed at that.

"No, you are certainly not Muhammad, my friend. Regardless, I think something unusual happened to you out there. Maybe one day you will share it with all of us."

"Yes, sir, maybe one day." I took a long pull on my canteen. "But not today."

He patted me on the back. "Fair enough, my friend, fair enough." He turned to walk away.

"Sir?"

"Yes, Captain?"

"Do you believe the valley is haunted—I mean, like your men do?"

"No, I don't believe it, I *know* it. My father knew it, as did my grandfather and his father before him. The truth of a place like that doesn't wander. The truth may be built upon, or the interpretation of it may change. But it never vanishes. It is unchangeable, as your spiritual ideal should be. The world that spoke to you is the same yesterday, today, and forever." He turned and walked slowly away. After a few steps he turned and said, "Unless your mind is fixed on Allah, the giver of all things, you may find yourself chasing shadows in your search for glory."

"Wait a minute. . . . What does that mean?"

"It means you have a purpose, and I think it is being made known to you. Listen to the message or chase shadows all your life. I must go now. I have a battalion to command. *Salaam aleikum,* Captain." He saluted and turned away.

I returned the salute. "*Aleikum salaam,* Colonel."

We jumped back into Savannah with all our families watching. Those were great homecomings, almost circuslike. After the standard formalities of equipment and personnel accountability we released the troops to visit for a few minutes with their families. First on my knee was Michaèl, followed by Mariah. I stood there anchored by my loved ones while Debbie approached me carrying Danielle. She had a troubled but eager look on her face.

"Oh, thank God." Still holding Danielle, she flung an arm around me. "I'm so glad you're home. I was really worried this time. I just knew something was going to happen. . . . How's your head? Captain August from Regiment called the other night to tell me about it. He said you were fine." She slapped me on the arm. "Why didn't you let them tell me about it when it happened?"

"I'm fine, honey. We didn't want you to worry. Look, it just put a big hole in the helmet, that's all. Sergeant Hanley has it; I'll show it to you later." I said nothing else, just hugged her and kissed my babies. "I'm glad I'm home, too, honey. What's for dinner? And please don't tell me, Goat."

After a weekend with my family it was almost as though I'd never left. I didn't bring up the topic of spirits or God or any of the paraphernalia that goes with them for a long time, and I didn't have any visions either, at least not like the first three. Life seemed pretty much back to normal.

And yet . . . things were not the same. Most nights I would dream lucidly; faces and images of distant friends would come to me even though I knew they were thousands of miles away. I began seeing things in my mind—imperfectly at first, but with increasing clarity. As the months passed, I actually came to believe that I could see forward in time or predict the outcome of certain events. It was an odd feeling having my mind's eye open all the time. I began referring to it as the television in my head.

One night in June of 1987, I couldn't sleep. The visions were too fierce and rapid. I got up and went into the living room. I sat there for hours trying to rid my mind of the images darting endlessly in and out. As I rocked gently back and forth, I was startled by a presence in the room, and a hand clutched my shoulder. I snapped around, chilled and frightened.

"Honey? What are you doing up so early? It's two-thirty in the morning."

"Christ, Deb, what are you doing sneaking up on me like that? You scared the living daylights out of me. Don't do that."

"I didn't sneak up. I've been calling your name out loud from the doorway for five minutes. I thought you had headphones on or something. What's wrong?" She sat down beside me, held my hand, and pulled me to her shoulder. "What's wrong, David? I've never seen you like this."

I took a deep breath. "I'm scared, honey . . . real scared. That bullet did something to me, something strange. I can't turn it off. I can't stop these goddamned images from coming into my head, and they're driving me out of my mind."

"What images? Images of what? You never mentioned—"

"I know, I know. I haven't said anything to anyone. I don't want to end up in a psycho ward."

"Well, what are they?"

I tried to regain my composure. "It's difficult to explain. They're always different. Sometimes they're images of what I think is the future, sometimes of the past, and sometimes of things that are happening right now, in the present. At least that's what I think they are." I leaned forward, burying my face in my hands. "Oh, God, I don't know what they are. I just want them to stop."

"I want you to see Dr. Mellin about this."

"I can't, honey! Don't you understand? If I do that, it's all over for us. Everything we've worked for will be gone. The army doesn't promote people who see things in their heads." I looked at her, and we both burst out laughing. "Well, I guess that's debatable, isn't it?"

"Yeah," Debbie said. "I think we've known some folks who saw things pretty routinely."

"Maybe so. But I'm not willing to run that risk right now. I'm willing to bet that it'll go away eventually."

"David! It's been over two months now. Just when do you think it's going away?"

"I don't know. Maybe if I change my ways like the angel said. Maybe—"

"What angel? David, you're making me very angry." She pulled her hands away and folded her arms across her chest.

I smiled at her pose. "Aw, look, I didn't tell you these things because I didn't know how to tell you. Hell, I don't know what they mean. I don't have any idea how to tell you what I saw and heard or how it even happened. I'm not sure I believe any of it myself, so cut me some slack here, all right?"

Reluctantly, Debbie nodded. "Well, all right. . . . But what did you see and hear?"

I took another deep breath. "I saw a being. Actually I saw several, but only one spoke to me."

"What did he say?"

"He said that what I was doing was wrong, or something like that. He said that I should choose a different path, a path of peace. Now what the hell am I supposed to make of that?"

"I don't know," Deb said softly. "Have you prayed about it?"

I shook my head slowly in the darkness of the room. "No, I haven't. I haven't prayed about much since it happened. I'm afraid to. I have this strange notion that if I open myself up, all hell will break loose. I have enough hell in my head now, thank you."

"I'm worried. You can't go on like this; you have to get someone to help you sort this out."

"Will it make you feel any better if I promise to do that, when I feel the time is right?"

"It will. You've never broken a promise to me yet." She smiled, and I felt her grip my hand more tightly. "I love you," she said.

"And I love you. Let's get back to bed and try to get some sleep."

I was never the same after that trip to Jordan and the bullet. Something in me changed, turned me inward. I thought perhaps I was spending too much time analyzing myself and the world around me. I thought that I needed to get on with the business of soldiering. But something kept telling me I had to prepare. I couldn't put my finger on it yet, but that bullet meant something. The mysterious figure meant something—and so did the message.

THREE

THE SELECTION

Regretfully, we left the Rangers in May of 1987. I was given orders to attend the Defense Language Institute in Monterey, California, to learn Italian. I would then serve again as a general's aide-de-camp, this time to an Italian general at CENTAF headquarters in Verona, Italy. The day I changed command and gave up my company, my Ranger battalion commander, Colonel Keith Nightingale, put his arms around Debbie and me to tell us that he had just received a phone call from the Department of the Army. The general had opted for an aide who was already in Italy and already spoke the language. That was his prerogative, and I would simply have to find another job. I was a free agent for the first time in my career.

Several colonel and general officer friends whom I've already mentioned helped me find a new home. Within a few days, I received a phone call from my assignment officer in Virginia, who had found a possible placement for me in the Washington, D.C., area. He couldn't talk about the assignment over the phone, he said, because it was classified. He quickly arranged a flight from Savannah to the District of Columbia for me to interview with what I considered a very odd unit. I stayed at the Holiday Inn next to the Hoffman Building in Alexandria, Virginia, where I received several cryptic phone calls during the night telling me what I was to do, what I was not to do, and how and where I would be contacted the following morning. This was a real cloak-and-dagger act, which I found comical. I thought these guys were kidding when they told me to walk out the east entrance of the hotel at precisely seven A.M. with a copy of *The Washington Post* under my right arm.

I was an infantry officer, and in my wildest dreams I'd never imagined that there were parts of our army that conducted business in this way. I knew lots of intelligence officers, but they never mentioned crap like this. And then I remembered having dinner with Colonel Bartley E. Day, the professor of military science at BYU, and his wife back in Provo. The dinner conversation had centered around which branch of the army I should choose: artillery, armor, infantry, and so on. I had already unofficially made my choice to be an infantry officer, but we were kicking the issue around nonetheless. Colonel Day said to Debbie and me, "Whatever you do, don't become an intelligence officer. There are aspects of that career choice that are very dark and without honor or integrity. Do anything but that."

Unfortunately, I didn't heed Colonel Day's warning. My choices over the next few days set into motion events that would bring to an end all that I considered normal.

I was interviewed and examined by a group of military intelligence folks, assigned to a bizarre unit called the Secret Army of Northern Virginia, or SANV. Its actual code name was Sacred Cape, and I'd never experienced anything like it. Actually, if someone had told me, while I was still in the Rangers, that a unit like this existed, I would have laughed in his face. But it did.

I underwent numerous psychological tests, written as well as oral. Supposedly, these were intended to enable the unit's psychologist to develop a "psychological profile" on each member of the unit. This profile, used to determine the candidate's emotional and psychological well-being, gave the commander inside information into exactly what made each member of his team tick—how far he could push you, what he could reasonably ask you to do before you balked, etc. It was peculiar, but I went along with it, as much out of curiosity as anything else.

I guess my appearance and psychological profile fit the unit's mold; I was asked that day to join. I agreed, again as much out of curiosity as anything. The day I arrived back at Hunter Army Airfield in Savannah, two young men in cheap suits showed up at the Ranger battalion head-quarters. They were there to initiate the processing of my orders to a classified assignment. This was my first awak-ening to the power of such units. Under normal circum-stances, it would take weeks to get permanent change-of-station orders. These guys got it done in a matter of hours. I was out-processed and en route within two days.

Once again, I left Debbie alone with the children to pack up and move while I spent six weeks at the Combined Arms and Services Staff School at Fort Leavenworth, Kansas, before reporting to D.C. for my new assignment as a "spook."

As I settled in, I found the new unit intriguing for a while. But that soon wore off. For the first time, I wasn't able to tell Debbie exactly what I was doing in the army. I was expected to lie to her about what the unit did and how it did it, as well as what I was doing there. And I didn't just grin and shuffle my feet when she asked ques-tions about the unit, I did exactly what they wanted me to do: I told her bald-faced lies. I also lied to my father and mother; they thought I was testing new weapons systems for a unit called the Systems Enhancement and Evaluation Office. I was actually working for a unit that trained and inserted operatives into Tier I and II countries—that is, po-tential "hot spots" in the world—to establish an infrastruc-ture that would support clandestine or covert military operations in that country should the need ever arise.

Debbie and the children were suspicious from the begin-ning. They hated this new life. There weren't any wives' organizations; there was no mutual support; there were no family days at which the spouses and families of the service members became involved. Dad didn't wear a uniform, and his hair grew long. This was not the army any longer, and it was frightening for the family.

My parents visited after a few months and were guarded as well. At one point when we were alone, my dad told me, ''I don't expect you to tell me what your new job is. Your mother and I know it's classified. Just be careful. These people are not like what you and I grew up with in the army. They're cut from a different cloth, and you can't trust them. Everything you say or do is captured by them for use against you.'' I filed Dad's message away for the time being, but his words never left me.

I have to admit that some extraordinary noncommissioned officers and officers were assigned to this unit. Not like the Rangers, but good nonetheless. However, there was a lower moral and ethical standard that would not have been tolerated in the army Debbie and I knew. I saw a lieutenant colonel and a sergeant major get in a fistfight over an enlisted woman they were both sleeping with. Both men were married, and yet their punishment consisted of a very pleasant reassignment for the officer. Nothing was done to the sergeant major; he was allowed to remain in the unit.

Expectations were strange, and methods of management and leadership were even more bizarre. People here were not members of any team. They were loners, independents who merely tolerated authority and had even less respect for the notion of comradeship. That went against everything I'd ever experienced in the infantry; but this was the new school, and I had to learn how to behave. In retrospect, I picked up a lot from the Sacred Cape people: I discovered that there is a dark and perverted side to our army.

In spite of our best efforts, everything began to change for Debbie and me. From the moment I entered the unit, our life together simply started to unravel. I can't explain why. Perhaps it was the mystery and the lies deemed necessary by the unit; maybe it was just me and my inability to assimilate myself into this new army I was discovering. Or maybe it was the nightmares and the message. Whatever it was, I was uncomfortable. Almost everyone in my workplace was a manipulator or liar by trade. I was out of place. Would I become like them, or would I hold my own?

As I said, these kinds of units come equipped with psychologists to keep track of the mental stability of the unit's members via frequent assessments of their psychological profiles. It was during one of these updates that I confided in Dr. Innis Barker, a command psychologist, concerning my personal experiences with the bullet, the visions, and the nightmares. Barker was a tall lanky man with a brisk walk and a snappy voice. His face, as narrow as his body, was framed by a well-groomed blond thatch and gold wire-rimmed glasses. He had a Ph.D. in psychology from somewhere . . . he didn't have anything on his walls. Oh—and he was quick on his feet. He had to be: he had been called to the Pentagon on numerous occasions to explain "clinically" the activities of several of the unit's operatives. It must have been difficult to explain away all the bad stuff these guys were capable of, but Barker managed.

He was a good man and appeared to have a kind heart. Sometimes he would confide in me, criticizing the unit and its methods. He became one of the few people there I trusted. When I decided to tell him my story, I half expected him to contact the Walter Reed Army Medical Center and arrange for a padded van to pick me up and deliver me to the psychiatric ward. Instead he listened intently as I described the events that took place on the day of the shooting, and everything that followed.

"Have you had any of these hallucinations—I'm sorry, 'visions'—recently?" he asked.

"I had something happen the other day while I was camping with my son and his Boy Scout troop. Only it wasn't really one of the visions. It was more like an experience."

"An experience?"

"Well, it wasn't like the others. . . . It was very odd."

"Okay, tell me about it."

His words sent a chill through me that I couldn't explain. I trusted him, but something about his eyes spoke betrayal.

He had something up his sleeve, and it concerned me. I sensed it. Don't ask me how—I just did.

"Well, it's fairly difficult to explain. I was with my son—"

"Michael, right?"

"Yes, that's right." How did he happen to know that? I wondered. There were over three hundred people in the unit. "It was very cold that night. A fresh snow had fallen covering everything in the forest. We set up camp and spent the day working on different skills for the boys. I really enjoy that—I mean, I enjoy being with my son and his friends. This was a beautiful setting, winter in the woods. But something strange happened."

"Come on—what do you mean, 'strange'?" Barker asked, obviously growing impatient.

"Well, it's difficult to explain. I went through the day . . ." I shook my head, trying to figure out a way to explain without feeling stupid. "I just felt closer to everyone, to everything. It was like I was tuned into a different frequency or something. Hell, I cried looking into my son's eyes, for no reason. I thought I could see into his life, into his future. It was all a jumble of visions and signals. I couldn't make anything of it, but it was there, just like the other nightmares I'd been having."

Barker put in, "I think I like the word 'vision' much better than 'nightmare.' It doesn't sound to me as if these are nightmares."

"Okay, Doctor, visions it is." I took a deep breath. "When we all went to bed I slept outside the tent, alone in the snow. There was a full moon, and a starry sky. I distinctly remember thinking how dark the sky was with all that light in it, and how the snow beautifully carpeted the forest floor.

"Suddenly, I felt myself rising slowly off the ground. It was strange—I wasn't frightened, I was oddly calm. I felt weightless and free as I watched the tree branches come closer and closer. I was completely horizontal, and then I began turning slowly to my left, until I saw a dark body in the snow below. The body was mine. I wasn't scared, just intrigued, as if I'd known that it was going to happen. Almost as if I had done it before.

"I rotated back toward the sky, and then I sped toward the moon so fast that it made me physically ill. I mean, I actually felt my stomach roll from the acceleration, and I thought I was going to vomit."

I paused briefly to see if Barker was still with me. He looked up from his notebook and smiled. "Please go on."

"I stopped above the earth and looked at everything around me. I could see for miles in the moonlight; the rolling hills, the forests, the lights in houses. But, strangely, I couldn't see any darkness. The moon was still there, but the stars were awash in some other light. I couldn't see them any longer. It was the same kind of light I'd seen in the desert. The night of the bullet."

Barker shuffled through his notes. "Yes . . . you mentioned apparitions in the desert. Were there any here?"

"No, there weren't. But I remember feeling that this was the end of the journey, and then I began slowly descending back to where my body was. I watched myself all the way back down, but I lost everything just before I became me again."

Barker laughed.

"I guess the whole thing is kind of funny. I certainly feel funny sitting here telling you about it, not to mention everything else. What the hell do you think it was?"

Barker turned the page in his notebook. "I'd like you to tell me what *you* think it was."

"Goddamn it, Doc, if I knew what it was I wouldn't be sitting here telling you about it! I'd be enjoying it."

"All right, all right. It's nothing to get excited about. If it's any consolation, I've seen this sort of thing before."

"Yeah, I'm sure you have." I started to pace the room. "In your textbooks on lunatics. This crap is not normal, and don't try to make me feel better by trying to convince me that it is. I know better."

"No, it's not normal. But what is?"

"Don't give me this 'what is normal?' bull. Nobody I know or have ever known sees things in the night or in their head. I'm spending parts of my life in the borderland, somewhere between this world and some other. I know that! What I want to know is why, and how to control it or fix it."

"Calm down, David, just calm down. You're correct: people don't go around having visions like you are having. But that doesn't necessarily mean that you are abnormal."

"What the fuck do you call it, then?" I snapped.

"I know some people who call it a gift." He paused, staring at me. "Did you hear me? They call it a gift."

"Who calls it a gift?"

"For now, let's just say some friends of mine. For them this kind of experience is part adventure . . . and part miracle." He dropped his notebook onto his desk, walked to a four-drawer safe, and began spinning the tumblers on its lock.

I sat there staring at the wall while he opened the safe and rummaged through one of the drawers. He pulled out several blue folders and tossed three of them onto my lap.

"I want you to look at these, all of them, from cover to cover. We'll discuss them in a day or two."

"Discuss what?"

"Well, I will want to know your perceptions—what you think about them and what's going on in them. You'll notice they're classified Secret. Please deal with them accordingly."

"Okay, I'll take a look at them."

"Good. I think that should be all for now. I'll call you tomorrow or the next day. Okay?"

"Okay. Thanks, Doc."

I walked back to my office, stunned. I couldn't believe that I'd talked to Barker the way I had. I couldn't believe he didn't have me taken somewhere for observation. I know *I* would have if I'd been him.

I walked into my office and turned on the lights. I was

shocked to see one of the other officers in the unit sitting there in the dark, waiting for me.

"Wondered when you'd show up." He took a drag on his cigarette and stared directly at me.

He outranked me; otherwise I'd have told him to get out of my office. I just wasn't comfortable enough with the first-name protocol of this unit to do that yet, so I stuck to what I knew best. "Can I help you, sir?"

"Yeah—you can help me and everyone else here."

"How's that?"

He motioned at the walls of my office with the hand that held his smoke. "I'm here about this."

"About what? My pictures and awards?"

"Oh, is that what they are? I thought it was more like a self-aggrandizing museum. Yeah, that's what it is, a fucking museum. Get rid of it."

"Why? They're just pictures."

"Yeah, pictures of the army. You're not in the army anymore. You're in a classified assignment and you are not supposed to expose yourself as a special operations soldier. You're supposed to be pretending like you're an acquisitions officer, not a fucking Ranger! Got it?"

"Yeah, I got it!"

He stood and placed his cigarette hand on my shoulder, letting the thick haze build up around my head. "That's real good, that you understand. I'll pass that on." He moved past me, pausing at the door. "I don't expect to see this tomorrow, right?"

"It'll be gone."

"Good. See ya, Morehouse." He opened the door and disappeared down the hallway.

I slammed the folders down. "*Fuck!* I hate this place."

I stayed late that night packing up my "museum" and carting it out to the car. It was ten o'clock before I sat down to look at the folders Barker had given me. I poured myself a fresh cup of coffee and inspected the outside of the first folder. It was stamped SECRET—GRILL FLAME in inch-high red letters top and bottom. Typed on a label on the lower right of the folder were the words NOT RELEASABLE TO FOREIGN NATIONALS—ORCON, followed by the words; CLASSIFIED BY: MSG, DAMI-ISH, DATED: 051630ZJUL78. I opened the folder to the first page. After the words SUMMARY ANALYSIS, REMOTE VIEWING (RV) SESSION D- , was a brief explanation of the target. I noted that no names were used in the folder; everyone was referred to either by a number or the title of "monitor." In this folder, two people were working the target. The monitor began.

"Viewer Number 66, I want you to shift your awareness in present time to the intersection of the target shown to you in the photograph. Describe the southwest corner of the target to me."

"Ah . . . it's like a . . . building, but not an office building . . . it has large doors, large swinging doors."

"Change your perspective so that you can see your left hand extending down one street, and your right hand extending down the other street, so you're facing the corner of the target itself, right there at street level. One street should be going off to your left and one off to your right. Describe the scene on your left."

"Um . . . I see, uh, large posters, signs, vehicles parked there. There is a corner of a building, a corner entrance, doors and a staircase. That's all I see."

"Okay. Move over the top of the intersection now, so now you won't be standing at street level, but you'll be gently floating at about a hundred feet above the ground, and as you look down you can see underneath you the sidewalk and the street extending off to your left. Describe it from this perspective."

"I see a great deal of activity. People running all over the place, shouting, chanting and waving banners and signs in the air."

"Do you see an entrance into the building below you?"

"Yes, I do."

"Move to it now."

"Okay, I'm here. What do you want me to do?"

"I want you to describe the exterior of the door, its surroundings, and the lock on the door if there is one. Is there a lock?"

"Yes there is, I do see a lock. . . . Here, I'll sketch it."

At this point I looked at a parenthetical entry that directed me to the back of the session analysis, where I saw the sketch provided by the viewer. It included the Arabic writing on the door's face.

The monitor asked, "Is this all you can see here?"

"No . . . wait a minute! I see—No, there's something dark next to me, moving toward me. . . . Jesus!"

"Sixty-six, move away from the darkness. Disregard it! I want you to pass through the door and describe the contents of the room for me. Tell me what you see there. Do it now!"

"Okay, I'm passing through the door now. . . . I see tables and chairs . . . and some kind of cooking place."

"Is this the kitchen?"

"No. No, it's not the kitchen . . . this is a makeshift place. Some old man is standing there cooking."

"Is anyone else present?"

"I don't see anyone. No, wait! There is someone else. There is someone helping him."

"Okay, I want you to move into the next room. Tell me when you are there. Stay at this level. Move to the next room."

"I'm there. It's a large conference room. There is a huge table with about two dozen chairs around it."

"Is anyone there now?"

"No, it's empty."

"Okay, I want you to move forward in time about twenty-four hours. Tell me what you see."

"Moving now. I see a gathering of people now."

"What time do you think it is?"

"It's about eight A.M., and the room is full of people. There is a mix of about fifty percent old and the other half are relatively young. They are getting ready for a meeting, I think."

"I want you to access the mind of the key individual present and tell me what he or she is thinking. Do you understand?"

"Yes, I understand. The key individual is an older man sitting at the head of the table. He's very bitter about something, very angry at some of the people in the room. He's pointing his fist at them, shouting at them."

"What is the meeting about?"

"It's about the Americans . . . I think the hostages. Yeah, that's what this is about, the hostages."

"What are their intentions? Do they intend to kill the hostages?"

"No! No, they are not talking about that. The conversation seems to be centering on what to do with them . . . let me see . . . to keep them here or to put them somewhere else. In fact, the old man is upset about the way some of them have been treated. He thinks the younger people have abused them, and he is cautioning them to take better care of the hostages. I'm getting tired now. . . . I think I want to come back now. Is that okay? I want to come back."

"Okay. You can break it off and return. We'll monitor your return. You may begin at any time."

I sat there, shocked by what I had read. I quickly thumbed through the other two folders, each of which contained similar accounts of floating above city streets, passing through roofs and walls as an apparition would. It was phenomenal. These guys were living what I had been calling a nightmare. They were doing it for a living—for the government. Who the hell were they? How did they get there?

The night was cold and drizzly, with wet and sloppy fog.

It was just what I needed to wake me up for the drive home. All the way I was as jittery as they come. I could have sworn that someone was in the backseat. I kept turning around to check, but there was nothing, of course. The trees lining the road blurred, seeming to encircle the roadway. I began to get claustrophobic. I pulled to the side of the road and stepped out of the car.

Inhaling deeply, I tried cleansing myself of the toxins in my mind. I sucked in the cold air, trying to exhale the haunting images that plagued me. After several purifying breaths I leaned over the hood of the car, resting my head against the warm metal. God, I *had* to get a grip. Why was this bothering me so much? What was the big deal? I slammed my fist into the hood. I knew what the fucking big deal was. I was reading about human beings who turned into fucking ghosts, and as if that weren't enough, they traveled in time to look at stuff and come back again. They fucking hovered above the ground, walked through walls, and spoke to evil spirits . . . and that's just what I'd read about! I had talked with an angel, exited my body and returned again, seen things in my sleep and in the dark for six months now. What was wrong with that? Why should I be alarmed? It was fucking normal to do that . . . wasn't it? I flopped back down on the hood, weeping. "Somebody help me," I sobbed. "I don't want this. . . . I didn't ever want this."

I stayed there for a long time, feeling the heat of the engine on my forehead and the frigid dampness soaking into my back. Dragging myself off the hood, I flopped behind the wheel and drove home. I fell asleep downstairs, staring into the darkness of the room.

I walked into the office the next morning looking raccoonish around the eyes, still numb from the night before. I grabbed a cup of hot coffee from the secretary's office and thanked her profusely for it.

"You look beat," she said. "You'd better grab two cups before the hordes get in here and empty it."

"Thanks, Margaret. I think I will."

The hot coffee poured life back into me. I walked into my office and spun the tumblers on my safe. I wanted to take another look at the files. I swigged deep and pressed the warm cup against my forehead. The phone on the desk rang, piercing the quiet of the office.

"David? It's Dr. Barker. I just wanted to know . . . did you get a chance to review those files?"

I hesitated momentarily, thinking that it might be best if I told him no. Maybe I needed some time to get my head screwed back on straight before Barker dragged me any further into this. Finally I answered him. "I did. I looked at them last night."

"Great! Can we talk about them?"

"Yes, sir. When?"

"Let's say today, about one o'clock. Will that be okay with you? Oh, and bring the files with you. I need to return them to the safe."

"See you then, Doc."

I sat there for a long time, staring at the files. Then I thumbed through the pages, looking again at the unearthly images sketched by the viewers. Their drawings were so detailed, their descriptions of the target so chillingly vivid. I shook my head in disbelief. *I've got to keep these,* I thought. *I can't just let them disappear.* I spent the next few hours in front of a copy machine. Whenever you duplicated classified documents in this building you were required to record the nature of the documents and the number of copies with a classified-document manager. But I didn't want anybody to know I was investigating this stuff. I also had the gnawing feeling that I needed to protect myself with this information. Something didn't smell right. I needed an insurance policy.

At one I came scrambling out of a command group meeting in the boss's office. I collected the files from my safe and headed down the hall to Barker's office. I knocked frantically at his door, but there was no answer. I checked my watch; I was fifteen minutes late. "Shit!" I muttered to myself, still pounding on the door. "He'd better be here! I'm not that late."

"Just a minute! I'll be there in a minute!" Barker shouted from inside.

I paced the hall, waiting for him to open the door. I must have looked anxious, or paranoid, or something. It seemed to me as if everyone walking by the office eyeballed me. Maybe they just wondered why I was visiting the shrink two days in a row.

The door jerked open. "Hey! Welcome, come on in. I was just talking to some friends about you." Barker motioned me into my usual chair as he took his place behind the desk.

"Friends? About me?"

"Sure! Your experiences provoke a lot of interest in my line of work. You can understand that."

"I guess I can understand that. It just concerns me—"

He cut me off. "Don't be concerned about anything. All this is confidential. I didn't mention you by name, only by your operative number, and they have no way of knowing who or what that means. Okay? Shall we get started?"

I sighed, looked briefly at the file folders, and handed them to him. "Those are quite interesting, to say the least."

"Yeah, I thought so. How did they make you feel?"

"They scared the hell out of me, that's what. How did you think they would make me feel?"

"I assumed they would be a little shocking at first, but I also thought that you would find a resemblance to some of your experiences. I guess what I really wanted you to see was that this sort of thing, while being unusual, is in fact a reality. I was concerned that you might begin thinking yourself an anomaly."

"I think I'm a goddamned freak, that's what I think!"

"That's precisely what I don't want you to think. The men you read about last night are not freaks. They are highly trained individuals who perform a very needed intelligence-collection service; they are a national intelligence asset. There is a great deal of information that only they can provide, and they are very difficult people to come by.''

"What's that got to do with me? I can't do what they're doing in those files. Hell, I'm nothing but out of control, and those guys—well, they go where they want to go, see what they want to see. They're special.''

"They are *now* . . . but they didn't begin that way. Yes, some of them have grown up with some semblance of this ability, but not with the refined capability we're talking about. Some of them had encounters that frightened them, just as you've been frightened.''

"Have they been shot in the head?''

Barker stopped mid-sentence and smiled. "Come to think of it, no, no one has been shot in the head. Frankly, I don't see how that changes things much. I can't imagine what a blow to the head of that severity could or would have done to you. But it obviously did something, since you didn't have any inkling of this ability before. That fact alone sets you apart from the others. But that's immaterial. What's important are your options. And they are: I can arrange for clinical assistance. That is, I can either try and help you here in the office with this perceived problem. Or, I can arrange for you to see a psychiatrist at another facility. Those are two options.''

I was indignant. "And?''

Now Barker was serious. "There is no 'and.' However, I can and will arrange an interview with some people. Some people who might be willing, if you qualify, to help you put this newfound ability to some use. The choice is yours.''

"No offense, Doctor, but those are pretty limiting options. If I read you right, you're saying that I can either end my career and seek clinical help for this 'problem,' or I can try to join a group of people who define this 'problem' as an 'ability' and spend the rest of my life trying to harness it so it doesn't kill me someday. Is that it?''

"You've distorted what I'm saying a bit, but that's essentially right. You wouldn't be doing it the rest of your life.''

"How long?"

"That depends."

"On what?"

"On how well you do, or whether you decide to stay with it, and on about a dozen other variables. But I'd say those are the most important. Dammit, David, I'm offering you a chance at a new life. Are you interested?"

I began to shake my legs nervously, thinking. Then I realized that Barker was watching me twitch and I forced myself to stop. "I'll have to give it some thought. Can I take a few days?"

"More like a few weeks would be better. I don't want you jumping into this; that wouldn't serve my purpose any more than it would yours." He stood up from the desk and walked to the same file safe as yesterday. "I want you to look at some material." He pulled a thick stack of papers from the drawer and handed them to me. "That should hold you for a while."

"What is all this stuff?"

"It's documentation pertaining to the unit you read about yesterday—some historical stuff, branch programs, more session summaries, and so on. It should give you a fairly good overview of the program. We'll keep in touch, and I'll be happy to answer any questions you might have about any of it. You know where I am." He laughed, thinking his last comment was a joke. "Now let's break this up, shall we?"

"Sure, Doc . . . but we didn't discuss any of the files."

"That's okay; I have a fairly good sense of what you thought. That's all I needed." He raised his eyebrows, said, "Thanks!" and motioned me to the door of the office.

I said nothing else. Lost in thought, I quietly walked back to my office, my head low. I closed my door and sat at the desk, staring at the pile of documents. *I can't do it*, I thought. *I just can't do it*. I placed the documents in the safe, closed the drawer, and slowly spun the tumbler.

Several days passed and I never opened the drawer. I

refused to spend time worrying about the future. Instead, I concentrated on my family.

Debbie planned outings for the entire family. I'd never had the chance to be involved in those, back when I was in the Rangers, and I wanted to get to know my children. It was a struggle at first, trying to adapt to a quasi-civilian way of life. It seemed I was in the way more than anything else. I guess it's difficult for a family to contend with Dad being home so much, when for years they've barely seen him. I think I was cramping their style, but they were as tolerant of me as they could be.

Michael started taking skating lessons, which eventually led to his playing ice hockey at an arena near Alexandria. It was a lot of fun for me to take him to the arena for practices and games. His gear bag was bigger than he was at the time. On Saturdays and Sundays the entire family would go to his games in the arenas about the capital Beltway. It was a tremendous escape from the events of the office and a fair diversion from my nightly journeys into the unknown.

I was beginning to feel I was fitting into the family again, to feel that Debbie and I were gaining confidence in each other. We seldom talked about what went on in my head at night, but I knew it troubled her. She was the one who comforted me when I became frightened, who wiped the perspiration from me, and who often shook me awake from my screams. There was no avoiding it, I was slowly losing ground with her on this issue. She was concerned about me, and angry that I wasn't seeking professional help. The career didn't matter to her. All that mattered was for me to be rid of these nightmares—these visions.

It was Easter weekend, 1988. We attended church as we usually did and picked up my parents at National Airport immediately following the service. It was good to see them again. I always felt comfortable around Mom and Dad. They made me feel safe. We spent time together catching up on family and friends; we even looked up some of Dad's old army buddies and spent an evening laughing over stories of World War II and Korea. It was without a doubt one of the most pleasant times I'd had in quite a while. Dad and I enjoyed a small glass of wine before retiring.

"How's the new job?"

I looked at him and grimaced. "It's interesting—and that's about it. No matter how good it gets, it'll never be as good as the infantry was. I'd give a month's pay just to see some dirty-faced troops for a week or so. I wouldn't call this the army, Dad; it's more like a highly paid, expensive boys' club. Some of the guys in this organization are drawing extra-duty payments of over eight hundred dollars a month."

"For what? Being spooks?"

"It's a bit more criminal than that. The other day I was sitting in a meeting when the unit training officer informed the various commanders that there were still some people drawing demolition pay who hadn't yet completed their quarterly qualifications. If they didn't, they'd lose their pay for a month. The good part is this: the qualification involves detonating a simulated blasting device. Can you believe that? These guys are drawing demo pay for blowing up what amounts to an M-80 firecracker. It pisses me off to see it. I remember young Rangers who jumped in five gallons of fu-gas with a claymore mine taped to it to incinerate the objective. And hell, they did it every other week. I couldn't have gotten them demolitions pay for that if I'd tried. And these guys get it for lighting firecrackers. It's bullshit, Dad, pure bullshit."

"I don't understand how they get away with it. Isn't somebody watching for that type of abuse?"

"I assume they are, but it's a big army, and we tend to concentrate on what we can see, not what's hidden from view under a cloak of secrecy. I saw a watch in a safe the other day that cost the taxpayers more than I made in three years. It was a prop that somebody in the unit used on a mission, as part of an alias. That would have bought me a lot of training ammunition when I was in the Rangers."

Dad touched my shoulder. "I know, son. It's a pain in the ass when you see stuff like that. But I'm sure it has a purpose, somewhere. They're probably working with the Agency when they pull some of this stuff—aren't they?"

"I don't know. I doubt it. There seems to be a running battle between this unit and the CIA. If you were to ask me to vote, I'd vote to let the CIA do it. They know what they're doing when it comes to this stuff; we don't. Yeah, we've got some good people in the unit, but for the most part it's a bunch of guys trying to play James Bond, and they aren't any good at it. As a matter of fact they stink at it, and it's embarrassing to the army to own these guys. The damned secretary of the army doesn't like 'em or trust 'em. But I told you that story already." I glanced at my watch. "Look, it's getting late, and tomorrow's a workday. Let's hit the sack. Good night, Dad. I love you, and thanks for being here."

He smiled and drained the last of his wine from the glass. "I love you, too. See you in the morning."

I checked on the children and finally lay down beside Debbie. She moved closer to me in her sleep as I lay on top of the covers, my hands behind my neck. I watched the fan on the ceiling spin as I lost myself in thought and quietly drifted into sleep.

My eyes opened to the darkness of the room. Above me the fan stopped cold in its tracks. I lay there for a moment, staring at the ceiling, trying to see the rest of the room with my peripheral vision. I couldn't feel Debbie next to me on the bed. I was alone. I tried to call her name, but nothing came from my mouth, as if some powerful thing refused to let air or sound escape from me. Again I tried to speak, but my throat only grew tighter.

I tried to raise myself, but the pressure of a dozen unseen hands pressed me back into the bed. I tried to scream, but couldn't make a sound. All that came from me was a gagging hiss of air. My arms wouldn't leave the position they were in, and I felt as though I were sinking into the bed, deeper, deeper. I could see nothing but blackness, like the blackness I'd seen in the desert—a blackness that brought with it a light from an unseen source. It filled the room. In sheer terror, I rolled my head from side to side, desperately trying to free my body from whatever held it fast to the bed. I tried to sit up or move my legs or roll, but I could not move. My heart raced, pounding so hard it felt like a foreign object, attached to me but not *of* me. Suddenly, the sound of a harsh wind pierced my ears. As I watched in horror, the room and everything in it folded upon itself and me . . . and then there was utter darkness and silence. It lasted only a blink, and I found myself resting on all fours in some unknown place. The ground was crimson and magenta and it sparkled from every angle. Not moving my arms and legs I raised my head to the horizon to see a torn and broken landscape, everything washed in strange mixes of blue and crimson.

Everything in sight, even the sky, was a swirling mass of color and movement. A dull, hot wind touched my face and dragged across the landscape, bringing with it small crystals the size of coarse sand. They stung my exposed skin, and I raised my arm to protect my face. Peering through the crook of my arm, I squinted hard to survey my position. I was alone, as far as I could see. There were no structures, no mountains, no trees, nothing but the cracked surface beneath me, and the crystalline dust. I felt my body to see if it was real.

A sound unlike anything I'd heard cut through the constant rush of the wind. I snapped my head, cocking it as a dog might, straining to get a bearing on its direction. Again I heard it! I spun on my heels, facing into the wind, pointed my body in the direction of the sound, and leaned forward, pushing my way toward it, my face protected by my arms. The sound grew in intensity as I weaved along. I thought several times that I could make out what it was saying. Every time I seemed to be within a few feet of it, close enough to seize it, the wind washed it away, leaving me to change direction once again.

I could barely make out an opening in something ahead of me. As I drew nearer, the mouth of a small cave presented itself. I entered it, leaving much of the noise behind. In front of me, a strange glow replaced the darkness. Ahead of me—at a guess, about twenty feet—I saw a blurred figure standing in the cave, its image moving wavelike in the glow. The noise came again. It was my name. "David," the figure called. I could see nothing but the pale outline of a being. It looked transparent, even hollow, yet it was not. Again it called my name.

"Who are you? What do you want?" I screamed at the being. It made no movement. It did nothing but call my name again.

Again I screamed, "Who are you? Where am I?" I clawed toward it, screaming as loud as I could. "Who the hell are you?" I stumbled and fell at the creature's feet, snapped to my knees, and looked up at it in contempt. My eyes burned into it and I swung at it with my fists, fighting to stand as I did so. My limbs passed through the being, leaving no trace. I swung and struck out at it again and again until, exhausted, my arms dropped to my sides. I stood there, head down and beaten, as though I'd tried to fight a scarecrow.

Emotion overcame me. I began to weep, dazed and muddled. I slowly raised my head to look into the face of the being and the shock of the vision stung my heart. It was *my* face that the being wore. "Jesus!" I screamed, striking out again. I plunged my fists into it once, twice, three, then four times, and then reeled to run away out of the cave and into the storm again. As I ran, I could hear it laughing behind me. The farther I ran from it, the louder the laughter became until I was certain the being was running after me, trying to overtake me. Turning my head to look over my shoulder as I ran, I lost my footing and fell hard. My face smacked on the flat surface, and my eyes closed at the impact. Stunned, I tried to climb to my feet, the laughter all around me . . . an evil, hideous laughter. Instantly, hands were all over my body, grasping at my arms, my head, my legs. I kicked and screamed aloud, fighting off whatever had hold of me.

"David! David, stop!" The air grew cold and the noise of the wind was gone. "David, stop kicking—we're trying to help you. David!" The voices came from different mouths all around me. "David! Open your eyes, son. It's Dad. Open your eyes!" I stopped struggling and lay there feeling the coolness and moisture of the ground on my cheek. I opened my eyes to see concerned faces: my mother's, my father's, Debbie's.

"Are you all right, honey?" Debbie stroked my hair with one hand resting on my shoulder, ready to push me into the ground again if she needed to. I heard my father's voice.

"He must have been walking in his sleep!"

Groaning, I rubbed my eyes and tried to find my voice, "What happened?"

Debbie caressed my back. "You're outside," she said, "on the back lawn. You had a nightmare or something; we heard you screaming out here, and you were thrashing around on the ground like you were fighting something. Your mother heard you first."

"I thought there was a prowler or something—I didn't know what to think. You scared me to death," my mother said. She stood next to my father, holding his hand.

I raised myself to a sitting position, head down and arms folded in front of my knees. "Jeez," I grumbled, still somewhat dazed. "I've never had anything like that happen before. I'm sorry to scare all of you. I don't know what happened. Must have been all that Chinese food, huh?" Everyone gave a guarded chuckle.

"I've eaten a lot of Chinese food in my life," Dad said, "but I've never ended up on the lawn because of it. You need to get this checked out, son."

Debbie put in, "He's been going through this ever since he was shot in the head."

"Shot in the head?" my mother shouted.

"Aw, Debbie! You didn't need to say anything about that, goddamn it."

She snapped back, "Oh yes I did. You've been having problems since it happened, and it's time people know about it, and you get some attention for it. I can't go on shaking you out of your nightmares, or quieting your screams, or picking you up off the lawn every morning. Damn it, I'm tired of it. You need to get some help."

Mom pointed at me, her words cutting the way they did when I was a child. "I can't believe it, David. You mean you got shot and you didn't bother telling us about it? Do you know how angry that makes me?"

"Christ, son. Why didn't you tell us?" Dad shook his head in disbelief.

"Well, I didn't—"

Debbie finished the sentence for me. "Because he didn't want anyone to worry about him. He'd rather you chase him through the woods like a lunatic than get medical help."

"Damn it all," I said, forcing myself to my feet. "It wasn't this bad at first. It's just been getting worse lately, that's all. I've been talking to the psychologist at the unit about it."

"Oh? And what's he say?" Mom asked. "You probably ought to be in the hospital."

"No! I don't need to be in the hospital. That's the last place I need to be. I just need to get some rest. I'll tell the doctor about this in the morning." I walked toward the house. "Good night, everyone. I apologize for getting you all up."

I lay down on the bed I had unconsciously left, and stared at the moving fan. I didn't close my eyes again that night.

The next morning I was nursing a hot cup of coffee outside Dr. Barker's office door, waiting for him to arrive. When he did, I spent an hour relating the events of the night to him.

"Well, it sounds very interesting, although I'm not sure

what to make of it. Have you ever experienced somnambulism—sleepwalking—before this?''

"I don't know. Nobody's ever had to wake me up before, but who knows what's happened when I don't make so much noise? I mean, who's to say this hasn't *all* been a symptom of sleepwalking?''

"That's a good point, but everything you've talked about so far fits the mold. . . . You say it was your face you saw?''

"That's right. What did it mean?''

"Actually, I have no idea what that might have meant. It was unlike anything you'd experienced prior to this. It may be some manifestation of the tempest inside you, the fight that is happening in you every day. You're confused about what you were shown, what the message you were given means. If I were to hazard a guess, I'd say those unanswered questions are prompting these visions. The cave and the being itself also interest me, but we'll save the discussion of those for another time. Okay?''

"Fine, but I have to do something about it. I can't go on living like this. In fact, I don't consider this living at all—it's more like existing. I don't know from one minute to the next what is going to happen. Every time I close my eyes I wonder if I'm going to end up in the woods or on the street, in some shopping mall, or stepping through some portal and going into a world I might never come back from. Did that ever occur to you, that I might not come back?''

"Hmm.'' Barker frowned. "Stay right here, I want to make a call. But before I do, I want you to know that I'm encouraged by this, and I want you to be as well.''

"Encouraged? What the fuck is encouraging about it?''

He raised his hand to me as if to say, Calm down. "Just wait, you'll see what I mean. I think I have the right answers for you.''

With that he picked up the phone and called a number I couldn't make out. "Hello, Bill? It's Innis. Do you remember the individual I told you about? . . . I'd like to bring him over to meet you, tomorrow morning if possible. . . .

Good, we'll be there around eight-thirty. Looking forward to seeing you.'' He hung up and smiled broadly. "Let's meet here early tomorrow, and we'll take a trip to Fort Meade. I want you to meet some people there.''

I had a pretty good idea who he wanted me to meet, but I wanted it from his mouth. "Meet who?''

Barker paused for a moment as if he were thinking that perhaps he had rushed too quickly into this. "Well, I didn't want to alarm you, but I've been talking to these people about you ever since our first meeting.''

"You have?''

"Yes, I have. In fact, I must confess that I've been watching you out of the corner of my eye ever since I reviewed your psychological profile. You have all the indicators that would lead me to believe that you would do well in this unit.''

"What unit?''

"The unit responsible for the files you have been reviewing.''

"You want me to join them.''

"The thought did cross my mind, but it's not that simple. You don't just walk in there. They have to want you. If they do want you, then nothing can stop them from getting you. On the other hand, if they don't want you, then we will have to explore some other options for helping you cope with this new gift you have.''

Barker and I drove to Fort Meade the next morning. At eight-thirty we pulled into an asphalt driveway that led toward two long one-story buildings partially obscured by giant oak trees. Barker stopped in the small parking lot adjacent to them. There were six other cars scattered around the lot. We approached the building on the left, the longer of the two. It had a large, heavy metal door guarding the entrance, and security screens were bolted over all the windows. Paint peeled off the surface of the building as though it were a snake sloughing its skin. Frankly, it looked like hell. Weeds snarled the sidewalk and clung to the green wooden stairway leading to the front door. I remember that as Barker knocked, I thought to myself that a kid armed with a small hammer would be capable of penetrating this building to reveal the secrets inside. Maybe they protected it with their minds, I laughed to myself.

The door opened slowly, and a round chubby face peered at us from the small opening. "Dr. Barker. Hello, hello, hello. Come on in, Mr. Levy is expecting you."

"Great! Jenny, this is Captain Morehouse, the young man I've been telling Bill about. Dave, this is Jenny Eastman." She glanced at me and smiled politely. "Hi! Nice to meet you. Come this way; I'll see if he's ready."

I tried to catch my breath as I looked at the scene I'd walked into. In front of me was an enormous mural, an image of a galaxy filled with crimson and magenta gas clouds. It made the hair stand up on the back of my neck. A couple of men stood next to a coffeepot to the right of the mural. They stared at me as I walked with Barker toward the office of the man we had come to see. A dark-complexioned man with a slight build emerged from the door to an office. A wide smile spread across his face at the sight of Barker.

"Welcome, Dr. Barker." The man snatched Barker's hand and pumped it up and down. "It's been a good while since you were here to visit."

"Oh, well, yes." Barker pulled his hand away from the man and took his glasses off to clean them, as if it were an excuse to reclaim his limb. He motioned to me with his elbow. "This is the young man we've been talking about."

I didn't know what to do. I tried to look intelligent, or humble, or something. I stuck my hand out to shake his, but I was too late. He had looked me over and turned to haul Barker into the office. He told Jenny to introduce me around to the rest of the office.

She came out from behind her desk and swiped her hand through the air. "This is it. It's not much to look at, but we call it home."

The building was long and narrow, consisting of one big

open bay that was sectioned off into cubicles. You could stand at one end and see all the way to the other without obstruction. The floor was covered with brown commercial carpeting and the office furniture was the standard Defense Department gray metal. An entire wall just to the left of the front entrance was lined with five-drawer file safes for the storage of classified documents. There were two small offices on either side of the building, about a third of the way down from the receptionist's desk. One of the offices was inhabited by Mr. Levy; the other was a collection of boxes plus a copier and a shredder used for classified documents.

Jenny walked me over to where the two gentlemen were still standing, obviously talking about something they didn't want me to know about. One of them saw us approaching and nudged the other to get him to change topics. Both men turned and looked at me with flat and curious smiles. I caught some of their conversation as we approached. Some of the words they used were familiar to me from the folders Barker had given me to read.

"This is Mel Riley," Jenny said, handing my arm to him as if I were a child.

"And you are?" Riley responded, shifting his coffee cup over so that he could shake my hand. Riley had a kind face with pale blue eyes. He was a medium-sized man, a little thin, with gray hair parted on the side. As he shook my hand I noticed the strength of his grip and the intense warmth of his flesh.

"Dave Morehouse. Nice to meet you."

"Are you sure about that?"

Jenny slapped Riley on the arm. "Always trying to be funny, aren't you? Don't you pay any attention to him." She turned me toward the other man.

"And this is Paul Posner." Posner was tall, trim and muscular, his hair slicked back against his head like a mobster's.

"Hi. Dave Morehouse," I said, reaching for his hand.

"Call me Paul," he said expressionlessly. "We've been

expecting you. Heard some interesting things about you, too.'' The way he said that made me uncomfortable; he had one of those I-know-something-you-don't-know looks. It kind of pissed me off. His handshake was firm but brief. It was as if he had some energy he was protecting, and he was afraid that I might steal it if he held on too long. I later learned he was the senior captain in the unit.

Both slurped their coffee noisily as they watched Jenny drag me farther back into the office. I could feel their eyes on me the entire time.

Jenny led me past the receptionist's desk and into a small cubicle where a man sat staring at a computer screen. Recognizing a new presence in the building, the man awkwardly tried to free himself from one of those back-saving computer chairs. Jenny started to chuckle as he fought his way out of the chair's grasp and nearly fell in front of us.

''That thing's gonna kill you yet, Lyn,'' she laughed.

''Yeah,'' the man said, looking back at the chair that had nearly laid him out. ''The damned thing's looking more like firewood every day. Hi! I'm Lyn Buchanan.'' Lyn was a kindly man, a bit older than me. His eyes sparkled with goodness; it gave me a wonderful feeling just being next to him for that short while. I looked down at his feet, and his eyes followed mine to the floor. His bare toes wiggled a friendly wave.

I snorted a laugh, pointing at his feet.

''Oh, yeah. Forgot my socks this morning.''

Jenny folded her arms across her chest. ''That's like anyone else saying they forgot their shoes at home, since socks are all he wears in the building.'' She glared at Buchanan.

He looked at me. ''It's more comfortable this way.''

''I don't blame you . . . I may give it a try myself,'' I said, offering some political support. He grinned.

Jenny snatched my arm and pulled me toward the next cubicle. ''This is where—Hello? Are you guys in here?'' She stuck her head around the corner. ''Ahh, there you are. I want you two to meet David Morehouse. He's the man Dr. Barker was telling us about.''

The two were sitting at their respective desks; a man and a woman. Both stood almost in unison to greet me. I reached for the man's hand first. "Hi. Dave Morehouse . . . how are you?"

The man stood a good four inches taller than me, with a bearlike posture and physique. He smiled warmly from behind extremely thick glasses. He had huge hands and thinning hair. More than anyone so far, he expressed genuine pleasure at the meeting. "I'm Pratt Orsen. I've heard about you."

I nodded. "That's what everyone's saying. I hope it's not all bad."

"Not a word of it." He motioned toward the woman. "This is my officemate, Kathleen Miller." Kathleen was a pretty brunette, thin and timid. She refused to make eye contact as we shook hands.

As we stood there for an awkward moment, I glanced at Pratt's desk and surroundings. His desk was barely visible under a cascade of books and papers on art, music, and the paranormal. The floor was littered with crumpled papers and snack food wrappers, fast food bags, and old soda cans. The expression on my face must have been obvious.

He turned and glanced at the mess. "Oh. I like to read. But I admit I'm kind of messy." He grinned, his eyes magnified by his thick glasses.

Kathleen chimed in with a shy smile. "Actually, he cleaned it up this morning because he knew you were coming."

"Well. I didn't clean it up"—Pratt snorted—"I just shoved it all into one pile."

Jenny said, "That's it! That's all of us. Let's go back up to the front and see if Mr. Levy is ready for you yet, shall we?"

I waved at the pair and backed out of the cubicle. "I'll see you later, I guess."

Jenny sat me down in front of that bizarre mural, in a small cluster of chairs that they called the lobby. I waited there for several minutes, watching Paul and Mel, who were still standing at the coffeepot, carrying on their conversation.

A few minutes later, Barker and Levy came out of the office. Barker motioned for me to come to them. "David, Mr. Levy would like to have a word with you now."

"Yes, David, won't you please follow me?" He led me into his office.

The entire room was lined in dead plants. Not a thing was alive in the office, nor had it been for some time. There must have been twenty of the shriveled, dry things around the room. He motioned for me to sit in a large overstuffed chair directly in front of his desk. As he sat down, he picked up a pencil and began playing with it, spinning the eraser on each of his fingertips in succession, over and over again.

"So! I have to say that I'm always amazed there are still young military people who are willing to give it all up to become a part of this effort." He focused on his fingers, never once looking at me.

I cleared my throat and shifted my weight in the chair. "I'm not certain of any of that, sir," I said nervously. "I'm not sure I understand what I'd be giving up—or, more important, what I'd be giving it up for. I mean—"

Levy cut me off. "And just what is it that you think we do?"

"Well, I think you engage in some sort of out-of-body experiments . . . or something like—"

He cut me off again. "No, that's not what we do." He leaned forward and stared directly into my eyes. "What we do here is train individuals to transcend time and space, to view persons, places, and things remote in time and space, and to gather intelligence information on them." He paused, still staring into my eyes. "That is what we do here. Now, your next question will most likely be 'How do we do that?' which is something I will not answer unless you are fortunate enough to join us. What I want to do now is determine if you are the caliber of individual we would want. What you'd be giving up is your life as you know it today. You would not leave here the same man as you arrived.''

"Exactly what does that mean?''

"It means just what I said: you will be changed, permanently. I'd like to believe for the good, but there have been some exceptions to that; however, they are few and far between. You needn't worry about that now. All I need to know is whether or not you are interested. Beyond that, the decision is very much mine.''

As he spoke, the hair stood up on the back of my neck and my palms began to sweat. This man made me more nervous than anyone I'd ever met. He rambled on for several minutes, but I can't remember what he said. I only tuned in again toward the end.

"So, we have a few tests for you. Pratt will give those to you; you may take them home. Dr. Barker will see to it that they are returned to us, and we'll let you know something as soon as the results are in. Okay? Now before we proceed, I want to know if you are interested in the program. Again, I realize that you've been given limited information, but that will have to do for now. What do you say?''

I stood, wishing I'd paid more attention. "Uh . . .'' I tried to review the consequences of what I was about to say, but I couldn't tally them fast enough. Finally, I followed my instincts. "Yes, sir, I'm very much interested.''

Levy took a deep breath, letting it out slowly. "Fine, then. We'll be in touch.'' He motioned toward the door.

"Thank you for your time, sir. I hope to see you again.''

Barker said his farewells as I moved toward the front door. Pratt Orsen pulled some documents from one of the safe drawers and hustled toward me.

"Here, David. Mr. Levy would like you to complete these.''

"Thanks,'' I said, taking the papers. "I hope I get to see you again.''

"I'm sure you will. One thing that might help: answer the questions on those documents as though you were the person you'd like to be, as opposed to the person you are.'' He could see I didn't understand. ''Put yourself into a mind-set free of any hostility or animosity. Answer the questions in a spirit of humility.'' He slapped me on the shoulder. ''Don't look so worried—you'll do fine.''

Barker and I climbed into his car as the heavy metal door of the unit clicked shut behind us. We sped down the driveway and made our way back to the Beltway. Barker was in a hurry to get back to the unit; he had a meeting later in the afternoon at the Pentagon. He checked his watch several times, mumbling to himself about the length of time we'd spent at Sun Streak.

''I know you're a little preoccupied, but I have a question,'' I said. Barker just stared ahead at the road. ''Levy alluded to a downside for all of this. What's the downside?''

''Well, there are risks—emotional, physical, and spiritual risks, to name the most critical ones.''

''Those are pretty significant!'' I said. ''Exactly how are they risks?''

''Let's save that for when and if these guys select you. Then I'll fill you in on everything else. Just understand that nothing in life comes without consequences. There are tradeoffs—and if you trade your 'nightmares' and visions for a little peace and understanding, you'll have to give up something in return.''

''Well, is it deadly?''

Barker glanced at me. ''I don't know. I'm not sure anyone knows the answer to that, really. We suspect that some trainees have had problems as a result of the training, but those people should have been screened out before they got to that point. We've gotten a lot better at picking the right candidates.'' He smiled. ''Don't worry, you have what we're looking for. I'd bet anything that you'll have nothing but good results from this. I think it will really help with everything going on inside your head.''

''Okay, I bow to your judgment.'' I settled back and closed my eyes for the rest of the trip.

That night, I said nothing to Debbie or my parents about the meeting at Fort Meade. Weighing the impact, I figured I'd wait until I knew more.

I completed Levy's tests and turned them in to Barker at the end of the week. I heard nothing from Sun Streak, and as far as I knew, Barker didn't have any contact with them either. He gave me more documents to review. They concerned the Soviet Union's involvement in remote viewing and related parapsychological studies. The documents were all old classified messages, many of which pre-dated Sun Streak's inception in the 1970s. Most of them were CIA traffic about a program funded by the government and conducted at Stanford Research Institute in California. From the documents it was clear that this was where our program had originated.

Barker supplemented my classified reading with open-source literature from various research programs, as well as books written by some of the early researchers like Dr. Russel Targ and Harold Puthoff. These books illustrated what a remote viewer could do, but the authors were careful never to mention any involvement with the government. At this stage it didn't matter. It was obvious when you took all the information in context that the U.S. government was heavily involved with parapsychological research on many fronts, not just in the area of remote viewing. They were focusing efforts on anything that might enhance human performance potential: sleep learning, subliminal messages, psychokinesis, and a host of others. Several general officers were mentioned prominently—officers like Major General Bert Stubblebine, the former commander of the U.S. Army's Intelligence Security Command (INSCOM) housed just down the road from the Pentagon, and Lieutenant General Mike Thompson, the former Deputy Chief of Staff for Intelligence. Thompson was the number one intelligence officer in the U.S. Army. Stubblebine appeared to be one of the bravest and most visionary of any of them, a man who recognized the potential of all the paranormal "technologies" and was willing to put his career on the line to support them. In one of the INSCOM memorandums I was shown, he stated that we "have no reason to exclude any science or body of knowledge that might enhance our intelligence collection capability . . . any degree of information is better than the absence of information." The rumor supplied by Barker was that Stubblebine paid a very high price—he was forced to resign—for supporting work with the paranormal. In short, he had been too up-front about what he was doing. He had opened too many doors for everyone's comfort and he had become too visible in his involvement. Because he believed in what he was doing, and supported a controversial science, he was sacrificed. The once fairly visible research programs went quickly underground, never to surface again. It was obvious from reading the documents that Sun Streak had its enemies, from prayer groups in the Pentagon to congressmen and general officers willing to kill it at all costs. I asked myself time and again what had kept it alive for all these years. The government was funding paranormal research in half a dozen private and as many state and federal research centers across the United States. They were pumping tens of millions of dollars into remote viewing and various related techniques. But the project and those affiliated with it were set into a class by themselves, no longer part of the intelligence community. They were feared, ridiculed, scoffed at, mocked, and ostracized. Yet somewhere, someone in a position of power was intrigued. Something fueled the program's fire, and from my readings that could only mean one thing: it worked.

But weeks passed and I heard nothing from the unit. I kept having nightmares, which were taking their toll on the family. Mom and Dad had returned home to California shortly after my nocturnal visit to the cave, so now Debbie was alone in dealing with all of this. I felt that I was growing sicker, and I was convinced that Sun Streak was my only help.

*   *   *

"Hey! Guess what?" Barker came running into my office slamming the door behind him, his eyes huge behind his glasses. "They want you! Can you believe it? Of course you can believe it. I told you so!" He shook the message in front of him, holding it with both hands. "They want you to report right away. As soon as I got this from the S-1, I called Levy. They want you tomorrow, if they can get you. Do you realize how exciting this is? Aren't you excited? We did it!"

I smiled, more at his reaction than anything. "Yeah, that's great news." But I immediately thought about what I was going to have to say to Debbie and the children, and the smile left my face.

"What's the matter? You still want to go, don't you?"

"Sure, I want to go. I'm just running over everything I'll have to do to get ready, that's all."

"Great!" he said. "I'm going to go tell the boss right away. You can go and see the S-1 and get your orders taken care of." Barker flung himself out of my office and darted across the hall to the command group to present our chief, Colonel Tony Messina, with a copy of the memo from the Defense Intelligence Agency.

I saw that memo later. It read: "The undersigned (Commander, Defense Intelligence Agency) authorizes the assignment of Captain David A. Morehouse to the Directorate of Technology and Science of this headquarters effective immediately. Report date to be not later than five days from receipt of this message. Direct coordination with this headquarters and DT-S is authorized. Early report date is authorized."

I can only speculate what happened after Messina read the message. What I do know is that he screamed at Barker for about fifteen minutes before demanding that I report to him. It was obvious he was unhappy about Barker making arrangements for the reassignment of one of his officers behind his back; it was also apparent that he was a bit taken aback by my choice of units. Regardless, Barker took his ass-chewing as well as he could and gladly passed the baton to me when Messina demanded my presence.

"Get in here, Morehouse!" I opened the door and walked toward his desk to stand at attention. Nobody ever did that here, but under the circumstances I couldn't help myself.

"Captain Morehouse reporting as ordered, sir!"

"Close the fucking door, Morehouse, and let's talk," he snapped back at me, never returning the salute. "Just what the hell is going on here? Barker comes in here this afternoon and presents me with some fucking orders for you to report to this unit called Sun Streak. Do you have any idea what you're getting yourself into? Do you have any idea how pissed off I am that you and Barker have been working this thing backchannel, behind my back?" He paused for a moment to glare at me and catch his breath.

"Yes, sir, I think I do. However, I didn't realize that—"

"Didn't realize what? That I might be pissed?"

"No, sir, that you knew nothing about it, sir."

"All right, let's skip over all that shit. It doesn't matter much anyway at this point—you have orders, and I assume you have accepted the assignment. That leaves me with only one option, and that is to tell you how fucking stupid I think this choice of yours is. Do you have any idea what this unit does?"

"Yes, sir!" I responded still standing at attention.

"Morehouse? Sit the fuck down and let me try and talk some sense into you. This unit is nothing but a bunch of fucking freaks. Do you hear me? They are fucking freaks and nothing good has ever come of anybody or anything affiliated with it. Now please tell me why you, with your service record, want to go to a unit like this. Please tell me what you were thinking when you said yes."

I couldn't look him in the eyes. He was so full of rage— and, oddly enough, I felt pity. "Sir, it's a combination of things. I'm not the happiest camper here. It's got nothing to do with you or anything. . . . I just don't fit in, in this unit. I'm not a spook, I'm an infantryman."

Messina jumped on that. "Do you realize how asinine that sounds when you're on your way to a bunch of out-of-body fuckers?"

I dropped my head, realizing that it did sound pretty foolish. "Yes, sir, but it's something I'm convinced I want to do. I really want to be a part of this unit and learn what it is that they do."

His fist hit the center of his desk. "Damn it, Morehouse! Your record has 'Destined to wear stars' written all over it by general officers; you're an above-center-of-mass officer and you will be commanding a battalion someday if you keep up the current performance level. Don't you realize that you're giving all that up if you go to this assignment? You don't just go to something like this and then walk away three years from now—it's crazy."

"Yes, sir, I understand that there will be changes. But I'm ready to take my chances on everything else." I wondered if Messina was right, and I was wrong for listening to Barker. I mean, a man I respected a great deal was re-affirming that I was going places in the army . . . and I was arguing with him. All I knew was what Barker and Levy had told me. Was I making the right decision?

Messina scowled at the orders once again, and threw them into his hold box. "I'll tell you what I'm going to do. I'm going to make you sit on this for a few days while I try to knock some sense into your head. I don't have to release you until I get ready to, so you take two or three days to think about this. Have you told Debbie about it yet?"

"No, sir, I've been waiting for the right moment."

"You'd better include her in a decision like this, or else step across the hall and see the lawyer, because this unit has a reputation for breaking things up. Yes, sir, you'd better make damned sure she knows exactly what you're getting yourself into—damned sure!" With that Messina dismissed me abruptly.

Over the next two days Messina summoned me into his office repeatedly for brief sessions during which he would all but beg me not to end my career by joining Sun Streak. Sometimes he was pleasant about it; at other times he would extract a pound of flesh. But each time I politely refused his offers to stay at Sacred Cape.

Reluctantly, on the third day, a Wednesday, he bade me Godspeed with these words: "I told you, nothing good has ever come from that unit. I've watched it destroy lives and careers. I can't imagine why you want to do this." Those were his last words to me. I began out-processing that afternoon.

I still hadn't told Debbie about Sun Streak; it was just too far out on the fringe for her to be comfortable with. I'd thought it best to lie low until all the decisions had been made. We went for a walk that evening after supper.

"Remember I told you and Mom and Dad that I was looking for some help with the nightmares?" I asked her. She only nodded, never taking her eyes off the sidewalk. "Well, I talked to Lieutenant Colonel Innis Barker, the psychologist at the unit, about them, and he—"

"I know who you've been talking to, David. Colonel Messina called me on Monday and told me all about it." She went on to say that he'd issued prodigious warnings that I would never be the same if I went to Sun Streak. He testified to her of the horrors he had seen in that unit and he urged her to put a stop to the transfer if at all possible.

"Shit!" I muttered. "Why didn't you—"

"Tell you? Why should I have to tell you? Don't you think it's important enough for you to approach me with? My God, David, you're going to a unit that plays with people's minds, and you didn't even tell me about it. Didn't even ask my opinion! What the hell's gotten into you?"

"I'm sorry, honey, I didn't think—"

"That's right, you didn't think. How could you plan something that dangerous and not include your family? Don't you realize that every decision you make, good or bad, affects us directly? And what about your mother and father?"

I started to get angry. "Oh, so you don't want me to do

it, either, is that it? Just because I didn't talk to you about it—which I would have done before I ever committed myself to the job."

"David, that's a bunch of crap! Colonel Messina told me that as far as he was concerned you'd already made your decision. So as far as I can see there's no use in our even discussing it, is there?"

"That's not true, Debbie! I held off making any decision or even talking to you about this until all the decisions outside our family were made. I didn't want to frighten you or bother you until I knew for sure what my options were. That's all I was trying to do!"

"So," she asked, her eyes tearing, "are you going to do it?"

"That depends."

"On what?"

"On what you think. But before you make any decisions, I want you to understand that this may be my ticket out of the nightmares. This unit knows how to control that stuff. Debbie, these guys do some of the most awesome stuff. Come on, honey. Isn't it intriguing and exciting?"

"No! It sounds too farfetched to be true. They're still playing with your mind."

I took a deep breath, kicking a pine cone off the walk. "Look, I understand why you're worried. But this is a chance to explore something only a handful of people have ever gotten the chance to explore. I just can't pass this up— and, quite frankly, the more people argue with me about it, the more sense it makes to me that I should just do it. Think of it: I can be trained to traverse time and space, to see and experience anything and everything I want to experience. How the hell can I pass that up? I'm going to do it, honey. I've got to do it!"

"Then for the first time in our marriage you are doing something without my blessing. And God help us," she said sadly.

I turned her toward me and I kissed a tear away, staring into her eyes and seeing the warmth and love. "I know you're worried about me. I can't tell you how comforted and secure it makes me feel to know you're always there for me, you love me, you support me. I can't imagine doing something without you by my side . . . all the way. Please think about it a little more before you shut me out completely.'' She nodded slightly. ''When I report in, I'm sure there will be something they'll share with you, and if not, I'll bring home anything I can to let you know what's going on. I'll keep you posted every step of the way in the training process. Okay?''

Her lips pressed tightly together, Debbie fought back the flow of tears. Her intuition told her that this wasn't a good thing. But she believed in me and she had always supported me . . . how could she not support me now? ''I'll give you some time,'' she said. ''We'll see what happens after you get there. But you have to promise me that you'll leave it if I ask you to. Do you promise?''

''Cross my heart . . . I promise.'' I kissed her.

FOUR

THE TRAINING

That winter of 1988, the first snow fell on the day I started at Sun Streak. We hadn't moved from Fort Belvoir yet, so I was making the long drive to Fort Meade. The trip took me an hour and a half in that first snowfall because I didn't really know where the office was. I missed the turnoff to the Baltimore–Washington Parkway and had to double back. When I finally exited the parkway and made my way down the small back road to Meade, I had to fight another car for the right to merge. It was some little bluish gray Mustang, and the woman driving it refused to let me in. We glared at each other, each struggling to hold ground. Running out of road, I was forced to step on the brakes and let her pass. She glanced at me in her rearview mirror and flipped me the bird as a victory salute. *Great fucking day!* I thought.

I made my way onto the post, trying to figure out where the unit was hiding. All I remembered was that it consisted of two old white wooden buildings nestled in a clump of huge oaks. With every turn, I was still in back of the little Mustang. I passed the post library, which I half remembered, and the theater as well. Finally the two white buildings came into view. I was only thirty minutes late on my first day.

My heart stopped as the Mustang turned left into the long driveway that led to the front of the buildings. I turned down the drive and parked alongside the bluish gray car, then got out and walked around it to face my tormentor.

"What the hell do you want, asshole?" A barroom growl from a rather innocent face. She had long straight brown hair draped over a petite frame. She clutched her purse in her right hand, ready to use it as a club if needed.

"Next time you try to cut someone off, you'd better have more car than you've got."

"So what do you want? Why did you follow me here?"

I wanted to give her a piece of my mind, but I bit my tongue. "I work here."

"Bullshit! You don't work here." And then it became clear to her. "Oh, my God. You're the new trainee from across the river, aren't you?"

"I'm afraid so." I smiled. "Sorry about back there at the parkway. I didn't mean—"

"Oh no . . . *I'm* sorry. I had no idea who you were." She smiled, extending her hand. "Hi, I'm Carol Bush."

"Dave Morehouse. I'm from Sacred Cape."

"I know, over there near Fairfax, right?"

"Yeah, right. I really mean it, I'm sorry about trying to merge on you like that. I just didn't know where I was going, and I was in a hurry."

"It's okay. Everybody gets crazy driving around here. Comes with the turf. Want some coffee?"

"Sure, that would be nice."

I didn't realize it then, but my first encounter with Carol was a harbinger of how things would be. I followed her to the door and watched as she punched in the key code. Once inside I recognized the painting of the galaxy on the wall, the massive file safes on the left, and the small waiting room and coffeepot to the right. Jenny Eastman jumped up from her desk, leaving behind a half-eaten bagel.

"Look who I found in the parking lot," said Carol, "ran off the road, flipped off, and cussed out."

"What?" Jenny asked. "You did *what?*"

"Oh, it wasn't like that," I countered. "We just fought for a little road space, that's all."

"And she flipped you the bird?" Jenny began to chuckle. "God, Carol, you really know how to make a person feel welcome." She reached for my arm and led me to the coffeepot. "Come over here with me and let's get some food into you."

Carol had left the welcome scene and was making her way to her desk. Over her shoulder she called, "Oh yeah—he'd like some coffee, Jenny. Could you take care of that?"

"You bet I can. Now, look, we have bagels, doughnuts, and some crackers here. And here's coffee and juice. We all pitch in five dollars a month, and I shop at the commissary to keep the fridge stocked. The coffee is half and half—that's half real stuff and half decaf. Now, since you're new, I'll let you slide for the month, and you won't be expected to contribute to the fund until the first. If you ever want a soda, they're pay-as-you-go. Just throw the money into the can here." She rattled the can for me.

"Now over here is the copier and right next to it is the shredder, that comes in handy given what we do here." Grabbing my hand, Jenny dragged me across the room. "This is the latrine. A cleaning team comes in on Tuesdays and Thursdays and you have to keep all classified put away until they leave. Over here next to it is the office supplies room." She paused. "Staying with me on all this?"

"Yeah, I think so."

"Good, because I move fast. I don't like to slow down for routine stuff. These are the safes where we keep all the training and operational materials. Every session ever done by this unit is right here. Yup, every one since 1978 is right here." She slapped the top of one of the ten file safes. "Back here is Mr. Levy's office—you remember that, I'll bet." She smirked. "And back there are the rest of the offices. Your desk is right here." She pointed to a gray metal desk sitting in a corner near a dirty grille-covered window. "Over here through this doorway is the back office. Oh, and there are some people I want you to meet. They weren't here when you visited."

I followed her through the opening to the right of my

desk, into a smoke-filled back room half the size of the space we'd just left.

Carol Bush sat puffing away at her desk. She had a black cloth spread out in front of her, and on it were about a dozen or so large cards with figures on them. She didn't look up but kept flipping and moving the cards from one stack to another.

"Playing a little solitaire?" I asked.

She looked at me, cigarette hanging from her lip. "Hardly." She broke her gaze and returned to the cards.

"Those are tarot cards, my dear. Some of us use them to keep a little polish in our work." The voice came from behind me, and I turned. "I'm Judy Kessler." She lofted her hand, palm down and pinkie extended. "And you must be . . ."

"Dave Morehouse," I said awkwardly. "I'm sorry, I didn't know what those were. I've never seen them before, except on television."

"Well, they're nothing to be frightened of; they're just tools. They help us do our job."

"Really?"

"Yes. If you'd like to learn how to use them, I'd be happy to show you."

"Sure . . . I'd like to know what they're about." Sitting next to Kessler was Mel Riley. Glancing at him, I noticed that his intent stare at the beads he was working on had turned into a frown. "Hey, Mel, how are you doing?"

He looked up slowly. "Good, Dave, really good. And you?"

"Well, I'm here, and that's where I wanted to be. So I'm happy." He only nodded and returned to his work. Mel, it turned out, was a student of just about everything relevant to American Indians. He knew their cultures, their religions, and their artwork and crafts. He would spend hours sewing tiny glass beads onto brain-tanned deerhide and other leathers. It was simply unbelievable what he could do. As the years passed and we became close friends, I would spend many an hour just watching him do beadwork. It was almost a spiritual experience; his demeanor and calm spread to everyone near him when he worked. He was always an anchor in this new world I was entering. Whenever I felt on the edge, Mel was there to bandage me, to help me understand the ways of the ether. He was, and is today, a true friend.

"Come on!" Jenny said. "We need to get you back up front to see Mr. Levy; he should be in the office now." We walked back through the cubicles to the front of the building.

After a few minutes, Levy appeared. He poured himself a cup of coffee and nodded for me to follow him. With the door closed behind us, he took a seat in the chair next to me. "Let's talk about your training program, shall we? I've assigned Mel as your trainer; he seems to like you. He was one of the very first viewers and I've not found anyone who grasps the theory the way he does. I plan on him taking you through the lecture phase; after that he'll pass you on to Kathleen. She's an excellent viewer and has the patience of Job. She'll take you all the way through Stage Seven training. I may switch you around from time to time, so don't be alarmed."

"Switch me around? I'm afraid I don't understand."

"I'll switch trainers and monitors on you, to round out your exposure. I've not done that before and I think it's time we give it a try. So, periodically, you'll be assigned one of the other operational members of the unit. 'Operational' means that they've completed all their training and are currently validated and are working real targets—I mean intelligence targets. Your first targets, during training that is, will be selected at random from the training files. They are targets with a significant signature and a good deal of known data. The data allow us to give you immediate feedback." I must have looked confused. "Are you getting any of this?" he asked cautiously.

I laughed out loud. "Well, I'm certainly trying."

Levy laughed too. "I guess I'm giving you the firehose treatment. I'll back off a bit. Mel can fill you in on every-

thing you need to know from here. Right now I want you
to read the historical files and get a feel for how and why
this program came into existence. You should come away
from the building today having a general idea of what the
Soviets, Chinese, and Czechs have going in this paranormal
arena. The rest will come in due time. Okay?''

"Yes, sir.''

Levy led me to a couple of stand-alone file safes and
dialed in the combination, mouthing the numbers to himself
so loud that I could almost make them out. "Start here,''
he said, "and work your way back and down to the last
drawer. You can pull the folders out, and carry them to
your desk for reading. Just make sure you replace them in
order. Got it?''

"Got it.'' I grabbed a thick slab of the folders, carried
them to the desk, and began to muddle through the musty-
smelling things. Soviet programs, KGB cover-ups, names,
faces, places, the Central Intelligence Agency, Stanford Research Institute . . . I couldn't believe it—this program had
been in existence since early 1974, for nearly fifteen years.
It wasn't experimental any longer. Christ, they knew it
worked—they'd proven that at Stanford, and all the evidence was here. There were books written on the stuff by
the researchers involved; nobody paid any attention to
them. The books didn't mention the intelligence involvement, but evidence of government funding and management was all over the place. There were illustrations of
machines manufactured in the Soviet Union that allegedly
could disrupt human brainwaves, causing nausea, stupor,
vertigo, even death. There were diagrams of "energy
alarms'' for detecting the presence of remote viewers or
other foreign energy sources. There were descriptions of
"remote mental manipulators,'' whose principal focus was
to access the mind of another human being and kill him.
I'd thought I had a grip on what I was getting involved in,
but now I realized I had only the faintest notion.

Several hours passed as I pored over the files, making

trip after trip to the safe for new ones. I'd lost all track of time.

"Are you ready for some lunch?" Mel asked, coming up behind me.

"Sure. I'm getting a little burned-out looking at these files. What did you have in mind, Burger King?"

"Hell, no! I don't eat fast food. You like chili?"

"Chili sounds great. You have a favorite greasy spoon somewhere?"

"Yup, my house. You can eat some of the best venison chili God ever put on this earth. Grab your coat, it's in walking distance."

We walked out the front door and headed across a field to Riley's place. He lived in military housing at Fort Meade, about a half mile from the office.

At his house, Riley made me feel like a king. "Sit here," he said, pointing to the lounge chair that was obviously his place. I tried to decline but my new friend insisted. "We'll have to be quiet, Edith is asleep upstairs." He noticed the puzzled look on my face. "Edith's my wife; she's a critical care nurse—works all night, sleeps all day. She's also very psychic. Almost as good as me"—he smiled—"but not quite."

"Oh."

"Well, you watch the news, and I'll warm up the chili. Keep the volume down, though—Edith will kill us both if we wake her."

Mel scurried into the kitchen to prepare lunch while I watched CNN.

"The top stories today," the anchor began. "President Bush canceled several top-level meetings due to illness. Sources say that the President is suffering from the flu, and that he should be able to resume his schedule in a few days."

"Mel, did you hear that?" I asked as I poked my head into the small kitchen. "They said the President was canceling some of his meetings because of illness."

"What did they say he had?"

"They said it was the flu. Can you imagine that, the flu? I don't think I've ever heard of a president getting the flu and canceling meetings because of it. Don't they give him flu shots and stay on top of that kind of stuff?" Mel handed me a bowl of chili. "I read this morning," I went on, "that one of those weapons the Soviets built could bring on flu-like symptoms. Do you suppose that had anything to do with it?"

"Sink your teeth into that, and try to talk about anything else." Riley said grinning. "Hope you like it hot!" He took a big mouthful and thought as he chewed. "You'll be surprised what you see happening in the world around you as you progress in your training. It's a very strange sensation to have a different kind of knowledge about everything. I don't want to muddy the waters for you right now, it's way too early. Suffice it to say that what you thought was normal, what you and everyone else in this world around us takes for granted, just might not be what you think it is. I mean, already you're speculating on whether Bush is really sick or one of our many enemies is targeting him with viewers or machines." He took another mouthful of chili. "See? Five hours ago, that possibility would never have entered your mind."

I swallowed a spoonful of chili as I walked back into the living room, and my mucous membranes screamed. My eyes teared and my tongue seemed to swell out of my mouth.

"Too hot for you?"

I was determined not to show weakness. "No . . . just right." I ate in a hurry.

"That was fast," Riley said when my bowl was empty. "Want some more? There's plenty."

"No, thanks," I said hoarsely. "I had a big breakfast." I sat there watching the rest of the news as my belly churned. I tried to remain more or less still.

After three bowls of chili, Riley looked at his watch, "Better start heading back. We don't want anyone to start looking for us."

I walked gingerly back to the office with Mel, trying not to slop the contents of my stomach. "What is this tarot card thing? Do we all learn how to do that?"

Riley's face turned red as he clamped down hard with his jaws. "Nope! That's purely individual choice. And if you're asking, I don't recommend it."

"Why—I mean, if it works?"

"Who the fuck knows if it works or not? That's the question. There haven't been any studies conducted, no research. Everything else you'll learn here has been scientifically tested and validated, and the training protocols have been documented and tested over time. There's no mystery there. But we don't know where this other crap, like channeling or automatic writing or tarot cards, is coming from. Shit! Most of it has been a circus act for Gypsies and now we have it in a scientific intelligence program. It's bullshit, and I know it; but you'll have to see for yourself, I won't be able to convince you."

When we arrived at the office, I walked straight to my desk and dived into the remaining files. For the rest of the afternoon I carefully read and reread the historical foundation of my new future.

It was about five and the office was emptying for the day. Everyone was gone except for Levy, Mel, and me. I had about five more files to look at before calling it a day, when Levy approached my desk.

"I've brought you some papers to sign. You can do it here and I'll do what is necessary with them."

He laid them in front of me and the first heading caught my attention: "[Human Use Agreement]." "What's this one?" I asked.

"It's your Human Use Agreement. Everyone here has signed one. Essentially it states that you understand that you are participating voluntarily in an experimental program using humans, and that you will not hold the federal government responsible for any damage that might occur."

I sat there staring at him for a moment. "What sort of damage?"

Levy seemed a little put out, as if I should have figured this out before now. "It should be obvious what sort of damage. You are involving yourself in the phenomena of time and space travel, in the viewing of events from a perspective that no other humans have ever experienced." He paused for a moment. "Some people who have undergone this training didn't fare well."

I continued to stare at him blankly, which meant to him that I wasn't satisfied with the answer.

"We have had some hospitalizations, and some removals from the training. If you are not well rooted in your belief structure, or if you have trouble comprehending what you see in the ether . . . well, you can have problems. You can suffer some emotional damage—a breakdown, if you will. That seems to be the worst of it, but it has happened on occasion. I'm sure you will not have any problems."

"Jeez, Bill, why didn't anyone say something about this to me before now?"

"Would it have made any difference in your decision? You had to know that this involved risks; common sense would tell you that. Are you trying to say that you wouldn't be here now if I'd told you there were risks involved in the training? Come on!"

"Where do I sign?"

"At the bottom of the second page. The rest of this stuff is simple nondisclosure documentation and some other administrative paperwork. The only critical one is the Human Use Agreement."

I signed each of the documents as Levy stood there watching me. I couldn't shake the strange feeling the Human Use Agreement gave me. I began to wonder if I should tell Levy about all the dreams and visions I'd been having. I thought Barker had done all that, but perhaps he hadn't; then where would I be? Could that make it worse for me, could it screw me up in some way?

"Bill . . ." I hesitated. "Am I in any real danger here? I'm already on thin ice with Debbie as a result of everything that's happened since the gunshot. I'm not backing out; I'd never do that. I want to do this more than anything I've ever done. But I want to take any necessary precautions.''

Levy gathered the papers and stacked them neatly in front of himself. "It's like I said the first day we met, David: this training will change you for the rest of your life. Neither you nor your family will ever be the same. You agreed to this training, and you must understand that and never forget it. No one is forcing you to be here, and you can say the word and walk out that front door today; nobody will ever say a thing about it. Or you can stay, and learn what every man only dreams about. It's your decision; you need to be comfortable with it, and your family does as well. We have lost many because they weren't ready. We are going to teach you to transcend time and space, and we will teach you to come back and report to us what you have seen.''

I was numb, my head spinning with a thousand different questions all over again. "How do I know if I'm ready or not?''

"I think you already do. I don't think there's a doubt in your mind that you are ready.''

I nodded. "You're right. I'm ready, and I think you know I'll give it everything I've got.''

"Good. We'll begin tomorrow.'' He collected the papers and walked back to his office. "You need to get out of here. I make it a rule to be the last one to leave the office, and I'm ready to leave now.''

Later that night, with the children gathered and kneeling around me, and Debbie by my side, I tried my best to explain my new adventure. I began as if telling a bedtime story, "You all know that I've started a new job, don't you?'' I waited for their little heads to nod before continuing. "Well, this new job is a little different than anything Daddy has done before. They say that I . . . I mean, we, as a family, will be going through a dramatic change, and we all need to be prepared.'' I struggled to make the nature of the assignment clear. "Daddy is going to learn how to walk with the angels."

"Walk with angels? Really?" Danielle and Mariah's eyes lit up.

"That's right."

Michael, now ten, tried to be more sophisticated and critical than his highly impressed sisters. "So, what else you gonna do?"

I noticed tears in Debbie's eyes, and I held her hand tightly.

"Let's see . . . I will travel to other worlds, see things that happened long ago, and learn to see things that haven't even happened yet."

Debbie asked in a quiet voice, "You mean, walk through time?"

I looked at her troubled face. "Honey, I know that my spirituality is going to be shaken, even redefined. I'm counting on you and the children to be my anchor. If you're not there to support me, I'm not certain I can go through with this."

She said, "I'm not sure I want you to go through with this! I'm sure this is fascinating for you, but it's scaring me, and eventually it will scare the kids as well." She stood and stomped away. "You children go on and play now, Daddy and Mommy want to talk to each other. Go on! Go and play!" They scattered, looking worried. Danielle began to sob. "It's okay, Danielle, stay with Mariah. Mariah, take your little sister and go up in your room and play. I'll be along shortly."

"Honey, come on." I tried to defuse her. "I didn't mean to frighten them."

"You probably didn't frighten *them,* but you're scaring *me* to death. This problem you've been having has been going on far too long, and now you nonchalantly come home and announce to the children and me that you are going to walk with angels and waltz back and forth through time. Just what the hell do you think you're doing, David? I asked you to get professional help for this problem and you assure me that this new unit will be just the thing for it—well, damn it! It just doesn't sound like that to me. It sounds to me like you are going stark raving mad and you've found some military unit willing to watch you do it while they take notes. What the hell's gotten into you? Don't you think of us at all?''

"Of course I think of you. What do you want me to do? It wasn't my fault that I got shot. I didn't want the visions; I didn't ask for them. All I want to do is be a soldier and get on with my life."

"Damn you!" She lashed out at me, striking my arm. "That's not what you're doing. You're off on another mission—another assignment from your precious army. You don't give a damn about us or you'd be getting the help you need for your problem, not using it to venture into some bizarre bullshit unit that will only make you worse."

"If that's the way you feel about it, then pack your bags and leave!"

"I'm not leaving! I love you and you are my husband. I'm angry and frustrated and I feel alone in this. You have a problem and you need help. Now all you've done is get into a place where everyone has a problem."

"Debbie . . ." I tried to hold her. "You're making more of this than it is."

She moved away. "No, I'm not, David." Her voice calmed and took on a serious tone. "No, I'm not blowing this one out of proportion. I talked with a therapist today, and he thinks you need to see him now."

"That's crap! I don't need a goddamned therapist, don't you understand? Sun Streak will help me learn to deal with this . . . it will explain it!"

Debbie let out a shuddering sigh. "I can see that you're going to do whatever you choose, and I have nothing to say about it. I never believed we'd be at a crossroads like this."

"Look," I said, "we've been through all this before. You agreed to give it a chance. If it doesn't work out, then we'll try something else. Right? Didn't you agree to that?"

I pulled her close to me and looked into her eyes. "Come on, honey, just give it some time. I'll live up to my end of the bargain; just support me in this. Okay?"

"We'll be there for you, David. We'll be there to pick up the pieces, too, when there's nothing left of you to love. But you owe us more than that." She turned and walked away. "When Levy said this unit would change your life forever, he was right. It's already started to."

The next morning I arrived at the unit bright and early. Jenny was there ahead of me and had already made a pot of coffee.

"Big day for you, huh?"

"Yeah, and I'm excited, too. My first day of lecture."

Jenny chuckled. "Well, don't get too excited, it's the part of training everybody hates. It's long and boring and there's a lot of writing involved. Most of the viewers would rather get a sharp stick in the eye than have to endure lecture again."

"That bad, huh? Well, I'll probably be the first guy to repeat it. I hate sitting in a classroom for anything. I'm more of a doer."

Mel popped in the door, his cheeks rosy from the cold outside. "Morning. Are you ready?" He winked at Jenny.

"He's chomping at the bit," she said. "Been here waiting for you."

"Well, give me just a few minutes to get some stuff pulled together and we'll go get started." He looked at the scheduling board next to the door. "We've got the garden room all day, all week. Good!"

"What is that?" I asked.

"Which do you mean, this board or the garden room?" Mel asked. "Levy fills out this board every night before he goes home. It tells you where and when you'll be working—you know, viewing. These red Ts and blue Os next to the session time tell you whether it's a training or an operational session. And this check here, in the 'monitor' block, indicates whether you have a monitor for the session.

You'll find out what all that means here in the next few weeks, so don't be confused.

"Great. I'll just hang out here and wait for you, okay?"

"No, not okay. You need a notebook and several pens from the supply room to take notes with, and you'll need another cup of that stuff Jenny calls coffee."

"Ahh, I brought a tape recorder, if that's okay. I'm not the best note-taker in the world."

There was a brief silence. "Yeah, there's a problem: you can't record the lecture, it's classified. You'll have to take notes, and we'll store them in a safe drawer. Jenny? Did you assign Dave a drawer yet?"

"Oh, no, I haven't, have I?" She sprang from behind her desk, carrying a green ledger book with her. "Okay, here's the combination to the safe." She showed me the open page. "Don't say it out loud! People might be listening—you know, the bad guys. You can write the combination down, but you can't carry it with you. Learn it quick or check this book. I keep it up-to-date. The combination changes every ninety days. When you get a new combination, you have to sign here acknowledging that it has been given to you. Your drawer will be this one"—she pointed—"the third one down, fifth from the right. That's the best way to remember it. Got that?"

"Yes, I think so."

"You keep all your notes and session records in here. It's your drawer to keep anything classified in. But, remember, Mr. Levy checks them periodically, so don't be stupid and put anything in here that you don't want to have to answer for. Okay?"

"I understand. Thanks."

"All right, let's get to it," said Mel. "Let me introduce you to the world beyond."

We walked across the parking lot and paused at the entrance to a long single-story building. Mel punched in the combination and then used a key to unlock the second lock. "After you," he said.

I stepped into a strangely barren lobby. There was a desk

with a phone on it, and two couches separated by a coffee table. Nothing hung on the walls. The floor was covered in a thin gray carpet, and the room was cold. There were two doors directly across the room, one on the extreme left, one in the center of the wall. Riley led me to the door on the left.

"This is the monitoring room. It's usually manned while you are doing an operational session. This is where they monitor your body signs: respiration, pulse, temperature. This is your lifeline back to reality. If you ever get into trouble out there in the ether, they'll know it in here, and they'll break the session to get you back home."

In the room were three chairs facing a large electronic panel filled with closed-circuit TV monitors, microphones, and cassette- and video-taping machines. In a small closet were hundreds of cassettes and videotapes, neatly catalogued and labeled.

"The joysticks let the monitors control the cameras in the viewing rooms. They can zoom in on you to see what you're writing if you're doing coordinate RV, or just to look at your eyes or anything else they want to see if you're doing ERV."

"What's ERV?" I asked.

"Extended remote viewing. Don't worry about that for now. The tape players pipe music of your choice in for your cool-down and then record your session so that we won't lose anything. Everything is recorded and monitored. This little gizmo here will monitor your brainwaves during your first few months of training. When we're certain that you can achieve the desired frequency in the appropriate amount of time, you won't have to wear the electrodes anymore. But at first you're gonna be wired for sound, and sweat, and farts, and anything else you decide to do in the ether. Fucking scary, huh? Come on, I'll show you the rest of the place."

We entered the other door which opened on a long, narrow hallway. There were doors on the left and right, and Mel popped one open.

"This is ERV Room Number One, and the other is Number Two, there on the left. They're identical, but you get so sensitive doing this stuff that you'll develop a preference."

The room was completely gray: carpet, walls, fixtures, desk, chair. There was a strange couchlike object, and that was gray, too.

"What's this thing?"

"That's an ERV chair. You sit in it like this." Riley jumped into the device and began pulling wires and belts into position. "You plug *this* in to monitor your pulse, and you wrap *this* around your chest to record your respirations. *These* are light and volume controls, here on this console, and you wear these headphones. Here's the microphone; you don't have to do anything with it, it's activated automatically from the monitor's room. Let's see . . . anything else? Oh, yeah, sometimes a close monitor will sit at the desk. Levy may do that, so he can lead you to the target and back. He likes to see up close and personal how you're doing. You have to watch the bastard, though. He's been known to separate and join you on the mission from this chair. There's not really any harm in that if you know he's going to be there; otherwise it can scare the hell out of you. He showed up in one of Kathleen's sessions, dropped right into her sanctuary and she damned near had a heart attack over it."

Mel saw that I didn't have any idea what he was talking about. "I'm getting a little ahead of myself again, huh? Just keep all this in the back of your mind. It'll be several months before you actually have to mess with any of it."

"I figured as much. Why is everything gray?"

"To avoid mental noise, incorrect information in the signal or transfer. It's kind of like TV interference; the same thing happens in your head—if there's a lot of color, light, or noise in the room where the viewer is working, the chances are high that it'll interfere with the session. By eliminating all that mental noise, we can keep the chances of a 'pure' session fairly high.

"In the old days, the plan was to train us to be able to do this stuff on the front lines of combat. Can you imagine? Squatting in a trench somewhere and jumping into the ether—that would be wild."

Mel led me three doors farther down the hall. "This is a dowsing room. It's where you'll be trained to find a moving target on the map. You'll learn any number of methods to do it, but whatever works best for you is obviously what you'll use. The large drafting table will have a flat map of a suspected location on it." On the wall was a map of the world. "In the closet there you'll find pendulums, rulers, dowsing rods—hell, anything you'd need. Over there against the far wall is a map storage box; it has just about every large-scale map of every target we've worked."

"Who picks the map?" I asked.

"Levy, usually. Sometimes he'll let someone else play program manager, but not often. When you're asked to work a dowsing problem, this room will be set up and waiting for you. All you have to do is find the target." He smiled and led me across the hall. "This is a CRV, coordinate remote viewing, room; that door over there is to Room Number Two. Again, they're identical, but you'll have a favorite."

The CRV room was longer than the ERV room, with a narrow table, eight feet long, in the middle. A row of track lights was centered over the table and a control panel sat next to the place the viewer worked from. The walls were gray, as was the carpet, the table, the chair, and all the fixtures. Mel pointed out that the room was absolutely soundproof and lightproof, just like all the others.

"This is the CRV chair," he said. "It has all the hookups the other ones did, plus it adjusts to whatever height you want. When you start CRV you'll see—it's critical to be comfortable." He pointed out the cameras' locations. "You adjust lights and sound here. That podium is called the target podium. It stays there, behind the monitor."

"What's it for?"

"The location of your target, training or otherwise, will

be sealed in a manila envelope and placed on this podium by the monitor. It's there more for your subconscious than anything else, but it's always there. We've done some experiments to see what effect switching the target folder might have, and the results were fairly astonishing. If I were working you on Target X, and during a break I substituted Target Y's folder without telling you, you'd start describing aspects of Y.

"That's very strange. Why would that happen?"

Riley shrugged. "It just does, that's all. If we waited until we could explain everything we do, we wouldn't have accomplished a thing in the last fifteen years. We know it works; we don't know how. So we just do it!"

"I see. I suppose this last room is the garden room?"

"It is indeed, and it is where you get your first dose of lecture."

"Hell, I thought I'd already gotten it as we walked down this hallway."

"I'll go easy on you—you won't have any homework tonight. This room is called the garden room because it has plants growing in it. It's the only room in either of the two buildings where anything will grow."

"Yeah. I noticed. Why the hell is that?"

Riley scoffed, "Beats the hell outta me. It's been that way for as long as I've been here on this tour, going on eight years."

"You were here on a tour before this one?" I asked.

"Yeah, I was one of the first viewers—me, Joe Mc-Moneagle, and a few others. Lyn Buchanan's been here for a long time as well." Mel's eyes sparkled. Perhaps those early days in the unit were a better time than now, because now he looked tired. "Shit," he said, smiling, "you keep wasting time like this, and I'll have to give you some homework."

"Levy didn't say anything about homework when he hired me!"

Mel slapped me on the shoulder. "Come on, we have a lot of ground to cover today."

*   *   *

In lecture, Mel laid out the historical evidence of time travel and out-of-body travel, from ancient Egyptian hieroglyphics to Scripture. Man, Mel argued, is more than his physical self. Each day flew by, and yet I hardly remembered it. It was as if I checked reality at the door each time I entered the unit, and picked it up later when I went home to my family. I strangely enjoyed the loss of time, the absence of the world around me. As the weeks rolled by, I felt more and more at peace with my environment. Everything around me seemed vibrant, clear, and meaningful, as if to a dead man suddenly revived. Life was a process of absorption. I drank in everything Mel said. I questioned nothing; it all made sense to me. I no longer felt strange about believing in remote viewing, but I felt apart from the others because I hadn't yet received my "eyes." The eyes of the Watcher. The eyes of the viewer.

Every night I told Debbie all the particulars of the day's training and let her read my secretly copied notes. Mel taught me small games. He'd have me concentrate on a color, for instance—"Swim in it," he'd say—and then he'd name the color, having plucked it from my head. I showed Debbie and the children how they, too, could reach into the minds of others. Debbie seemed to be growing more comfortable with the unit as the weeks passed, and as for the children, they thought the circus had come to town, because every night Dad had another game or drawing exercise to teach them. I was making progress, and we were all pleasantly happy about it.

One night, after many weeks of lectures, the phone rang just minutes before dinner. Mariah sprang up to answer it. "Mom, it's for you. Somebody named Mr. Levy."

Debbie looked at me. I could only shrug; I had no idea why he would be calling. Debbie picked up the receiver, pausing to remove an earring, and tried to speak.

"Hello, Mrs. Morehouse?" Levy's sharp voice cut her off.

"Yes?"

"This is Bill Levy. I just wanted to call and formally welcome you into the family, so to speak. I usually do this a bit earlier, but time seems to have slipped by. I wonder if I might convince you to pay us a visit at the office sometime in the near future. I'd like to discuss the unit with you, and some of the changes—well, little things that you might start noticing about David. Different things.''

Debbie looked frightened. "Of course, I can come in to talk.''

"Splendid. Would tomorrow morning be convenient—say nine or nine-thirty?''

"Nine would be fine. I'll ride in with David if that's okay.''

"Yes, of course. I'm looking forward to meeting you. Good-bye.''

"Good-bye.'' Debbie set the receiver down. "That's a very strange man! I can hear it in his voice. . . . Well, I guess you heard—I'll ride in with you and keep the car for the day when I'm finished. I have some errands to run. I'll pick you up around four-thirty.''

I was glad to see that, at least for the moment, Debbie could keep it all in perspective. "Sounds great to me. I wonder what sort of lecture you're in for tomorrow?'' She looked at me as though I'd set her up. "I swear, I had nothing to do with this, and I know nothing.''

The next morning, we pulled into the parking lot and I led Debbie to the front door.

"Dumpy place.''

"Be quiet!'' I scolded. I opened the door and shouted from the entrance, "Hello, everybody! Debbie's here with me. If you have anything on your desk she shouldn't see, you'd better put it away. She has instructions from the Kremlin to photograph everybody's desktop.''

Jenny laughed. "Make sure you get a shot of Pratt's desk. I want to send it to the *Guinness Book of World Records* for the Trashiest Desktop in the Known World category.''

"Ah, Mrs. Morehouse.'' Levy scurried out of his office.

"Welcome! Can I get you some coffee or tea? Anything?"

Debbie offered him her hand. "No, thank you. I'm afraid David is the only member of our family who drinks it." She glared at me. Mormons aren't supposed to drink coffee, but I'd picked up the habit in the infantry.

"Well, I think we should get started, then. David, I believe you have some lectures to attend. If you will kindly loan me your wife for a few minutes, she and I have some things to discuss." He motioned Debbie toward his office door and followed her in, closing the door behind.

It wasn't until years later that Debbie told me what happened. Levy began by thanking her for coming in on such short notice, then said: "I asked you to come here because I want to talk to you about David. Please don't be alarmed; this has been standard procedure for some time now. Our psychologists feel it's important to let the family know exactly what is going on with the service member and what might happen to him."

"Please do tell me what could happen to my service member, Mr. Levy."

"Yes, I'm sorry. I'm trying to find the proper words—"

Debbie interrupted, smiling politely. "I assure you, the proper words in this case will be the truth about what my husband is involved in and what might potentially happen to him. Please continue."

"I see. Well, then. I'll be blunt. What we do here is select and train people in a very unusual intelligence-collection method. We call our staff viewers. The training usually takes anywhere from twelve to eighteen months, but I believe that David will become operational much sooner. He is doing remarkably well." Levy paused and looked away. "The training is rigorous, and the emotional makeup of those being trained is very fragile. So I'm constantly on the prowl for variables in the trainee's day-to-day routine that might make the training more difficult or perhaps more dangerous. I'm aware of your husband's frequent nightmares. While they present no immediate cause for alarm, I want you to know that I believe they eventually will.''

"In what way?''

"First, I want you to understand that David promises to be one of the very best viewers we've ever produced. But he is extremely vulnerable to outside influences.''

"You're talking about me, aren't you?''

"Yes—but please don't be offended; that's not my purpose in bringing you here. It is also not the only thing I'm concerned about. I think that the visions David is having suggest that many of the conduits normally left closed at birth have been damaged in some way. They have been forced open and are not reclosable. While that will make him a natural and excellent remote viewer, he will also be operating in a way, and in a world, very foreign to him. David is not what I would call the usual remote-viewing personality. He is accepting of the training, but very confused about the visions. I think he believes that we will make them stop. I'm afraid the opposite is true. The more capable a viewer he becomes, the more frequent his contact with the ether will be, and the more chances for spillover through the 'conduits.' ''

"What you are telling me is that he runs the risk of not being able to tell where reality stops and the ether begins.''

"Exactly; you're very astute. Now, this curse is also a blessing.''

"I tend to think of it as a curse.''

"Well, that is true only if you limit David by the usual definition of normality. He is an exceptional human being; he will only become more exceptional. If he has your understanding, and if you help him establish and keep a solid belief structure, then I think we can minimize the negative impact. However, if he doesn't have your support, I would fear—I'd *expect*—the worst.''

"I have to be honest, Mr. Levy: I don't want him here at all. I want him to get professional help at a hospital, with doctors who know what to do for someone like him.''

Levy leaned forward. "I'll tell you what the doctors will do. They will very carefully document his descriptions of the visions, perhaps even ask him to draw sketches. They will put him through some simple tests. They will classify him as delusional, maybe even psychotic. And then they will prescribe all sorts of drugs. They will want to control his visions with a chemical straitjacket. They will not be understanding; they will not care; and his career will be over. The best you could hope for would be a medical discharge for psychological disability. Not a very fitting end to an otherwise exceptional career, is it?''

''Maybe that's not what they'd do! Maybe they'd find a cure for what happened to him. The bullet must have caused some damage. Maybe they can find it and correct it.''

''Mrs. Morehouse, you're being far too optimistic. When it comes to the psychology of its soldiers, the army is downright archaic. They won't understand what is wrong with David, because there's nothing visibly wrong with him. We gave him a CAT scan at Bethesda three weeks ago; there is nothing medically wrong with him. They can't cut into his brain and take something out, or move something over and stitch it up again. Please try to understand what I'm telling you.''

''I do.'' Debbie's eyes filled with tears. ''I don't know what to do anymore. I have no options. All I can do is hope that you give him the tools to live with this thing. That's all I have. They took my husband from me, and I have no one to call upon, no one to help me.''

''I'll help you.''

''No! No, Mr. Levy, I beg to differ. You are not helping me. What you are doing is using my husband's sickness to your advantage. I can't say I fault you for it, but I'll allow you to do it only because I haven't any recourse. I'm against a wall in a very small box, so you can use David and I'll back you up. But don't you *ever* expect me to thank you for it. Good day, Mr. Levy.''

Debbie stormed out without speaking to anyone else. I was already in the other building with Mel. Over the next two years Levy never mentioned the meeting to me; when

I asked, he avoided the issue. I didn't find out what happened that day until Debbie told me, in June of 1993.

"I want to introduce you to the concept of time," Riley began. I was distracted, wondering how Debbie was faring with Levy. "Don't worry about Debbie," he snapped. "She's a big girl and she can take care of herself. You pay attention, okay?"

"Sorry." *How the hell does he know what I'm thinking all the time?*

"Connelly Wilson—who's dead, by the way—and Doctor Michael Rendell, an experimental laser physicist at Stanford Research Institute . . . Remember him? We talked about him several weeks ago."

"He was one of the first researchers, along with Dr. Harold Puthoff and some others."

"That's right. Well, the pair did some experimental work on time travel from a viewer's perspective. They weren't interested in actual travel, only in the ability of the viewer to project himself forward and backward along the time-space continuum. I want you to think of this continuum for a moment as linear. It isn't, really, but we're not going into theory. So just think of it as linear, like—"

"A fire hose?"

"Okay, like a fire hose. There are three critical points relevant to the viewer: past, present, and future time. Past time is easy; it's locked in and doesn't change. When you travel backward in time to a designated target, you are viewing that target as you would a snapshot. You can select any place, person, thing, or event connected to that snapshot, and view it. Everything about that instant in time will remain, infinitely. Every emotion, pain, thought, personality, horror, event, death—everything remains. Viewing the past is like opening an encyclopedia of the period, including all the relevant intangibles and aesthetics. A well-trained viewer can experience pain, temperature, everything. Can suck it right out.

"Present time is locked, too: you cannot change it; you

can only experience it.'' He paused. ''Well, Lyn is heading up some research on influencing present time, but you needn't concern yourself with that for now.

''Rendell and Wilson were experimenting with future time. They were convinced that Wilson could move forward in time to view events that had not yet occurred. Rendell asked him to explore the probability of a future event, and Wilson did that with a high degree of accuracy.''

''Okay, hold on. Look, I know we haven't talked about viewing into the future, but since you brought it up—well, I don't doubt what you're telling me. But I don't understand how he could view into the future with any degree of accuracy.''

Riley gave me a sidelong look. ''What do you mean, 'with any degree of accuracy'?''

''I mean just that—accuracy! How can you look into the future with any accuracy? I don't see how results could be valid.''

''I still don't see your point,'' Riley said, taking a seat.

''I'm sorry, I don't have the vocabulary for this. Let me see if I can find another way to put it.'' I thought for a moment. ''All right: as I understand it, when we tap into the unconscious mind, we are, in a sense, tapping into the time-space continuum; right so far?''

''So far, yes.''

''Then looking into the future means identifying a point in time, somewhere along this continuum, right?''

''Still right.''

I went to the chalkboard and drew a straight horizontal line across it. ''Okay, this represents time, all right?'' Placing a dot on the line's far left, I labeled it ''A.'' ''This represents present time.'' Mel nodded. ''So, if I remote-view a *future* event, that means I'm accessing a point somewhere out here.'' I placed a dot halfway along the line, to the right of ''A,'' and labeled it ''B.'' ''Let's say this represents that point in future time.''

''Go on.''

''Well, the future isn't locked, is it? Doesn't it fluctuate in accordance with the variables that affect it?''

"No, it isn't locked, but we can still see forward in time.''

"But the future is directly tied to countless variables. Wilson may have seen accurately into the future, but I submit that that was an aberration.''

"Why?''

"Because there must be too many opportunities for events to be skewed between 'A' and 'B.' In the time it takes one of us to write up a report about what we saw out there, the event we were looking at could change a million times.''

Riley sat in his chair frowning in thought. "So if I asked you, as a viewer, to tell me if there would be an assassination attempt on the life of the President next month, and you said yes—then I should pay no attention to it?''

I sighed. "What I'm saying is that it's a fifty-fifty chance that you'll be right. You might as well flip a coin. That's why your garden-variety street and television psychic isn't winning the lottery, isn't protecting the President, because predicting the future is just guesswork.''

"It's not a guess; they're seeing into the future.''

"Without a doubt, yes, they are seeing into the future. But the data can't be reliable! Too much happens between 'A' and 'B.' So if someone predicts an assassination attempt on the President, I say it changes nothing. The Secret Service still has to operate, every second, of every hour, of every day, as though an attempt were imminent. A remote viewer's data or a psychic's visions should change nothing.''

I could see that Riley wanted to get back to Rendell and Wilson, so I said, "Look, you're the professor here, let's get back to the lecture.''

Riley smiled. "Questioning theory is how we get better at what we do. Don't ever stop questioning the method or the data; the day that happens, you might as well start writing science fiction novels, because that's all you'll get for a product. Well done!''

I don't really know where my outburst came from; I just knew I was right. Viewers can't accurately predict the future; they can only describe a snapshot in time, as yet unaffected by the events of life. Riley knew that, too; he'd just wanted to see if I'd figure it out. It was a test and, thank God, I passed.

My mind wandered for the rest of the afternoon, poring over the issues we'd discussed. Time travel had its limitations, and the science fiction writers were all wrong. It wasn't like the movie *Back to the Future;* you couldn't change past time to affect future time. The past was locked and the future was an untethered fire hose, rocking and swaying, constantly changing, infinite variables affecting it as time crept forward.

Weeks passed and the long hours of lecture rolled on. I never tired of hearing Mel talk. He would often anchor unusual ideas by tying them to American Indian lore or legend. He was the wisest man I'd ever met, and I was thankful for the opportunity to know him. I often wondered what my life would have been like had I passed him by and returned to the Rangers; but that wasn't possible. I'd come to believe, more than ever, that I, like each of us, have a destiny. Mine had brought me to Sun Streak for a reason.

One night in June I awoke with a sharp pain at the base of my neck. Rubbing it, I stumbled out of the bed and into the hall; then something shot up the length of my spine, locking me in place, fixed and rigid. I was turned like a doll on a stick, looking this way and that as the house filled with shadows and strange light.

I heard the children calling me, frightened by the lights and the presence in the hallway. *Is it me they're afraid of?* I thought. *Is it me?* I decided to call out to quell their fears, but the voice of a beast left my mouth. The children screamed louder and louder, waking their mother. Debbie ran toward me, pulling on her house coat. She approached and horror filled her eyes. She screamed. A hand, not mine, came into view as if it were attached to me, an extension of me. It grabbed her by the throat; I watched helplessly as the beast I was a part of dragged her to the stairs and flung her to the bottom. Through foreign eyes I watched blood flow from her mouth and ears, forming a small pool beneath her head. Spitting and wheezing, she choked on the blood in her lungs as she lay there. Whatever had taken me over moved with me to the bottom of the stairs, floating effortlessly, like an apparition. Those hands grabbed Debbie's neck and snapped it. The children wailed above me. My form moved again; it was growing in evil, and with each heartbeat I was becoming more a part of it. I entered Michael's room and shook him by the throat, feeling his body grow limp and heavy in my hands. I dropped the child and turned to the screams of the others. Out of the bedroom and down the hall, homing in on the sound, I tasted what evil tasted and felt the power and hatred that drove it: the vileness of living flesh and the welcome feel of death. I clutched both living children in my hands and crushed them, dashing death to the floor, welcoming the silence and peace. The stillness and beauty of death and its light and song. I was at peace with my power. I understood the necessity to kill.

I sat up in bed, gasping for air. Debbie's hands were on me.

"David! David, are you all right? It's okay, you're all right now. I'm here."

I kept gasping for air, my throat closed off as if it had been clutched by the form in my hallucination. Drenched in sweat, I began to shiver. I could not speak, only gasp and moan at the horror and pain of what I'd done. My mind was clear and alert, chiming over and over: "You murdered your family. . . . You murdered your family. . . . You murdered your family!" In dismay and fear, I wept uncontrollably as Debbie held me; she too was weeping and crying out to God for help. I heard her pray aloud: "I command you in the name of Jesus Christ to depart. I command you in the name of Jesus Christ to depart!"

After what seemed like hours, I began to breathe more normally. Michael, Mariah, and Danielle had awakened; they came to our bedroom and stayed until dawn.

"Is Daddy going to be okay?" Mariah asked. "Did Daddy have a bad dream?"

"Yes, honey, he'll be okay," Debbie replied, still holding me and stroking my hair.

I lay there in shock, the images still clear in my mind as I relived each chilling second over and over. The children held my hands and helped their mother rub my head. They had never seen me cry before, and they didn't quite know what to make of it.

We rested together for seven hours. Debbie didn't let the children go to school, and she called in sick for me. By afternoon, I could speak.

"Why did you call the name of Christ?" I asked Debbie.

Tears fell from her eyes, and her lip quivered. "Because I was frightened, and that's what I was taught to do whenever I was frightened. Why?"

I was covered in a blanket. I pulled it closer at the neck, clutching it from beneath. "I don't know. I've just never heard you do it before, that's all. It was strange. Did it help?"

Debbie looked at me, troubled. "Strange? You think calling on the name of the Lord is strange? David, have you forgotten everything you were taught in school, in church? What do you think was happening to you last night?"

"I don't know."

"Well, you were flopping around like a rag doll, screaming and crying. I didn't know what was happening to you, or where you were, but it didn't matter: I needed some help. I believe that the Lord is there to help in times like that. That's why I called his name, because I knew He'd be there to help. Don't *you* know that?"

"I don't know."

"You don't know? You don't know if you believe in Him any longer, is that it? He's not current enough for you, all of a sudden? If that's what's happening, you are going to be lost. I don't know what your life will become.''

"I'm not giving up on God—don't exaggerate.''

"You disgust me!'' Debbie cried. "I don't know you any longer. You aren't my husband. I don't know what you are—but you aren't my husband.''

I went to work the next day, still a bit shaken. I didn't speak to anyone, but quietly made my way to my desk with a cup of coffee and tried to settle in to my lecture notes. Throughout the lectures I'd been preparing essays, as required by the training protocols. Each essay was reviewed by every operational member of the unit—that is, everyone but Judy Kessler, who was still in training. My work had passed the test and I was only a few short weeks, at most, from graduating into Stage One training.

"Ready for the day's bombardment?'' asked Riley, poking his head into my cubicle.

"Sure—you want me now?''

"Yup! But is something troubling you, buddy? You look a little peaked; maybe we should sit this one out, since you were sick yesterday.''

"No, I'm all right, really. I want to work. I'll be there in a few minutes.''

"See you there.''

In the latrine, I splashed cold water on my face and stared at the stranger's face in the mirror. Debbie was right; I was changing quickly, and perhaps not for the better. I made my way to the garden room where Mel was waiting.

"I have some good news,'' he said. "Levy likes your progress in lecture. He wants to bump up your Stage One training. I figure you have about three more weeks of lecture, but we'll start your first Stage One session next Monday. How's that sound?''

"I can't believe it—that's terrific. Who's going to be my trainer?''

"Kathleen. You'll like her, she's a neat girl.''

"Man, that's great!'' But the excitement left my face as

I remembered what had happened two nights ago.

"There's that look again," Mel said. "What's the matter? Is everything all right at home?"

"Yeah, everything's fine."

"Except?"

"Except that I had another hallucination the night before last. A terrible one!" My hands began to tremble. "Mel, in my vision I killed my entire family. What kind of man envisions that? I love my family more than life itself—how could I see myself killing them in cold blood?"

"Whoah." Mel put his hand up to stop me. "I know you're shaken up by this, but get a grip; there's an explanation. You might not like it, but there *is* an explanation."

"I'd sure like to know it. *Debbie* would sure like to know it."

"Well, it's not that simple. I'm not going to sit here and feed you the answer to the problem. I'm not certain I could, but even if I could, I wouldn't. You'll find it out for yourself eventually. All you have to do is hang in here until that time comes. Don't start beating yourself up because of this. I know it scared the hell out of you, and you think you're scum for even imagining it, but you aren't. We're going to drop this topic for now, but remember: you will soon find out that nothing in this world is as it seems. There are parallel worlds that touch and intersect with ours constantly, and there is a world of deceivers. You're dealing with them now! Just chew on what I've said and forget about anything else for now. You have a long way to go. Okay?"

"Okay. Thanks for the counsel." I was relieved to learn there was an explanation for all this, but I was frightened by the thought of an actual group or world of beings responsible for my illusions.

I could hardly contain myself through the weekend. It was difficult to stay emotionally in touch with Debbie; I wish I'd been able to share the excitement I felt, but she wasn't ready to hear it yet. I went to work early on Monday.

When Mel arrived he came immediately to my desk with a cup of java. "Are you sure you want to do this? It's not too late to turn back."

"No way! After sitting through your boring lectures, you think I'm gonna miss the best part? When do we get started?"

"Well, I haven't talked with Kathleen yet, but you're on the board for Room Two at 0830 hours. That gives us about forty minutes to get you hooked up and ready."

We walked over to the other building and Mel put the electrodes on my head. He took me to the CRV room and wired me into the monitor board. "I'll be in the monitor's room after Kathleen arrives. How you feeling, nervous?"

"Nervous as hell!" I replied. "Absolutely, nervous as hell."

Kathleen arrived ten minutes before the start of the session. "I'm going to let you cool down for about ten minutes before I come back in. I'll be in the monitor's room with Mel; if you need me, just ring the call button. Any questions?"

"No, I don't think so, at least not right now."

"Good. Go ahead and cool down, I'll be back in a few minutes. Oh, and good luck! You'll do fine."

I listened to one of the focus tapes I'd been given to help me relax. The tape carried both audible and subliminal messages; certain tonal frequencies on it were specifically designed to help merge the brainwaves of the left and right hemispheres of the brain. This helped the viewer to achieve an altered state. As I was cooling down, I could hear the tones in my biofeedback mechanism sounding the current wavelength of my brain. The target was theta wave; I was now functioning in beta.

Kathleen came in precisely ten minutes after she had left. "Adjust your chair for the session."

"Christ!" I thought, *I've been in here ten minutes and I've already screwed up.* I fumbled with the adjustment handle for a moment, setting the chair in the position I thought I wanted. But as I squirmed in it, I concluded that

I didn't like it. "Goddamn it!" I exclaimed.

"Is that how you want the chair?" Kathleen asked.

"I don't know if I want the damned thing lying back, sitting up, straight, or jacked up higher than the table. Where the hell *should* it be?"

Kathleen laughed. "Just make it comfortable. Make it high enough that your arm rests lightly on the table. That will help you with your ideogram."

As I fumbled with the chair, Kathleen placed a stack of white paper near me. She pulled one sheet off and carefully centered it directly in front of me.

I dimmed the lights slightly.

As Mel had explained, I would be given a set of coordinates—random numbers assigned to the target. When I received the numbers I would write them down as they were given, and after I had written down the numbers my hand would produce what we called an ideogram. An ideogram was nothing more than an autonomic response to the target in the matrix. In other words, the ideogram came from the unconscious mind and was somehow descriptive of the target. How this worked was all part of Riley's lengthy and cumbersome lectures.

"Whenever you're ready," Kathleen said.

"How will I know when I'm ready? I mean, I feel ready now."

"You'll know you are ready when you feel a peacefulness, a warmth come over you. When you feel that, place the tip of your pen to the paper, and I'll read the coordinates to you. Got that?"

"I've got it. Thanks." I tried to count down in my head, as I had been taught. I closed my eyes and relaxed. The audible tones of the biofeedback machine sounded, rapidly at first, then slowing, slowing . . . changing tone to alpha waves. Slower . . . slower . . . slower . . . finally, the flat tone indicating theta waves. Within seconds, I felt as if I had no arms, no legs; it was a centered and peaceful feeling. I was aware of nothing in the room, only Kathleen's breathing. I heard her heart beating, and the blood coursing through her veins. My head dropped forward and my hand slowly lowered the tip of the pen to the paper. As soon as it touched, Kathleen announced my first set of coordinates. I repeated them to her as I wrote them. As I reached the last digit, I waited . . . and waited . . . and waited.

"Dammit." I tossed the pen to the table in disgust. "Why didn't it happen? Why wasn't there a response?" I hoped Kathleen had an answer.

"It's all right, you'll get it. Just don't panic. Let's take a break and get some fresh air. Write the word 'break' on your paper, and put the time down next to it."

I did as I was told, but I didn't want a break; I wanted something to happen. Unplugging from the console, I followed Kathleen out of the room and into the sunlight.

"I don't understand it." I sighed. "I was right where I wanted to be; it should have happened, I should have gotten an ideogram."

"David," Kathleen said calmly, "you can't force the ideogram. You did exactly right; if it doesn't come, you simply declare a miss and ask for the coordinates again, or take a break like we're doing now. It'll happen, trust me."

"I guess I expected something more overt to happen. Maybe I thought something would grab my hand and drag it across the paper."

"Don't be disappointed. Look, here is what's going on. Your unconscious mind is trying to figure out how to talk to your conscious mind. You have to remember that there has been little or no conversation between the two for your entire life." She hesitated. "Physical life, that is. The two minds need to learn to communicate. That's what training is all about. Now, let's get back in there and give it another shot, what do you say?"

Back in the room, I sat down and adjusted the chair again. Kathleen said, "Now, I want you to write 'resume' on the paper directly underneath the word 'break.' Include the time there as well. Let me know when you're ready."

I began counting down again, feeling myself slip deeper and deeper until I reached the altered state again. I noticed that it happened much more quickly this time. When my pen touched the paper, Kathleen gave me the coordinates again.

My body seemed to move sluggishly, almost in slow motion. As I wrote down the last coordinate my hand quickly skipped several inches across the paper.

I looked up, half dazed. "An ideogram!"

Kathleen didn't smile; she simply asked, "Is it manmade or natural?"

I tried to focus on her question. From somewhere deep inside my mind, pictures began to push through the darkness, as if someone were flipping a light switch. Briefly, I felt as though I were falling in a bright tunnel; then the sensation ended abruptly. It came and went over and over, the images always following it. Faint images of a white sparkling substance, brown jagged objects, and a greenish circular star—no, snowflakelike things. The images passed by me as though I were flying and looking down from maybe inches above the surface of something. I felt cold on my face and warmth on my back. Looking up, I thought I briefly saw a brilliant light like the sun, but I returned my attention to the surface. Now I knew the answer.

"No, no . . . it's not manmade."

"What is it, David?"

"It's rising up sharply. It's natural." I was just verbalizing my perceptions of the images passing before me. "Definitely natural."

"Trace the ideogram and describe it to me."

"Rising up sharply, peaking, dropping sharply . . . it's natural," My mind assembled the pieces of the puzzle. The white sparkling cold substance—snow, perhaps? The brown, jagged objects and the green snowflakes—lichen-covered rocks? "It's a mountain!" I called out, astonished at the revelation. "It's a mountain, isn't it?"

Kathleen made a few notes on her paper without looking up; then she reached behind her to the target podium and retrieved the folder containing the feedback. "I'm supposed to make you do your summary before seeing this, but I'm going to violate the protocol just this once." She tossed the envelope across the table to me.

I hesitated, and then tore open the envelope. A chill ran up my spine as I stared at the photograph inside. "Mount Fuji!"

"And you were just there; how about that?" Kathleen was grinning from ear to ear now. "Okay, give me the folder back and you go and write your summary. Levy will want to see it before the day is out. You did great! I've never seen anyone get the images you did—that was excellent!"

Kathleen left the building and headed for the office, but I sat in the room for a long time, thinking. Finally, shaking my head, I muttered to myself: "It's got to be just luck. How could it be anything else?"

"No such thing as luck in this business!" I'd forgotten Mel was in the monitor room. "Don't forget, someone's always listening, so keep your comments to yourself. Hey! *Great* fucking session. I'll see you in the office." And he was gone, just like that. *Never pick your nose in here,* I told myself.

I felt as if a moment ago the world had opened its darkest secret to me. As I stood alone in the room, I stared at the ideogram and remembered the sensation I'd felt. Bill Levy was right; my life would never be the same.

I hadn't completely escaped Mel's lectures; I found myself in a mix of classroom and viewing room over the next three weeks. It seemed Levy was experimenting on me, trying new protocols and combinations of procedures to see if he could expedite the training process. It was July 1988, and I'd been in training for almost six months now, with about twenty-five CRV sessions under my belt. Kathleen and Mel were excellent viewers, and their skill rubbed off; I was getting better all the time. There was still a great deal I didn't understand; so far I hadn't been expected to converse with the monitors, and I was also not able to move in the target area. Many of the lectures concerned those issues.

I'd had a few more nightmares, but nothing as hideous as the one involving the family, and I was feeling pretty sure of myself at this point. Yeah, I still had my doubts about how and why this stuff worked, but one thing was certain: work, it did.

"You gonna be ready in ten or fifteen minutes?" Mel asked.

"Forgot to check the board. What time am I supposed to be viewing?"

"You're on for 0900 hours; I'll monitor and Kathleen will take the monitor room. Did you happen to notice the target designator on the board? Oh, that's right—you didn't bother to look, did you?"

I ran for the board. There it was, the big blue "O" staring me right in the face.

"All right! Operational! The real thing!"

Mel smiled. "I knew that, but you didn't. Next time make sure you look at the board. See you over there at a quarter of for hookup and prep."

In the viewing room, Mel set up the target folder and slid me a sheet of paper. I adjusted my chair, dimmed the lights, and began. Off the biofeedback monitor now, I had to get to the desired brainwave frequency on my own. It didn't take long these days; in a few minutes I was ready. I picked up the pen and my eyes closed. My head dropped as I fell deep into an altered state.

"When you're ready, Dave," Mel said. As soon as my pen touched the paper, he read the coordinates: "Zero one four three one one . . . one one three two one one."*

---

*Without jumping into a full-blown explanation of coordinate remote viewing, coordinates, the matrix, and so on, let me just say that the numbers assigned to a target are inconsequential; they are randomly generated and assigned. What, how, and where they come from means nothing. However, once they're assigned to the target, they become an address for that target (wherever it is) in the matrix of the mind.

The theory stems from Dr. Carl Jung's concept of the "collective unconscious" of the human mind. If an individual is cognizant of the

My hand jumped across the paper, leaving an ideogram behind.

"Decode it."

I turned my head, cracking my neck as I put the pen back on the ideogram. I methodically probed it slipping deeper and deeper into the ether. Time had nearly stopped. I felt myself rising into darkness, away from the table and the room. Up, up . . . I tried to gain some sense of what and where I was. There was a rushing sound in my ears, like a cold wind passing. I felt blind, lost, helpless, and cold. Pinholes of light came into focus, like stars in a black fog.

Am I in space? I've got to get to the target. I can't miss the target.

The "stars" suddenly blurred into horizontal streaks of light. I felt myself accelerating, faster and faster, falling toward the target as if through a tunnel of light. My speed began to create heat around me, and I closed my eyes and fists, expecting to burn; but I didn't. I looked in the direction of my descent, and there, looming at the end of the tunnel, was a moving field of dark blue mist. I struck it full force and punched through into something else. The air was

---

target, or aspects of the target, and then assigns a number to that target, then, in theory, those numbers will represent an address for that target (or for the knowledge of it, or for the concept of it). These coordinates make the target accessible to any human being capable of entering an altered state and searching for that particular address. In theory, and practice, if I am given the coordinates of 12345 67899 on Monday, and if those numbers are assigned to a hidden bag of rice, I should be able to describe the bag of rice and its surroundings. If Mel is given the same coordinates on Tuesday, he, too, should be able to describe the same bag of rice. If Lyn were given the coordinates one year from today, in theory, he would be able to describe the same (now moldy) bag of rice.

You see, the numbers mean very little. In earlier years they were in fact actual coordinates: Cartesian, grid mercator, or even latitude and longitude. As the years passed, it became clear that the numbers didn't need to pin the location down to some specific "earth surface" address. In fact, these forms of coordinates could even be limiting in some respect. The coordinates became computer-generated numbers, assigned to specific targets without any additional consideration.

warmer now, and I felt more in control. Without warning, a voice invaded my sanctuary.

"David?" It was Riley.

At first I choked, trying to find a way to speak with this phantomlike body. And then it came, as if I'd been doing it all my life. "Mel, this is very strange. Damn, did you hear that—I talked!"

"I know it's strange, Dave, but you're doing fine. Try to stabilize yourself and tell me what you see."

"Stabilize myself? Hell, what am I supposed to do, hang on to something?" Warm air rushed around me; a white haze crept in, blocking my vision.

"Just relax, Dave. Get a sense of where you are. Let yourself find the target. Just think about the target." My friend was doing his best to guide me and help me keep control.

"This is unbelievable, Mel," Kathleen said over the intercom. "He bilocated within seconds of receiving the coordinates. Nobody's ever done it that fast before."

Mel replied: "Let's hope it isn't just beginner's luck. He's floundering around out there, you know, trying to figure out how everything works, but I think I can get him on target fairly soon." He turned his attention back to me. "What do you see, Dave?"

"Ahh, the haze is going away. . . . I've got all kinds of visuals coming in. . . . I think I'm outside some kind of building."

"Describe it to me."

I was struggling to remain stable, but I kept moving involuntarily around what I thought was the target. "It's still hard to see; there's a lot of stuff coming and going out here. It's kind of confusing."

"That's just visual noise. Pay no attention to it. Just focus on the target."

"I think I see it. . . . It looks like an older building, made of stone, maybe. Yeah, stone. I can see windows and— Wait a minute!"

"What?"

I laughed. "I still can't get the hang of this. One second I'm standing still and the next I'm two inches off the ground, staring at the sidewalk."

"You'll get the hang of it. Just concentrate on righting yourself and getting back to the mission."

Riley and I worked until, by focusing my thoughts into visual patterns, I could control my movements in this phantom state. If I wanted to stand, I visualized myself standing; similarly, if I wanted to move left or right, I pictured myself turning that way.

"Mel! I got it! This is like a platform diver visualizing the dive before it's executed—he basically moves from place to place visually."

"Exactly. And there is no other way for us to teach it to you than for you to experience it like this."

"Fascinating!" Experimenting, I shot straight up in the air till I was about a hundred feet above the building. "I'm above the building now; how do I get in?"

"The same way you did everything else."

"Do I use the door, or what?"

"No, just punch through the roof and describe the interior of the building to me."

I stared at the rooftop and concentrated briefly; my phantom body hurled itself down. I flinched as the roof passed by, but it felt like nothing more than a soft puff of air, like a mild aftershock or blast concussion.

Inside the building I found a puzzling scene. "I see a lot of junk." My emotions began to clash with what I was sensing. "Mel?" I called. "Mel?"

"Yeah, Dave."

"I'm a little confused again. I can describe the room for you, but I'm getting something deeper, something emotional."

"Tell me about the building first; then we'll move on to other aspects."

I slowly turned full circle in the center of the room. "I see wooden floors, and cases and boxes covered in glass. I think there are weapons here. Yes, that's it, I'm surrounded by weapons.''

Riley smiled, and kept jotting notes.

"There are smaller rooms off this one. This appears to be the central room in the building. There's a lot of wood and metal objects—mixed construction, not separate.''

"Explain that.''

"I mean the objects are made of both wood and metal.''

"Are these the large objects you described earlier, the ones with glass on top? Or are they related to those objects in any way?''

I struggled to answer. "They're related. . . . One goes inside the other, but I don't understand how or why.''

"What else can you tell me about the site?''

"Well, there's this emotional thing.''

"Okay, let's explore that. What's so strong that it keeps punching through to you on an emotional level?''

I closed my eyes and tried to absorb the unseen aspects of the site. The images and emotions came in a trickle at first, and then suddenly flooded me. "Jesus! That hurts!''

"Hurts?''

"Well, no, it doesn't hurt. I guess it's making me sick to my stomach more than anything.''

"Tell me what you sense, Dave.''

My phantom body dropped to its knees, while my physical body uncontrollably slumped onto the table. "This place is fraught with death,'' I sobbed. "Everything in here smells and tastes of death.''

"Touch one of the objects and tell me what you feel and see inside yourself.''

I reached for an object near me. "I see a man walking. He is filthy, covered in smoke and blood. He smells like an animal! His hair is long, and so is his beard; he's moving in a line with a lot of other men just like him.'' I paused. "He's a soldier.''

"What kind of soldier?''

"I don't know. I think he's old. His—his time is gone.

He's gone . . . gone away. I'm seeing something past, aren't I?''

Riley sat back in his chair and took a deep breath. "Okay, Dave, I want you to come back. Let everything go now, and come back.''

I began to breathe rapidly; small beads of sweat formed on my forehead and arms. My muscles twitched and jerked involuntarily as my phantom body fell through the tunnel of light again.

I could see Mel through eyes I couldn't control. It was frightening, like the horrible nightmare I'd had months ago, to look at Mel through someone else's eyes. But in a few minutes, I was able to raise my head and focus my eyes. As my vision cleared I saw Mel sitting in front of me and smiling.

"Have fun?''

I rubbed my eyes and wiped my face on my shirtsleeve. "Oh, great fun! Where was I, anyway? And why did I feel like I was looking through another set of eyes?''

"That's for you to tell me. I want you to go into the garden room and do your summary for me. Kathleen and I'll be in there in about twenty minutes. Okay?''

I nodded, but when I stood up I started to sway. I had to grab the table for support. "Damn!''

"You'll be all right in a minute or two. That was your first real bilocation. They tend to take a bit out of you at first—actually, they always take a bit out of you. Twenty minutes in the garden room.'' Riley walked out of the room.

"Okay.'' I felt awful, as if I had a hangover or maybe the flu. My legs wobbled and my stomach was queasy. I could hear Kathleen and Riley congratulating one another in the monitor's room down the hall, but I couldn't quite make out what they were saying.

In the garden room, Kathleen and Mel sat on opposite sides of the table and looked intently at me. I had the urge to say, "I didn't do it!'' Whatever "it'' was.

"So, give us your perceptions,'' said Riley.

I gave my notes and sketches a quick glance and began reading. ''The site has aspects of both old and new. It's a stone building that houses many objects. These objects—they're definitely weapons of some sort—have a military value. Most of them are made of wood and metal. There is a great deal of glass in the building, plus wooden floors, carpets, old furniture, and so on. The site has an almost domestic appearance.''

''What about the man you saw?'' Riley asked.

''I'm getting to him. There are paintings and posters on the wall, all reflecting combat of some sort. Heroes, villains, and victims are represented. The man I accessed was a soldier. I say 'was' because I got the distinct sense that he's dead.''

''What gave you that perception?'' said Riley.

''I don't know. It's just the way I felt when I looked at him. He was grubby-looking, wet and dirty; I could even smell him. But there wasn't any heart, any soul—it was like looking at a movie. All the physical attributes of emotion are there, but when you look inside, there's nothing. Just an empty frame.'' I set my notes on the table and looked at Riley and Kathleen. ''Okay, so where's my feedback?''

Riley pulled the target folder from his stack of papers and slid it across the table. I snatched it and hurriedly opened the folder.

''A museum?'' I was devastated. ''You sent me to a Civil War museum? I thought you were giving me an operational target.'' I threw the folder back on the table. ''A goddamned museum!''

''Calm down,'' Riley said. ''We had to be sure you could handle something simple before we could give you anything difficult.''

''So why the hell didn't you tell me that, instead of letting me believe I was ready to go operational?''

Kathleen answered me. ''We wanted to see if thinking you were going operational would pose a problem for you. I'm sorry for the deception, but we had to know.''

As angry as I was, I had to agree. "I understand. It's just a bit unsettling, not knowing when you're pulling a fast one on me."

"It had to be done. I'm sorry," said Mel.

"Okay. . . . Where to next?"

"Before you go anywhere, I want you to look at that target folder again," Mel answered. "Don't blow off good feedback just because the target wasn't what you expected." He tossed the folder back on my lap. "Open it and let's see how good or bad you were."

I opened the folder again and carefully analyzed it under the watchful eyes of my mentors. "Hmmm, pretty interesting."

"Isn't it?" said Riley. "Do you realize that you were in the target area seconds after taking the coordinates? And if that's not enough for you, take a look at your findings. 'A building,' you said. Well, this museum certainly looks like a building to me. 'With aspects of old and new,' you said. Kathleen, does a museum have old things in it as well as new ones?"

"Yup!" She grinned.

"All right, I get the message."

"Look, Dave," Riley said, "you were on target almost instantly. You collected information that would have cracked the target wide open had this been an operational mission. You saw weapons where there were weapons. You accessed a Union soldier who's been dead over a hundred years. You captured every critical aspect of the target. So what's your bitch?"

I was embarrassed. "I apologize. I deserve whatever you guys hand out."

Riley chirped, "I'd say you deserve a break today—like lunch at McDonald's. My treat."

"I thought you didn't eat fast food."

"Well, I'm making an exception today. Kathleen, you coming?"

"No, you two go ahead. I'm brown-bagging it."

"Yeah, and you'll live longer than the two of us because of it."

After lunch Riley promised to send me on a real operational target. I took my position in the chair and hooked into the control panel to begin the cool-down process. I emptied my mind and slowed my pulse to about thirty-two beats per minute. This time without prompting from Riley, I picked up the pen, ready to receive the coordinates. I called them out as I wrote them. And as I recorded the final digit my right hand lurched, forming a quick, roughly circular ideogram.

"Good; now decode it," came Riley's comforting voice.

I touched the ideogram with the pen; my physical body slumped in the chair and I "separated" again. I found myself spread-eagled, spinning into the stars. This time I felt better about what was happening. As I righted myself, the lights of the stars blurred into horizontal streaks. I felt charged with electricity; my skin crawled and tingled, and my phantom body grew cold as ice.

I could feel my limbs, and my inclination was to rub them to get some life and warmth back into them; but there was nothing physical to rub. I felt myself rising higher and higher, and I closed my eyes to absorb the sensation. Suddenly, I stopped moving upward. I felt myself casually turning to the left as though I were doing a cartwheel, and then I began plummeting down the tunnel of light. I accelerated toward the target, faster and faster. The silence of the ether grew to a huge roar, as if I had stuck my head outside a jet in flight. I tried to cover my ears, but I was still unable to manage my limbs. When I finally opened my eyes, I saw myself falling toward the strange light again and I braced for the impact. I felt the light puff-of-air sensation, followed by the immediate silence. I was there.

"I can't move! I can't move! It's like I'm stuck in molasses," I cried. The sensation was stifling; I was being held in position by something I couldn't see.

"Dave, calm down and describe what you see. Do you know where you are?"

I began coughing, choking, and flailing my arms about. I threw my head back, gasping for air and freedom; I felt as if I were fighting for my life. The pen fell from my hand.

"David! David! Get some height. Raise yourself above the target, David. Raise yourself!" I could hear Mel shouting and I struggled to comply. Gasping for air, coughing, I pitched backward in the viewing chair and sucked in a long, rasping breath, like a diver who's made an emergency ascent. I was filled with fear, my hands were balled into fists, and I was wringing wet. I tried to regain my composure. "What . . . happened?"

I think Mel knew what had happened, but first he had to stabilize me and get me to describe what I was seeing.

"Dave, I need you to tell me what you see. You need to get control, shake it off, and get back to the mission."

I sensed the confidence in his firm tone. I gathered myself and tried to focus on the target. In what seemed only a few minutes I was calm enough to begin talking again.

"Uh"—I swallowed hard—"I see a glassy surface below me."

"Glassy, as in flat and smooth?" Riley asked.

"No; it's smooth and flat, but there's some texture to the surface."

"How big is it?"

I turned in a slow circle above the plane. "It reaches as far as I can see in every direction, but it's hard to tell, because there's a fog or mist blocking my view."

"About how far can you see?"

"Oh, I guess about two, maybe three hundred meters."

"Smell the air, Dave, and tell me what you smell."

I closed my eyes and took a deep breath. "It smells like the sea, just like the sea!"

Riley sounded relieved. "Let's get back to the mission. What you're seeing is not the target; you need to find the target."

I closed my eyes and "listened" for anything, any perception, that might lead me to the target. Somewhere off in the haze I felt a vibration. Its pitch stayed constant, reverberating in my head.

"I feel a vibration, and I think I can find the source."

"Good. Move there now."

The vibration grew louder and more intense with each passing second. I stopped for a moment to get a better bearing, hovering a few feet above the glassy surface and listening. The sound and vibration increased. I turned from side to side, my eyes still closed, straining to get a bearing on the source. The vibration rapidly grew so intense that it shook my entire body.

Later, Mel told me he saw my hands shaking on the viewing table.

The sound grew to a roar, and I opened my eyes to see a dark mountain of steel coming at me. It hit me head on. I winced, but my phantom body passed through the steel. Reeling but uninjured, I hurled myself at the object, trying to catch it. In a few seconds, I was matching its speed, flying a hundred or so feet above it. It was obscured by the haze, so I moved in for a closer look.

"I see a large metal object moving quickly across the glassy surface."

"Tell me about it."

"Uh, it has an odd shape, angular on one end, and rounded on the other. The rounded end is the front, or, at least that's the direction it's moving in. The object is covered in boxes, tubes, and the like . . . let's see . . . and it's got two major features that I can see."

"What are they?" Riley asked.

"There is a large glass-covered box in the center of the object, toward the rounded end. I think it has some control feature. And on the square end there are one, two, three cylinders about five or six yards long. There is some sort of force coming from them, but I can't make it out—I mean, I can't see what it is. It's invisible to me."

"Can you tell me how fast the object's moving?"

"I can't tell. I don't know how to gauge it."

"Guess."

"Hmm . . . I'd guess about forty to maybe fifty miles per hour."

"Okay, I want you to come back now. Break contact and come home."

"On my way!"

It took several minutes to get back. This time the effects of the session were less severe, though I felt weak and had trouble focusing, as if I were still attached to the target in some way. I kept crossing the threshold, passing in and out of the ether without any control over the process. After a while this symptom passed, but I was to experience it after every viewing session. I learned that if viewers worked more than twice in a day, we had to be driven home. We weren't fit to drive ourselves; the chance that we would slip back into the ether was too great.

Riley went into the monitor's room and talked with Kathleen, returning to the viewing room just as I was getting coherent.

"Stay in here and work on your summary; as soon as you're ready, come into the garden room. Kathleen and I will be in there waiting, okay?"

"Sure."

"You doing all right?"

"I feel a bit weak, that's all. I'll be okay in a minute or two."

Riley left the room and met Kathleen in the hall. I could hear them talking.

"So, what did you think?" asked Riley.

"He's fast, first of all. But that's not where it stops; he's accurate, as well."

The two walked into the viewing room; I was just standing up from the table.

"Go ahead and get started on your summary," Riley said. "You can use the garden room and we'll join you in a few minutes."

"Wait a damned minute. You guys are walking around here talking about me like I wasn't even in the building.

Well, I am. And if you're going to talk about me, have the decency to include me. Now, what did I do wrong?''

"Okay," Riley said, "you didn't do anything wrong. I just wanted Kathleen to see what you left us on the table here. Look on the table there in front of Dave.'' He pointed to several small pools of liquid on the table. I'd coughed them up when I was choking early in the session.

"What is it?" Kathleen asked, keeping her hands in her pockets, but bending to get a closer look.

Riley looked at me. "Where do you think you landed at first? Don't think about it too much, just call it, tell us what it was like."

"Well, I couldn't breathe, there was a lot of pressure, and the environment around me was thick and restrictive. When you told me to move upward out of it, I did, and I could breathe and move."

"Yeah, but it wasn't that simple, was it? You coughed and choked on the thick stuff. You couldn't breathe for a reason. What was it?"

I looked at Kathleen, but she stared at me blankly. "I don't know. Honestly, I don't know."

"You landed underwater, and you started choking. You were spitting this stuff out like a drowning man. It was unbelievable!"

"That's ridiculous. I wasn't really in the water!"

"No, you weren't really in the water. But your physical body will manifest certain reactions to what your phantom body is experiencing in the target area. That's part of bilocation, and you're catching on to it very quickly, which is great. But the downside is you don't have enough experience to understand it, react to it, and deal with it quickly; and that can be dangerous."

I stuck my finger into a pool of liquid and smelled it. "It's not seawater?"

"No, it isn't," Riley said. "But it's liquid that came from you, and that's enough."

Kathleen said nothing. She gave the liquid another close look and then followed Riley into the garden room.

In a few minutes I joined the two of them with my notes and sketches.

Riley began. "So! Tell us what you saw."

I laughed nervously. "Well, I tasted more than I saw at first. And it was pretty scary coughing it up. I understand that I was in some sort of water, but I don't have any idea where."

"The Baltic Sea," Kathleen said.

"Really?"

"Really. Now tell us about the object."

"Well, it was constructed mostly of metal. It was largely gray, although there was a good deal of black as well. I was fascinated by the three cylinders at the square end of the thing. They were the source of the vibration I reported, and appeared to be a power cell or propulsion device of sorts."

"Were there people on this object?" Riley asked.

"I didn't see any, but then I didn't look for them. I kept my distance, pretty much."

"You mentioned a box, with glass—do you remember?" Riley asked.

"Yes . . . yes, I do. I remember feeling that it had something to do with controlling the object. I think if there were people on this thing that's where they'd be."

"Can this object turn or maneuver in any way?" Riley interjected. "Can it move on any kind of surface, or is it limited to what you saw?"

"I didn't see it do anything but travel in a straight line. But for some reason, I'm certain that it can do just about whatever it wants. It can travel over all kinds of terrain if necessary, but it's most at home where I saw it."

"You mean on water."

"Yeah, on water. Okay, what is it?" I asked.

"You tell me." Riley handed me the target folder.

I gawked in amazement at its contents. "Damn! So, that's what it was."

In my hand was an intelligence photograph of a Soviet *Pomornik*-class air-cushioned landing craft, fifty-seven meters long with a 350-ton displacement. In the photograph the ship glided along the surface of the water on a cushion of air, powered by three huge encased fans mounted on the rear.

I could only think of one thing to say: "Fascinating!"

"Yeah, fascinating," Riley and Kathleen said in tandem. Riley smiled and shook his head. "I take it back. I told everybody you were a dumb-ass infantryman and I was having to shove this stuff down your throat with a pitchfork. But I'm beginning to think you might be catching on. This is good."

I didn't know whether to be flattered or insulted. "So when do I get to give the lectures?"

"Oh, not long. Maybe in five or ten years."

We all laughed and headed for the office. I needed a good night's sleep.

FIVE

THE CHANGELING

My next mission time was posted on the assignment board, with a huge red "T" beside my name. *Another training target,* I thought. *Someday it won't be.* Kathleen and I entered the viewing room and started to hook up all the monitoring apparatus.

I'd been in the unit for eight months now, and I'd graduated from coordinate remote viewing a few weeks ago. That meant I was no longer required to sit in a viewing chair, or take the coordinates sitting up, or produce an ideogram. For extended remote viewing, ERV, all I did was lie on a specially designed platform bed, count down, and make the separation into the ether. I was still hooked up, and still monitored by Kathleen in the room as well as by the audio and video monitor.

ERV technique was to place the tasking sheet on the small table next to the platform. I would look at the tasking sheet, focus on the encrypted coordinates, and then lie back, adjust the lighting, and go. With ERV, I could stay in the ether a good deal longer than under coordinate remote viewing conditions. Some of the viewers, like Mel and even Kathleen, preferred the discipline of the CRV protocols, but I became attached to the free-form process of ERV; once I had made the switch, under Levy's tutelage, I never went back.

Adjusting her own light, Kathleen took up her position

at the desk overlooking the platform I'd call home for the next hour and a half. I looked at my tasking coordinates a final time: "Coordinates seven eight five six four, nine three four five two; describe the target and any significant events." Within minutes I was in the ether and on my way to the target. Paul Posner monitored the changes in my physical body which indicated to him that the separation was complete.

"He's gone," he said.

"I know." Kathleen had been with me so often that she could tell by my breathing rate when I was gone.

I made the long fall down the tube of light and passed through the membrane into the target area. I never got used to the sickening feeling of the descent; no matter how many times I did it, it was like making a night parachute drop with combat equipment. Your heart jumps into your mouth every time you step out of the aircraft and into the empty night.

I slowed to a stop some feet from a cold stone wall. Righting myself, I studied the rough granite and lines of mortar. Grass grew up against the wall, which stretched some hundred feet to my right. The surroundings were barren and drab, the air cold and damp. Kathleen interrupted my absorption with the place.

"Where are you?"

"I have no idea. It's cold and damp, and very lonely. . . . I feel very lonely here."

"What are you looking at right now?"

I turned slowly, surveying all that was around me, describing it to Kathleen as it came into view. "I see a large stone wall, maybe a hundred feet long. The grass is poorly kept, and the ground beneath me is wet and spongy-looking; there are large patches of muddy ground as well. I see a small but very old stand of trees in the distance. The bark of the trees is dark and the leaves sparse."

"Do you see any buildings?"

"From where I'm standing, I don't see anything but what I've described. Should I move?"

"Yes. I want you to move ahead through the stone wall and describe what you see."

"I'm moving now." The wall pressed against my phantom form with the sound of Velcro tearing open; in the center of the wall it was dark. It was at times like this that I learned that everything indeed has a spirit. The wall had its own history, and it seemed to weep as I passed through it. I left the darkness feeling as though I'd left a painful, clutching memory behind.

After this training, I never doubted that all things are animate. To hear or feel an object speak had been unfathomable only a few short months ago; now, it was a not so uncommon event. Every viewer experienced it at times; we learned to listen and trust what we heard. Levy had taught me that. A target's surroundings recorded the history of the place without prejudice and stood ready to bear witness to all who had the ears to hear.

When I left the wall, I felt it reaching for me; it was a feeling I had had as a child, of the unknown and unseen reaching for me as I left a dark room at the top of the stairs, and hurried down to light, safety, and the company of others. To me, the wall spoke, and it spoke of pain.

"I sense something wrong here."

"Do you see any buildings?"

I shook off the emotions and surveyed the area again. I had no idea what the target might be. Usually, my targets were things or places, but here I recognized nothing as yet. Nothing but stone and emptiness—and the small buildings in the distance.

"I see some buildings, maybe a hundred yards away. I'm moving to them."

"Good! Focus on the buildings. Go inside and tell me what you see and feel there."

I stood outside the closest building. They were aligned in a neat row, their corners matching perfectly, the pitch of their roofs the same. In all, I could see four, maybe five of them. Tall pillars jutted from them, scratching at the grayness of the sky.

"I'm standing at the nearest corner. The buildings are constructed mostly of stone, but there are a few walls of red brick. Some of the brickwork looks like repairs, patches. There are tall brick pillars sticking up from the buildings, maybe two or three per building."

"David, slowly touch the building."

"Okay . . . It's a rough granite; the only wood seems to be in the trim and rafters." In a few seconds I was overcome with grief. My phantom body quivered as I held fast to the building. My heart ached, and a sense of complete despair and depression enveloped me. Spikes of hatred and denial stabbed at me. "I—I have to let go. I can't touch it any longer. I'm sorry, I just can't."

"Tell me what you feel. Be specific, ask questions, search for answers; you have to work—work hard!"

"Uh . . . I feel hopelessness. I feel forgotten and I've given up. I don't fear anything any longer, although there is much to fear here. This place is filled with hatred and evil. . . . There is no goodness here, no light, only darkness and curses. The spirit here is gone, broken and empty. Everything here feels poisoned. Everything here feels dead. Everything here is horror."

"I want you to go inside the building. I want you to search in the same way you've been doing. Touch and ask for answers. Go inside now."

I passed through an arched stone doorway leading into a vacant chamber. "I don't see anything but an empty room."

"Look harder; touch the floor and the walls. Find the answers to this place."

I reached out to the nearest wall and let my hand pierce it. "Oh, my God, this place is sad and empty. The walls feel they are evil, but they aren't, I can tell they aren't. No, wait! They don't *feel* evil, they have *seen* evil—yes, that's it. This room has seen unspeakable evil and the stench will never leave. The spirit of this place is stained; it will never be cleansed."

Kathleen was impressed with these results, but I was still

missing the most important aspect of the site, and she knew why. "David, you're doing fine, but you aren't looking at the entire target. You are allowing yourself to ignore it. You have to open your eyes; you can't allow yourself to see selectively. Open your eyes!"

I struggled to see what she wanted me to see, but I couldn't. I felt too overwhelmed. "I'm trying, Kathleen, but I can't see anything else. I hurt from being here. I want to come back now. I feel filthy and I want to come home and wash. I don't want to be here anymore, do you understand? I want to come back."

"Okay, David, break it off and come back."

It took me twenty minutes to pull myself together. Kathleen met me at the front door of the viewing building with Paul in tow.

"Tough session, huh, buddy?" Posner said. "Don't feel bad, it's a—" He stopped in mid-sentence. "Well, just don't feel like the Lone Ranger on this one. Finish your summary and you'll see soon enough."

Kathleen patted me on the back and gently shoved me out the door and into the sunlight. I looked at her, but all she would do was smile back.

I made several sketches of the wall and the buildings, including the tall brick pillars and the stand of trees on the far side of the wall. I wrote my summary, which amounted to about four pages, and presented the package to Kathleen at her desk.

She thumbed through the sketches, frowning, read the summary, highlighting various passages and descriptions, then made two photocopies of my work. "Sit down," she said. "So—what do you think it is?"

I paused, trying to find the right words. "I think it is a very strange and evil place. I've never felt the place itself talk to me like that. I felt very odd being there, as if I was supposed to listen to the place get something off its chest. I felt as if it were grabbing at me, trying to get me to stay and listen to its tale of woe."

" 'Tale of woe'—you didn't include that in your summary."

"Well, it just came to me. I think the place has a terrible history, and the image of that history will never leave it. That's all I can think of; do I get any feedback?"

Kathleen smiled. "I guess so. You were fairly close." She pulled out the target folder and tossed it to me. "See what you think."

I sighed, pulled open the envelope, and extracted the first of five black-and-white photographs. A Nazi death camp.

"Dachau," I whispered. "I completely missed it, didn't I?"

"Whatever gives you that idea?"

"I missed it! I fucking missed it! I had no idea I was looking at this. And look, the ovens—I didn't even *see* the ovens where they burned the bodies. Thousands of bodies."

"Oh, no? What do you call these? Kathleen pointed at my sketches, then set them alongside the photographs. "These brick pillars look like the stacks for the ovens to me. And what about the emotion of the place? You damned near drained it all out. You did fine; quit beating yourself up. This is a difficult target; nobody waltzes in and waltzes back out. Every time you go to a place like this you leave something behind. Every time you go here you will experience something more evil, more lost, more godforsaken. You were right when you said the place was stained with evil."

"Why the hell did you send me there, anyway? What could possibly come from it, besides another nightmare for me?"

"Everyone gets sent there; it's part of the training program. Every person in this office has been there, and everyone here has been affected just like you."

"Everyone?"

"Everyone except Judy. She crawled around in the ash and bones of the ovens and never picked up anything out of the ordinary. She came back and described the place as a military post or something like that."

"Why is it important for us to go there?"

"You have to experience the extreme out there in the ether, in order to be able to understand the nuances of some more obscure targets: double agents, test pilots, politicians. In the near future you will learn how to reach the minds of these men and women and tell us what they are thinking and feeling. If you can't train yourself to grasp the extreme, overwhelming evil of Dachau, how can you expect to grasp the more subtle nuances of a pilot test-flying the latest Soviet fighter? Learning the extremes is the first step in the process of getting your eyes. You want them, don't you?"

"Of course."

"Then you will have to pay a price." She stood, collected the folders, and shook my hand. "You did very well; I'm proud of you, and you should be proud of yourself. Look, let's call it a day. This was a tough mission and I don't want to run you on your afternoon session. I'm going to tell Levy that I think you should hit the road and get some rest. Why don't you get your files cleaned up and I'll take care of him, okay?"

"I don't need—"

"Listen to me; if Mel were here he'd tell you the same thing."

"Okay, whatever you say, professor."

Kathleen was right: I needed to go home; the mission had really shaken me up. Levy understood completely. As I drove home, images of that place followed me; they lasted throughout the night. I'd never forget.

The next morning was uneventful except for a blowout between a couple of the remote viewers and the two channelers. There are a lot of arguments among remote viewers as to the effectiveness of channeling. By definition, channeling involves the use of either oral or written data transfer. The channeler invokes a so-called "spirit guide" during the session. Through the guide, the channeler will allegedly talk to the "thing" being contacted. Placed in the context of the military spy arena, this approach obviously has severe limitations. It appeared that Carol, who was essentially Judy's protégée, had turned in a poor-quality session summary. She had been working with Lyn on an operational target for about two weeks and had completed about five sessions. Now Lyn wanted a complete summary with sketches, but he was dissatisfied with the results, including almost meaningless conclusions like, "There is blue at the site." Lyn, who was a remote viewer, had every excuse to present this nonsense to Levy as evidence of the dangers of mixing channeling with remote viewing. Lyn was a consummate trainer of remote viewing and he hated to see potentially good viewers waste their abilities on the channelers' unproved methods. Whenever something like this happened, and it often did, tempers flared and opinions and accusations flew. I learned to ignore the blowouts, to stay the hell out or suffer the consequences. You couldn't talk quietly about anyone in the office—after all, in a group of remote viewers, how could you talk about someone without her knowing it? I kept my own counsel and kept my mouth shut.

Besides, as I saw it, nobody in the unit had any reason to second-guess anyone else about what they did or how. We were government-paid and government-trained psychics, spying on the enemies of the United States; why get riled up about the method used? At this point in my life, I was so overwhelmed by what I was learning that I didn't draw any lines. If someone had told me that I'd have better viewing results if I ate frogs before a session, I'd have been looking for a supplier. I didn't want any part of the cancer that was slowly eating away at the cohesion of the unit.

I was scheduled for a ten o'clock ERV session with a training target and Mel as my monitor. We walked to the viewing building together. Mel carried his coffee in a broken-down chipped-up mug about a hundred and fifty years old. I was surprised it held liquid, but he was never without it.

"I think you'll enjoy today's little journey," he said.

"I could use a little entertainment."

Once I was set up and ready, I started my countdown; in a few minutes I was entering the ether and on my way to the target.

"Give me your impressions as soon as possible. I don't want you wasting any time here."

"I'm someplace like a cave. It smells musty and the ground is cold. The air isn't moving at all, and it's completely dark. I can't see anything at all." I moved forward in the direction the signal line led me. "No, I see a small flicker of light in front of me."

Riley leaned back in his chair and watched the video monitor closely. "Good! See what the light is."

I moved toward the light as fast as I could, but it seemed to move away from me, as if I were chasing something in a dream. I chased the light for about ten minutes, but though I was moving in what I thought was a straight line, I just wasn't gaining any ground. Frustrated, I stopped.

"I've stopped moving toward the light source, Mel. I just couldn't close on it. I don't know if I'm not really moving, or if it's moving away from me. I'm just standing here in the dark now."

"Do you sense anything in the darkness? Anyone or anything?"

My first thought was, *Great! Just what I want to do, grab something in the dark.* "All I can say, Mel, is this target better not be a page out of the *Odyssey*. If I run into a—"

"Oh, be quiet and look around. You can't remote-view something that never happened, for crying out loud."

Suddenly, the cavern I stood in was flooded with brilliant light that came from *within* the surrounding stone. The light vanished as quickly as it had come. "What the hell was that?" I shouted.

"Tell me what you saw."

"I saw a light coming from the walls of the cavern. By the way, I *am* in a cavern; the light just confirmed that. But it's dark again and I see nothing."

Again and again the light pulsed and disappeared, like a strobe. The pulses seemed to pierce my eyes and ears, even my flesh. The temperature of the cavern began to rise rapidly, and it was increasingly difficult to breathe. I told Mel so.

"You need to move on out of there," he replied. "Take a look around for another passageway."

Sure enough, behind me was a wide arched passage into another room. I hadn't seen it because I was facing away from it chasing the light; in retrospect, it was as if the light had been trying to lead me away.

The next room was smaller, a rectangle about twenty feet by ten feet with a ceiling maybe fifteen feet high. Like the larger chamber, it was lit from within the surrounding stone, but something was different, as if the pulsing energy I'd felt in the larger chamber originated here.

"I'm in the smaller of the two rooms, and there seems to be no way out of this one except the entrance I used. I sense some form of energy here, and I'm having difficulty focusing my vision on the center of the room. There's something here that I can't see—but there's something here, for sure."

"An object, a personality, a definitive energy source?"

I struggled to see. "There's a low platform in the center of the room. It's carved out of stone."

"What are its dimensions?"

"About five feet by three feet, and maybe ten inches high. I can't see . . . it's like a mirage in the center of the room."

"You can't focus on it?"

"Exactly. It's vibrating too fast. The vibration's like a camouflage of sorts. Something's there, but I'm not supposed to be seeing it. Something very unusual and powerful."

"Okay, here's what I want you to do. Try and move to a time when there is less vibration and you might be able to see."

I understood; we'd worked on movement exercises like this before. The idea was that if I initiated movement in time the signal line would take me where I could view the target clearly. It had worked on some small training targets, but I hadn't tried it on anything like this.

I concentrated on the movement through time and closed my eyes to the events speeding by. I felt vertigo setting in, which indicated the speed of my movement. I'd found it best to keep my eyes closed so as not to vomit. Finally the sensation of movement slowed gradually and stopped. When I opened my eyes, I beheld the most bizarre scene.

In the center of the room a group of peasants chipped away at the stone of the floor, forming the pedestal I'd already seen. Now time scrolled forward, stopped briefly, then scrolled forward again: the signal line was moving me at will, allowing me to see the room at various points in time. Finally it stopped completely, at a point it must have "felt" was critical to the mission.

In amazement, I watched as four men dressed in ancient-seeming clothes carried a golden box into the room. One man at each corner of the object, they reverently positioned it in the center of the stone pedestal and retreated backward from the room, their heads bowed. Now a huge stone covered the room's entrance, and slowly all outside light was blocked as the men labored to seal the passage. Oddly, the golden box kept the room lighted. And the same strange energy I had felt before, when I could see nothing, filled the cavern. A sense of threat came over me; I felt I was being warned not to approach the box.

"What's going on, David?"

"I'm in the presence of the object and it's very weird, as though I were standing in the presence of some very powerful deity. The golden box is a symbol of that power, and it's warning me not to come closer."

"I want you to ignore the warning and get as close as you can. Touch it if you can, and describe the sensation to me."

I tried to move toward the object. "It's a golden box with animals on top of it."

"Real animals?"

"No, small statues, and they have wings that sweep

backward and up. The box itself is very powerful, or maybe it's something that protects the box that's powerful. Whatever it is, I can't get any closer. I feel I'm in real danger of being hurt; I don't like this.''

"Remember, you're not physically there. But tell me what you think would happen if you *were* physically there. Describe that sensation to me.''

"I think that nothing mortal can be in this presence. I couldn't even be in the same room with it; if I were, I'd perish instantly.''

"You'd die?''

"No, I don't think 'die' is the word. I'm thinking more along the lines of being vaporized. But I seem to feel that that would mean another movement to another place, only I wouldn't have any control over it. What I'm trying to say is, nobody's supposed to be here. Even *we* aren't supposed to be here; it's an invasion, an intrusion into something very powerful and sacred.''

"Ah, that word 'sacred.' Explore that a bit—look into the essence of the box. What's there that's sacred?''

I moved around the box carefully, never taking my eyes off it and never letting the doorway out of my sight. ''Well, I sense that this symbol is, or has been used as, a tool.''

"What sort of tool?''

"I don't know exactly. It had some very lofty purpose, and it served a great number of people for a long time. Then it was placed here until it was needed again. Many people lost their lives to be able to use it; even more died in order to get it here.''

"Why is it in that lonely place, do you think?''

"It's been hidden until called out again. Its purpose has been served for now, but not forever. It's being protected. If you try to unravel its secret you are dumbfounded and confused—that's one of its defenses. If you stumble upon it, you are destroyed or taken away to another place for fear you might reveal the secret.''

"All right; you've been there an hour and forty minutes now. Let's break it off and come home.''

Those were the words I wanted to hear. I felt very uncomfortable and vulnerable in the cavern. "I'm on my way."

An hour later I sat in the garden room with Levy and Mel and discussed my session with them. They began with the usual questions: "What did you think it was? What is this sketch of? How did you feel?" And so on. They marveled at my sketches of the box and the winged creatures that adorned it. They discussed the powerful unseen presence and the indications of a protective force. We talked for more than an hour without them revealing anything concrete about the target, but finally Mel suggested that I be given my feedback. Like a dog waiting for a bone, I waited for the envelope. Levy opened it first and looked inside, smiling. Of course, he already knew what the target was; he just wanted to amuse himself with another look at the feedback. Shaking his head, he tossed the artist's sketch from the envelope on the desk in front of me and walked out of the room.

"Well, aren't you going to look at it?" Riley asked.

I turned the paper over to see a painting and description of the Ark of the Covenant. "Oh, my God," I said slowly.

" 'Oh, my God' are the exact words I was looking for." Riley laughed. "I was sure you were gonna say 'em any time. But the damned thing is just too powerful. I had the same problem. The only person to ever call it in the air, so to speak, was Posner. I think it's because he's such a hardhead he didn't hear the thing warning him not to come any closer, or maybe he knew what it looked like before he got started—he's kind of religious, you know. Have you ever seen a picture before?"

"Nope! I've heard of it—I mean, who hasn't? But I never knew what it looked like. Or felt like."

"Some very important religious articles were carried around the desert in that thing. It went along with Moses in the wilderness."

"Yeah, I'm sort of familiar with the story. I had to take religion every semester at BYU."

"Did you know the Ark was part of a dimensional opening?"

"What do you mean, 'dimensional opening'?"

"I mean a portal that lets you move from one dimension to another. I think God dwells in a four-dimensional world; that's why He's omnipresent and omniscient. When the high priests went into the inner sanctum of the Temple in the wilderness, they tied ropes to their ankles so their buddies could pull them back. These guys were traveling somewhere, and I believe it was to another dimension, where they would commune with the Creator. The ropes on their ankles were their way of making sure they had a round-trip ticket. Cool, huh?"

I stared at him. "You never cease to amaze me, my friend."

Kathleen was responsible for my next mission. She had selected the target in accordance with Levy's wishes and was waiting in the monitor room when I arrived.

"Go ahead and get hooked up; here are your tasking sheet and coordinates. It's pretty simple today, no tricks or heavy stuff. Okay?"

"You bet. I should be ready to go in about five or ten minutes. I'll give you a holler over the intercom."

I hooked myself up in ERV Room Number Two and took my position on the platform.

"Okay, I'm ready to start the countdown."

"Fine," said Kathleen. "Start talking to me as soon as your eyes clear and you're in the target area."

I said nothing as her voice faded and I began my separation. The fall through the tunnel seemed longer this time and I never hit the membrane at all. It seemed to me that I'd traveled a great distance, or perhaps had missed the coordinates.

"My throat seems constricted, and there's a harsh chemical smell, like some caustic solvent."

Kathleen watched my respirations on the monitor. "Concentrate on your breathing, David; keep track of it, and remember, nothing can hurt you there.''

"I'm having trouble breathing; my throat's sore. It feels like it's being burned inside. All I see is a desolate-looking landscape, very lunar. The soil is amber and there is no atmosphere—I should say, no oxygen. Where *is* this place?''

"You tell me. Take a look at the horizon—do you see anything familiar? Look at the sun or whatever the light source is; does it look familiar? Do you see anything out of the ordinary that might help you determine where you are? Come on, now . . . you need to learn to look for these clues on your own.''

I looked to the horizon, a staggering landscape of jagged mountains and rock outcroppings. The sky was black, not blue, and I saw no moon. The stars had an odd shimmer, not like what I remembered looking into the night sky in New Mexico or Wyoming. And the sun was very different, smaller and colder.

"This isn't Earth, I know that much. I can see distant ranges of mountains, an open landscape littered with rock of all sizes and shapes. There's a fine dust covering everything, and a harsh wind seems to be kicking up in the distance, spreading the dust. A giant red cloud is climbing upward from the effect of the wind.''

"Are you alone there?''

That stopped me in my tracks. "I certainly fucking hope I'm alone here. Why? Am I not supposed to be?''

"I'm asking for your impressions of the target. Try not to second-guess me even if the question seems a little leading. I merely want to suggest that you look for something that might not be obvious.''

"I don't know. I don't see any structures or anything that remotely looks like a structure, not even any caves. I'll try to search backward in time.''

I let the signal line drag me into the past; present time gave me little information. I closed my eyes to ride the movement out, and I opened them to a landscape that hadn't changed a bit.

"I don't understand it. I just executed a fairly large movement in time and I still don't see anything. Nothing on the horizon has changed, nor in the atmosphere. I'm going to walk around for a while. I think I'm okay with the breathing now."

"You appear to be; I'm not seeing any adverse reactions on the monitors. Don't wander too far, though. I don't want to leave you here too long."

"I'm walking toward a large outcrop of rocks maybe five hundred yards away. The atmosphere is very strong and caustic; it makes my skin tingle. I'm dropping down into a small depression in the surface. It's maybe five feet deep and thirty feet across. I'm on the far rim now and still moving toward the rocks. I see nothing of interest here, and I find no indication of life, not even me. I'll keep on in this direction a little longer—" I stopped, noticing something in the soil. "That's odd."

"What?"

"There are two identical linear depressions running in front of me. They are parallel, maybe ten feet apart, and they run along the ground about sixty feet with a few short breaks. The depressions are about three quarters of an inch deep and about twenty inches wide. I can't see any reason why they start where they do or where they're headed. They aren't headed toward the mountains, but rather more or less parallel to them."

"Touch one and see what you get."

"I'm touching it now, and I . . . these are not natural. I mean, nothing fell out of the sky and skidded here; these were made by something or someone."

"Did the makers live there?"

"Yes, I think so. I think this was home to them, but they weren't there in present time. What happened to them?"

"Do you think you can answer that question?"

I kept touching the depression. "No, I doubt I can. It seems that whatever happened here took place over many thousands of years. What happened, and how, is a mystery to me. Perhaps with some other sessions and viewers we could figure it out, but I definitely don't have it in me to do it alone, now.''

"Okay, then let's call the mission complete. Break it off and come home."

I was back in the office preparing my summary when Mel approached me.

"How'd it go this morning?"

I showed him my sketches. "This is all I saw except for these two lines in the ground. I don't know; sometimes I think I'm getting worse at this stuff, not better. I can't seem to lock onto what I'm supposed to be looking at. I just wander around until I stumble on something, and even then I can't tell what it is."

"You're doing fine—hell, better than fine. Look, you're not being targeted against fixed installations like museums and churches anymore. You're moving up in the world to difficult targets with extreme emotional and intellectual impact. This is the stuff that separates talented psychics from remote viewers. You're learning to be a workhorse, not a sideshow. Nobody has the key to success here, and we all have good and bad sessions. You will, but from what I can see, this was not one of them. You get on target faster than anyone I've seen; you may not have the skills to pick things apart yet, but you don't fuck around when it comes to getting there. So stop pissing and moaning and finish this summary. I want to see the target folder."

Kathleen came around the corner and glanced at my sketches briefly. She looked at Mel and tossed the folder to me before I'd finished the summary.

"But—" I said.

"Just look at it, and don't tell Levy I gave it to you this soon. If I didn't think you were right on, I'd make you wait."

The target folder contained a series of shots taken from Mars orbit and from a lander on the planet's surface. There was a chemical analysis of the atmosphere, and some high-altitude photographs of the surface with captions indicating which spots had led several scientists to believe Mars was once inhabited.

"Interesting!" I said.

"Mel, I believe our boy is growing bored with his travels. 'Interesting,' he says about the surface of the planet Mars." Kathleen was a bit indignant.

"Ah, he just wants to branch out a little more, that's all."

"Branch out? Branch out from Mars? Well, I'll work on it." She snatched up the folder and headed for the door. "I expect the rest of your summary in ten minutes."

"I do believe you've pissed her off," Mel said. He took out a cigarette. "I'll leave you to your misery while I go smoke this thing."

I plodded my way through the rest of the summary and turned it in to Kathleen. "Hey, I'm sorry if I came across as an ass," I apologized. "I guess I'm looking for answers out there, and all I ever run into are more questions."

"I know how you feel, and I apologize for losing my cool. I have an agenda in mind for you, and it's frustrating when you don't realize the significance of what you're doing. Going to the surface of Mars and back in a matter of minutes is significant stuff; you can't just blow it off because it doesn't answer all your questions. One big question it should have answered for you was whether you can journey off-planet and survive. Another thing: we are not alone in this universe. That's the kind of lesson I want you to learn here. Everything else will come in time. Okay?"

I smiled at her. "You know, if you'd been my freshman math teacher in high school, I most certainly wouldn't be so bad at math now." I patted her on the shoulder. "Thanks for your patience. I know I'm a terrible student."

"You're an infantryman; I don't expect anything more. What's that saying? Arguing with an infantryman is like wrestling with a pig: everybody gets dirty, but the pig loves it."

*   *   *

One hot summer day Debbie managed to convince me to have a picnic with her and the children. Burba Lake, just across the road from the unit, was ideal. We enjoyed lunch and had a game of kickball in the grassy fields surrounding the lake. While the children played only feet from us, Debbie and I lay in the sun and spoke of happier times and better places.

"Sometimes I wish we were back at BYU just being students. We only had two hundred and fifty dollars a month to live on, but we were happy, weren't we?" Debbie asked.

"Yeah, honey. We were really happy. I remember what a night out consisted of after Michael was born. Remember that?"

"You mean the trips to the Snow White Drive-In for five-for-a-dollar hamburgers?"

"Exactly—and we could doctor those things until they put Burger King to shame, couldn't we?"

We both laughed, relaxing in the Maryland sunshine. A flock of geese paddled by our picnic site. Michael and Mariah tossed pine cones at them, producing a clatter of wings and water.

"We used to go to the BYU Film Society showings for a trip to the movies," Debbie reminisced. "Only cost us twenty-five cents apiece to see a movie."

"You mean *try* to see a movie, between taking our screaming kid outside or getting up so someone else could take out theirs. Remember we couldn't even afford a bag of popcorn? We had to bring our own from home and sneak it inside. I wonder what would have happened if they'd caught us."

She chuckled. "At BYU? Are you kidding? We'd have made campus headlines: 'Popcorn Smugglers Nabbed in the Act.' I can just see it, you and I expelled for violating the popcorn law: no education, no job, no future." She hesitated for a moment. "No army, no bullet, no nightmares."

"Come on, honey, things haven't been all that bad, have they? I mean, we have the house in Bowie, our kids get to stay in one place, I'm home most every night. It's not like it was in the Rangers.''

"I enjoyed the Ranger battalion. I liked helping the troops and their families. It made me feel needed, which I don't feel now. I was a part of a team there, our team. I loved Colonel Taylor and Keith Nightingale and their wives and kids. It was just a better time, that's all. And I miss it.''

"I know you do. Deep inside me, I miss it, too; I just can't afford the luxury of thinking about it any longer. Here is where I am now, and I'm changing because of it. I know you don't like it, and I'm causing you a lot of problems, but I think it will work out in the long run. Everything in life happens for a reason. You and I always felt that way about the army, we always felt that we would be put where we could do the most good, influence things for the better. I have to keep on believing that. I have to believe that everything in my life has led me to this point." I snuggled into her shoulder. "Now just hold me and tell me you love me while I catch a nap.''

"I do love you, husband. I always have, and I always will.'' She sighed a troubled woman's sigh. "You go to sleep.'' She stroked my hair until I fell asleep.

I opened my eyes to the bright sunshine. "Damn, Debbie, how long did you let me sleep?'' I reached for my watch and shoes but they were gone. I was alone. Panicking, I jumped up and ran this way and that, trying to find Debbie and the children. "Dammit, I can't believe she'd just get up and leave me lying here. Dammit! Dammit! Where the hell are my shoes?''

I turned toward the unit and my eyes met those of a familiar figure. It was the angel from my visions in Jordan. He stood looking at me, saying nothing.

"You again! Listen, I don't know who you are or what you're doing here, but you're not leaving until I get some answers out of you. First off, where the hell are my wife and kids?''

He spoke to me in a tone so loving and gentle that my

entire body filled with warmth and light. "They're still here, right where you left them."

I risked another look around me, but they weren't there.

Before I could speak, the angel said: "You can't see them because you are in another dimension, parallel to theirs. They can't see or hear you. I assure you they are perfectly safe, and unaware of your absence."

I nodded briefly, not losing eye contact with him. "Okay. But why are you here? Why am I here? What's happening to me?"

The angel smiled knowingly. "You are here to speak to me; I am here to speak to you. What is happening to you is entirely up to you."

"Why me? Why not Mel, or Paul or Kathleen?"

"Because you were chosen. Your father knew it long ago. He will tell you the story one day in the near future, when it is appropriate, and when he finds the courage to tell it to you. He was given information in a vision much like yours."

"What information?"

"That will be for him to share with you, in his time. I want you to know that troubled times await you. Everything you hold dear will hang by a thread, and you will feel alone and hopeless. You will be broken down and cast out. I tell you this so that you can prepare yourself spiritually for the encounter. I'll say no more except that I've been given to you by a very special person who loves you dearly. I will always be with you, even through your darkest hours. Remember that. *I will always be with you, even through your darkest hours.*"

His image faded in the sunlight until nothing remained. I awoke softly, still in Debbie's arms. I kissed her on the cheek and held her tight for a moment longer.

"I have to go to work, honey. Thanks for spending time with me." We embraced as the children gathered around us and hugged our legs. I left them and returned to my world.

*   *   *

The summer of 1989 faded into fall. One morning before work, I found Mel tossing stones into a small creek near the unit.

"You're in early today. Get in trouble at home?" I asked, tossing a small stone at his feet.

"Hey! Watch it. Nah, I just had some thinking to do, and this is as good a place as any to do it."

"Oh? What's so heavy it brings you out here?"

"Retirement." He tossed his final stone and stood looking at the spot where it broke the water. "You know, this old creek has kept me sane for about eight years now. I'll miss it when I have to go."

"Well, why *do* you have to go? You only have twenty years in. Why don't you stay for another ten and retire with a bigger paycheck? Damn, Mel, you never told me you were thinking about retiring. What the hell am I supposed to do around here without you?"

"Thirty?" He laughed loudly. "I wouldn't give the fucking army twenty-four hours past twenty years, and you'd better not either." He picked up some more stones. "Nah, twenty years of your life is more than enough. Especially when you've seen what I've seen. You came from the real army, Dave—the army where they use words like 'pride,' 'passion,' 'honor,' and 'comrade'; those words have been missing from my life since I was a young sergeant. I don't want this anymore. I want a life with Edith, somewhere in Wisconsin, where we can love each other and grow old together."

"It's still not right," I said. "I don't know what I'll do without you here. One thing I've learned in my short time here, you have to have a friend you can trust. You're that friend, and I'll really miss you."

Riley looked at me with less irony than I'd ever seen in him. "Thanks. I consider you a friend, too, and I know I can trust my back to you. That's rare in this business; one day somebody claims he's your friend, the next time he tries to leave a knife in your back. Because he thinks he's smarter than you." He threw his last stone, pulled a small leather bag out of his jacket, untied the top, and reached in. "I made this for you, to keep you safe."

In Mel's hand was a flat, perfectly round stone, in a supple, tightly sewn hide case that left only the top third of it visible. The case was adorned with an intricate pattern of beads and finished with a long strap that allowed it to be hung around the owner's neck. It was beautiful.

"What does this pattern mean?"

"It's your rock medicine—like mine, see?" He pulled his from inside his shirt to show me briefly. "You wear it next to your heart, always. I made yours to indicate that you are a member of the Bear Clan, a warrior class. The symbols on the front represent the bear in his cave. These colors and patterns here represent the piercing bullets of his enemies heading toward him, and the wavy lines here show how his spirit and power have made the bullets waver and fall. See, he's protected by his power, and his power comes from his bravery, and his bravery from his spirit."

"That's really . . . I don't know what to say. Nobody's ever given me anything like this. Thank you, Mel."

"You're welcome, brother, but there's more. Turn it over. The symbols on this side represent balance in all things, sort of an Indian yin and yang. The stone is balanced, as are the colors and symbols on this side of the medicine. The red represents adversity, turmoil, and challenge, while the blue speaks of depth and promise and goodness. The central yellow symbolizes the east-to-west journey of the sun separating the two powers and thus creating balance." He put his hand on my shoulder and smiled lovingly. "I think you need some balance in your life. If you wear this all the time, and believe in it, the medicine will provide what you need according to your faith." His gaze seemed to reach into my soul briefly. "Now, what do you say we get some fucking coffee?"

"Yeah, I could use some. And, Mel, thanks for this. I will never let it out of my sight."

"You know, I picked up that rock about twenty years ago, just before I came into the army. I've carried it all this time waiting for the right way to use it. You better take care of it, it's a Vietnam veteran.''

I wanted to say something important but all I could do was fight the lump in my throat, so I kept my mouth shut and listened to Mel talk all the way back to the office. That night, on my way home, I held the medicine in my hands, rubbing the beads with my fingers until they were warm. I wanted to believe that their power would always keep me safe. I prayed silently that this was my answer to the nightmares.

One day two weeks later, with Mel monitoring, I undertook what was called an open search. In an open search, you have no coordinates to guide you; you just invite the signal line to take you wherever there's something to be learned. Remote viewers did these every so often just so they could remember that there are more of *them* out there—more planets, more beings, more civilizations—than there are of *us* . . . I guess. This was my first such search. Mel had spent the last two days coaching me, but as I began, all I could remember was that they were always humbling experiences, full of surprises.

"Tell me where you are," Mel said.

"In the middle of a prairie. I can see a series of jagged rocks jutting out of the ground about fifty yards away. They're maybe a hundred feet high and they look like black crystals set at a forty-five-degree angle in the ground. It's strikingly beautiful.

"I'm next to the crystals now, and I can see my reflection in them. That's odd—I've never been able to see my reflection in anything on a search before. Also, the reflection looks as if it's a couple of meters *inside* the crystal.''

"Do you—''

"Whoa! I see other reflections in the crystals.'' I spun around, thinking something must be beside or behind me, but nothing was. These weren't reflections at all. "Mel! I see movement inside this black crystal wall. The images look human, but I can't quite make them out.''

"Move into the wall and find out who they are."

I pressed my hand into the crystal and followed it in. "This seems to be an entrance. There's a stairway leading down; it's about twenty feet wide and it drops from here maybe two hundred feet below the surface. I'm going to follow it."

"I want you to describe the beings to me. Tell me what they're thinking, how they look, and what they do."

I descended the stairway. All around me was a labyrinth of causeways and great arching entrances. Everything I saw was made of the black crystal; everywhere I looked, there were people on foot.

"They look pretty much like us, I guess—in fact, I can't see anything markedly different. Their clothing is something like what people wore in ancient Egypt, very loose-fitting and accented with gold embroidery and metal. It's white, which contrasts tremendously with the blackness of this place.

"I'm approaching a transparent archway. It covers the walkway I'm on for several hundred feet. I'm in a big room, and this archway runs the length of it. The damned thing is huge."

"Is there a central place where everyone's congregating?"

"I don't know; let me see." One walkway seemed to have heavier traffic than the others, so I moved there. "I'm following a large group now. It's a very strange feeling, walking among these beings. I get the impression they know I'm here—in fact, several of them have looked directly at me and sort of smiled. They aren't interested in me; they just seem to know I'm here."

"See if any of them will talk to you."

"Okay, whatever you say." Feeling stupid, I waved my arms at the beings, spoke to them, even stood in their way. All they did was look at me; I was in their path, they walked right through me. "Nobody's talking here, Mel. Sorry!"

"Fine, see if you can find some central hub."

"I'm still following this large group; they seem to be turning off . . . yeah, we're entering a large room, where everyone is standing shoulder to shoulder. It's like an amphitheater, very narrow at the bottom and wider at the top. Still made of the black crystal."

"What's going on in this place?"

"There's someone sitting in a big elevated chair at the bottom of the room. Everyone here is paying very close attention to whatever this thing says."

"Why are you calling this being a 'thing'?"

"Uh, that's a good question. I think because he or she or it is larger than the others, and dressed differently. They're in all white; this thing's in black. It has a large open hood over its head, with long flowing sleeves that mostly cover its hands. The hands are not like everyone else's; the texture is much rougher, and the color is darker. If I had to call it, I'd say this one is very evil."

"Evil?"

"Okay, not evil. He's some kind of lawgiver or something. He directs people to do things, and they do them without question. It's not really clear; he points to people, motions to them, and they leave, apparently to carry out some task."

"Can you speak to this lawgiver?"

"No! And I don't even want to try. I can tell he knows I'm here, but he couldn't care less, and I get the impression he'll be pissed if I try to flaunt the fact that I'm here."

"Okay. Have you seen enough?"

"Yeah, I think I have for now."

"Break it off and come on back."

I thought Mel might be disappointed by my timidity. It seemed he wanted me to really assert myself and let the beings know I was there, but I simply didn't feel comfortable doing that. I felt a certain fascination in visiting another world, but I also understood the need to treat it respectfully. I was an invader, not a guest. I saw them look at me; I knew they were aware of my presence, yet they chose not to speak. So it was clear to me that I was being

tolerated, not accepted. And I vowed I would never interfere in other worlds. It was their prerogative to acknowledge me, but I would never force myself on them.

Riley snatched my summary out of my hand. "Come on,
let's get out of here early and grab a beer. I want to talk
to you."

"I hope you're not pissed at me because of the session."

"Pissed? There you go again, thinking you didn't do
well. Dave, what you get out of an open search is up to
you; the unit doesn't have any expectations. Open searches
are freebies; you get to go where the signal line takes you
instead of telling it where you want to go. They're like an
amusement park, only the tickets are your RV training.
Ain't it great?"

"Yeah, I suppose so."

"So, did you learn anything?"

"I guess I learned that there are other worlds and other
civilizations, and that each one has its own agenda in the
universe. It puts things into perspective for me. I used to
think of the human race as God's chosen people, but I'm
obviously wrong."

"What makes you say that?"

"Well, who's to say where God's reign starts and stops?
I mean, He could be the overseer of that place I visited
only hours ago; what makes us any better than those beings?"

"You're catching on, my friend. We're nothing but a
little blue spot in a solar system, in a galaxy with a hundred
million solar systems, in a universe with a hundred million
galaxies. And the truth is we don't know where it ends, or
if it does. And we aren't even talking about dimensions yet.
Gives you a headache, doesn't it?"

I laughed. "It does, at that. Let's go get that beer."

We drove to a small pub off-post and sat at the bar. The
place was a typical military-town bar, plastered with unit
stickers and letters of appreciation from members of this
team and that detachment. There were plaques scattered

across the wall behind the bar, and dozens of bills and coins from around the world, a testimony to the bar's proximity to Defense Department globetrotters. Mel ordered up two dark German beers.

"I've been looking at some property in Wisconsin, and I want your opinion on it." He pulled out a worn newspaper article and some real estate papers, and spread them out on the bar for me to see, ironing them with his hands.

The photos were of an old two-story house in Scandinavia, Wisconsin, with lots of original woodwork and trim, all in hardwood. It sat on a lake with a quiet main street at the front. Giant oak trees wrapped the house in green shade.

"It's gorgeous, Mel. How much?"

"Thirty-eight thousand for five bedrooms and a detached garage, on the lake, with all the history you could ask for." He took a long pull on his beer, belching as he dropped it back on the bar.

"That's it? Thirty-eight thousand for all that?"

"That's it! Now you know why I want to go back home to live. A house like that would cost ten times as much around here. And who the fuck wants to live here? Not me, that's for sure. I want to give Edith a life. Hell, *I* want a life. I want to go fishing." He drained the last of his beer and ordered another. "Yup, it'll be a great place to live and die. And I can remote-view anything I want to, and I won't have to ask permission to do it. I'm looking forward to it."

I tore the label off my bottle as I listened to my friend plan his future. I had no idea what mine would be like. I wasn't even thinking about it these days. "What would you view if you could do anything you wanted?"

"No doubt in my mind. I'd look into the past of the Native Americans and try to find some answers for their future. I'd do anything I could to help them secure a better life. We owe them a lot, and I want to be part of the payback. There's got to be some application for remote viewing in that role, and I'm going to find it."

"I'd've thought you'd spend more time off-planet, looking for extraterrestrials."

"Is that what you want to do?"

"Hell, no! You know how I feel about that—I think it's great that we know they're there, and that they know we're here, but that's as far as it goes. I don't have a thing about it."

"Enough people in the unit do. I thought you'd jump on that bandwagon."

"Not me. I have my own troubles, and so does the rest of humanity. I think the solutions are right here in River City, not out on the edge of the galaxy. Every place I've ever been out there, the locals have been busy with their own agendas. They're mildly curious about us, and that's it. What about you?"

"Well, I'm not all that fascinated either. I think they're kind of like bored neighbors. They drop into our backyard to see what's up but they certainly aren't here to alter the fucking human race or anything. I mean, look at all the other races and species you've seen out there. We're nothing special, right? There are far more advanced and durable species out there—we've seen 'em, you, me, and everyone else in the unit."

"I know. People want to make extraterrestrial life more than it is. They want to market it, and sell everyone on the idea that our future lies in the hands of some wayward space traveler, when we should be looking for answers right here at home. We should be using remote viewing for science and medicine and education. Hell, it could—"

Mel interrupted me. "Hold that thought. Henry! Get my friend another beer; he's waxing philosophical and his bottle's empty. All right, go ahead."

I took a swig and picked up where I'd left off. "Look, we could use remote viewing to find a cure for AIDS, or cancer, or Alzheimer's. With the right controls, with a dedicated group of viewers and a team of technical experts to analyze the data, we could do anything with remote viewing. Instead, what do we do with it? We chase bad guys and spy on the enemy while they turn around and spy on us. It's criminal that we continue to sequester remote viewing as a weapon of war. I don't like it one bit.''

''Whoa, there, buddy, don't forget where you are. This is Meade, the rat's nest of intelligence. Some NSA geek is already playing a tape of those remarks for a counterintelligence officer, and by the time you get home tonight, your phone'll be tapped and one of your neighbors will have been paid off to keep an eye on you.''

We both laughed. ''I know, I know. It's how I feel, anyway. Look, I've got to get home. I'm in the doghouse enough; I don't want to show up with beer breath and have to sleep with the dog. She's not my type.''

We left the bar and headed our separate ways. I couldn't shake my thoughts about the potential of remote viewing, about all the lives that could be saved and all the dim futures that could be turned bright. I let it pass; there was nothing I could do about it.

My training was nearly complete. Levy said so, Mel even asked that I be stepped up. If he'd had his way, I'd have been on operational status for a month already. But, though Levy was pleased with my progress, he felt he'd have a hard time justifying a decision to let me stop training six months sooner than usual. He wanted to let things ride for another month or so.

The winter was upon us. The army at Fort Meade didn't contract for anyone to rake the leaves—I guess they were trying to save money—and the ground was covered with oak leaves. They fell so thickly in this part of the country that they actually became road hazards. People braking would slide on them, just as they would on ice. Being a Southern California boy, I'd never seen such a thing. Our entire office was out in force, raking. We worked our way around the building, scaring our pet cats, and Jenny even got to take a swipe at the squirrel she hated so much. It was the first time I ever saw everyone laugh and talk together; it was also the last. The next year some guy with a huge leaf-sucking truck just drove by the window vacu-uming. Jenny stood at the window praying her squirrel didn't get turned into mush.

I grew more attached to the unit every day; conversely, I grew more distant from Debbie and the children. I was losing my ability to talk to them. If your spouse was inter-ested in what you were doing, there was hope. When she opposed it, even if only deep in her heart, then it was hope-less. If the work hadn't been all-consuming, if I'd had a job that I could leave at the office door, I would have been okay. But I didn't. When I came home I tried to share some of my experiences, but I was the alien in my children's lives; I was a sideshow, a stage trick for their friends. As long as I maintained that role I was okay; my nightmares, though, made them cry and wish for a safer life. I fright-ened them, I frightened Debbie, and worst of all, my vol-atility frightened me.

I stopped writing my mother and father. All I could think of to say was that I loved them; nothing else seemed im-portant enough to write about. They called once in a while, but they were hurt; I'd all but abandoned them. Debbie tried to explain to them that I was, in her opinion, still in des-perate need of help, but I don't think they yet realized how far gone I was. And as for Debbie, I hadn't taken her out on a date in a year or more; we just stopped expecting that of each other. She found new friends, and I lost myself in the ether world. I read books on the subject; I kept notes and a detailed journal of every experience and nightmare I encountered. Involved in my explorations of the unknown, I no longer had time for people who couldn't appreciate that.

Cathy and Ashley Joyner, my closest friends from the Ranger battalion days, whom I loved as if they were my brother and sister, were little more than a memory to me. When I'd left the Ranger battalion—it seemed centuries ago—Ashley had had a beautiful knife custom-made for me, and I treasured it. The single most stunning thing about it was a scrimshawed handshake on the handle, the eternal affirmation of two friends. On the knife's hand-made oak case was the famous Theodore Roosevelt quote that reads, in part, "It is not the critic who counts. Not the man who points out how the strong man stumbled or where the doer of deeds could have done better. The credit belongs to the man who is actually in the arena. Whose face is marred by dust and sweat and blood. Who strives valiantly, who errs and comes up short again and again." I put the knife away; it reminded me too painfully of what I had been.

Debbie had always maintained that she could endure almost anything if I would remain faithful and attend church meetings, at least for the sake of setting an example to the children. But I abandoned the church, and it soon abandoned me. My last encounter with it was in a sacrament meeting one summer day in 1989. It's a custom in the Mormon church for members to speak periodically to the congregation on some topic set by the bishop. The topics are generally simple, in keeping with traditional belief, and members' talks are supposed to be testimonial, informative, and uplifting. Debbie and I were asked to speak.

Debbie gave a wonderful presentation. I, on the other hand, concluded that the congregation had been fed religious pabulum for too long. I ignored the assigned topic and substituted one of my own: "Temples—Beyond Ritual." My talk dealt with issues of dimensionality, astronomy, other worlds and beings, who God really was, and what motivated His dealings with us. I challenged the congregation to expand their minds, to reach beyond the books and spoon-fed teachings of the church, to be more than they'd ever imagined.

I think they thought I was insane. When I gave the concluding "Amen," maybe five people in a congregation of two hundred said it with me. At the time, I was furious. I thought the reaction was a perfect example of organized religion: don't challenge yourself, don't ask questions, just sit in the pews and breathe; God will reward you for it. I thought of *Hamlet*, Act III, Scene ii: "Some must watch, while some must sleep; So runs the world away." *Run away, little sheep, and be safe in your little world; I haven't time for you any longer.* I did not return.

It was the fall of 1990. Mel was getting ready to retire in a couple of months and I wanted to give him something to remember me by. I convinced Debbie to let me dip into savings, and I bought him a canoe. He needed something to fish from, something he could use to get away from it all. I found a place in Alexandria that sold them; by the time I'd learned everything there was to learn, and asked every question I could, the salesman had eleven canoes laid out in the front yard of the place. I sat in every one at least five times. I did some mock paddling, much to the amusement of the salesman and the people who were there to price yachts. I even picked each one up and carried it around the yard a couple of times. The salesman must have thought I was a basket case by the time I pointed at a canoe and said the magic words: "I want that one!" He had the paperwork done and the canoe strapped to my car so fast I thought I'd just bought a Big Mac.

It was worth all the work to see Mel's face when I dropped off the canoe. It was like Christmas, and he was twelve again. Edith, God love her, was naturally concerned about where the damned boat would go until the movers came to pack. Mel, of course, had a number of ideas he was more than willing to share with her. I left them standing at the curb in heavy negotiations, and I drove home with a big smile on my face.

It was Friday, time for the weekly staff meeting. Everyone trickled into the back room and plopped down, waiting for Levy to arrive. I always sat next to Mel; when the meeting got boring I could count on him to have two or three pages of drawings and doodles to glance at. It was amazing what the guy could create when he was bored. Too bad Levy wouldn't let him do beadwork during the meetings.

In meetings, Carol and Judy were their usual sarcastic selves. Pratt and Paul might have been asleep, but their eyes were always open and following whoever was speaking. However, if you asked either one a question about the meeting two minutes after it adjourned, they wouldn't have a clue what you were talking about. It's a knack, I guess.

Kathleen was always attentive and punctual. She even took notes, like one of those little girls I always hated in grade school, pretty, intelligent, teacher's pet. Lyn was like Kathleen, except that he was a guy, which made it worse.

Levy finally showed up, a diet soda in hand. "Are we all here?" Which is what he always asked, though he never got an answer. "Good! I have a few administrative announcements. First, someone has been taking sodas from the fridge and neglecting to pay for them. Whoever it is needs to put about twelve dollars in the soda kitty. Just get it done and nothing else need be said about it."

I elbowed Mel and whispered, "Pay up, asshole."

He just grinned. I don't think I ever saw a soda in his hand.

Levy continued. "Second, if you use the unit car to run to DIA for classes"—he stared at Kathleen and Pratt, who were the only ones taking classes at the Defense Intelligence Agency—"I'd appreciate it if you filled up the tank before returning the car for some unsuspecting soul to get in and try to run to headquarters only to have to hike to a gas station because some uncaring person or persons left it empty! Third, David is now operational. Fourth, we are expected to be at Dr. Compton's retirement next week. If you—"

"Hold on there!" I said. "Can we please go back to Item Number Three? Did you say I'm operational?"

Mel didn't plan on missing the chance to harpoon me. "That's what the man said—didn't you take notes? I think we should give Dave another month or two of training, Bill. I can't believe an operational viewer wouldn't take any notes; you took notes, didn't you, Kathleen?" She held up her paper, snickering. "See! Kathleen took notes."

"All right, all right! Let's get back to business," Levy said. He rambled on for another hour, but I didn't care; I was an operational viewer. No more training targets; from now on it was the real thing, and it counted.

I'd been running operational targets since about two hours after Levy's announcement, but Mel never got to monitor me on an operational mission. He'd left quietly that same day, though he stopped by now and then while he used up his leave and packed up his household. Six weeks later he was gone. He dropped in to say a final good-bye while I was out of the office on an errand, and when I called his quarters, the phone had been disconnected. I drove over there, hoping to catch him on his way out, but the door was locked and his truck was gone. In seventeen hours he'd be starting a new life.

I tried to be happy for him. It took me a long time to get used to his absence, though. Kathleen and Lyn were good people, and I was close to them, but never as close as I was to Mel.

In the next few weeks, Levy announced that he too was retiring, which came as a shock. Who would be his replacement? What would our unit be like without his supervision? It was during this time that a colonel from DIA showed up at the office. I was called in to the office that afternoon.

"David, this is Colonel Welch from DIA. He has something he'd like to talk to you about."

I started sweating bullets.

Welch adjusted himself in Levy's broken-down guest chair. "Something's come up and we need to talk to you about your future at DIA."

I was sure he was going to tell me that because of my nightmares I'd have to leave the program. I couldn't believe Levy would abandon me like this and let me go after I'd been through so much for the unit.

"You've been selected for promotion to major, and for attendance at the army's Command and General Staff College at Fort Leavenworth, Kansas." He offered me his hand. "Congratulations!"

I was shocked. What did this mean? "Thank you, sir,

but I'm not sure I want this. I mean, the Leavenworth thing. Can't I just get promoted and stay on here?''

Welch was obviously taken aback by this. ''What the hell do you mean?''

Levy tried to jump to my rescue. ''I'm sure what Captain Morehouse means is that he just needs some time for this to settle in. That's all.''

''No, that's not it at all,'' I objected. ''I don't want to leave here and go to Fort Leavenworth for CGSC. You can give the slot to somebody else, and I'll take the nonresident course.''

''Are you dumb or just plain stupid? The army's trying to tell you something by giving you this. There are young men and women out there who would die to be offered a resident position at CGSC, and you want to throw it away for a bunch of fucking freaks?''

Levy's eyebrows went up. ''Excuse me, Colonel—''

Welch cut him off. ''You hold your water, Bill. I'm talking to this boy—who, for starters, obviously doesn't know what he's gotten himself into. What's worse is he doesn't understand what's being handed to him on a silver platter. Listen up, Morehouse! You are not going to throw this chance away, especially not for an assignment to this unit. Piss and moan all you want, but if you think you aren't going to CGSC, just try to stay here and I'll see to it that your ass is moved. This is a fucked-up operation and it isn't being refunded or restaffed. You are an infantry officer in an intelligence officer's billet. You stand out like a pimple on a baby's ass. People know you're here—people you used to work for. They think you're being held against your will, and they want you back in the infantry. Because I know and like them, I'll spare them the misery of being told their boy wants to stay. You get the fuck out of here. You are going where the army needs you most. Now get!''

''Yes, sir!'' I was out the door before he got off another salvo, but Levy had to endure another ten minutes of the guy. I'd never seen Welch before that day and I never saw him again, but the wheels were in motion for me to leave the unit. It would take some time—maybe as long as a year—but I was going to leave Sun Streak.

One of my most interesting operational targets involved the search for Marine Lieutenant Colonel Higgins, the United Nations observer taken hostage in Lebanon. Our attempt to determine his location and condition for DIA's customers was one of the most complex missions we'd ever worked. Each of us did eight to ten search sessions; Higgins was being moved often, but we found him over and over and passed the information along. Nothing ever came of it— that is to say, nobody ever launched a rescue operation. It was difficult for members of the unit to tap into Higgins and feel his suffering and his worsening physical and emotional condition day after day without any relief in sight. Several people had real trouble living Higgins's pain so as to turn in intelligence that was never acted on. I understood their distress, and I tried to explain the army's reasoning. Nobody was going to launch a rescue operation and risk lives on no basis except information from remote viewers. It would be insane to risk lives in reliance on our intelligence product alone; things just weren't done that way. The information we produced was intended to augment and balance more solid, reliable, conventionally acquired data. If two or more "collection assets" could have confirmed our findings, I'm certain the rescue would have taken place.

If it's any comfort, our unit determined that Higgins had been dead for many hours before his body was displayed on video. He died of a broken spirit and a broken heart, not from the hanging. His brutal captors, frustrated by his sudden death, hanged his body in a show of defiance, doing their best to capitalize on their error. Higgins was of no use to them dead; he was a bargaining chip they'd failed to keep. If it's any further consolation, he is in a far better place than this world. He is happy, busy, and eternal. Seven remote viewers confirmed that.

Another operational mission took place over the nine days immediately following the destruction of Pan Am

Flight 103, which detonated over Lockerbie, Scotland. It was a frosty morning when we received the mission tasking. Only we could provide immediate feedback while the search crews and investigators slowly pieced the events together.

I watched an old acquaintance, a man we all called Tiny, die as I relived the event for Sun Streak. We worked the mission twice a day, each day presenting detailed sketches of the two explosive devices and two methods of detonation. Judy and Lyn and I sketched the primary explosive device months before the investigators announced their findings. We diagrammed the electronic device, the tape player and radio that contained the explosives. We identified the site of the explosion as the aircraft's left front cargo hold days before that was announced. We tracked the builders of the device to the point of transfer and even farther, to the place of assembly. We provided descriptions, phonetic spellings of names, and sketches of houses and meeting places for the terrorists.

The secondary device was hand carried aboard the aircraft by an Iranian woman on a suicide mission. She had lost loved ones on the airliner the United States shot down in the Gulf, and she was willing to die to avenge them. Her high explosives were camouflaged as commercially wrapped chocolate bars, which she was to have detonated if the automatic device failed. She sat very near the point of detonation, on the left side of the aircraft.

In the most painful of all the sessions, Lyn described being in the airliner just before detonation. In his phantom form he was, of course, not seen. However, the instant the bomb detonated, he stood in the presence of dozens of quickened souls wondering what had happened to them. Lyn wept as one small child approached him in the ether and asked him where her mommy was and what had happened to them all. Lyn had the tools to return; they did not.

During the War on Drugs, Sun Streak was called upon to determine whether certain ships were carrying illegal narcotics. In the ether, viewers boarded ships to pinpoint the illegal cargo, piercing bulkheads to find packages of marijuana and cocaine. We found the sites of planned open-water drops, and located buried base and paste on islands throughout the Caribbean. From the ether, we hunted Pablo Escobar and other drug kingpins, accessing their minds to reveal elements of their plans that could not have been obtained by any other means. Eventually, some members of Sun Streak were moved into the Counter Narcotics Joint Task Force headquarters in Florida, where they worked for nearly a year. The commander of the CNJTF sent DIA a memo saying that the remote viewers had saved the task force millions of dollars on search and seizure operations. The viewers were a tremendous success and a new power tool in law enforcement. However, this glory was short-lived. Things were heating up in the Gulf region. Central Command, a multi-service command whose specified theaters of operation include the Persian Gulf, spent considerable time on planning and in briefing Washington and the Pentagon on the escalating tensions there. Several weeks later Saddam Hussein's army invaded Kuwait and held its ground despite international demands that they leave immediately. In a relatively short period of time, funding, weapons, and observation platforms such as helicopters and observation aircraft all began to be diverted to the rapidly escalating situation in Kuwait. Emphasis on the drug wars by the Department of Defense and the White House understandably began to drift eastward into the Central Command region.

I'd been an operational viewer for nearly a year when I left Sun Streak, on the day of the Iraqi invasion. I was on my way to Command and General Staff College, with a one-year stop in a strategic deception unit. Levy departed several weeks after me.

I never went back to Sun Streak, but I heard that the successes of the drug wars breathed new life into the program. Two new remote-viewing trainees were brought in, as was a new program manager to replace Levy. It looked as if everything was going to be fine. I hoped I'd be able to come back someday. Perhaps DIA would unlock the potential of the program and let it help all of mankind.

I'd been gone from Sun Streak for about three months when I began having trouble with the nightmares again. I thought it was because I wasn't spending time in the ether. I couldn't focus on anything; I felt disconnected and empty. My head spun with images I'd seen in the unit; swamped by waves of emotion, I wept openly and often. I was slowly disintegrating emotionally, physically, and spiritually. Bitter and lost in a world that neither understood nor cared what I'd been through, I talked to myself and sketched the images that poured from my mind. I needed "hands-on" help, an intervention by someone who knew the ether. But Kathleen was gone, Mel was gone, Levy was gone—all the people who spoke the language of the ether were gone. I turned into a hermit, never venturing out of my office building during the day. On weekends, I seldom left the house or shaved. Afraid of sleeping, I stayed awake for long periods, and every night I played the television and radio together, trying to drown out the noise and the images that swamped my mind. I needed to be under the control of the unit again; I needed the ether; I needed friends who understood what was happening to me.

One night I curled up on the couch in a sleepless stupor, my hands covering my ears to keep out the noise of the darkness. I coughed and snorted my way into a disturbed sleep, full of images of Lockerbie and Dachau, all the haunting horrors of the world I'd come to know so well. I drifted in and out of consciousness, the faces of the past around me. I saw a young lieutenant who'd served with me in the Ranger battalion die in a plane crash with someone he loved. I felt him die as I had Mike Foley many years ago. I awoke long enough to see the shadows of the living room come alive. Every object in the room projected a living shadow that stood to threaten me. Screaming and wailing, I ran, bouncing off walls and stumbling. I ran out into the brisk October air and fell into the safety of the grass and leaves. Embracing the living things beneath me, I lay there until sunrise.

"You okay, Dave?" A voice came from above me. It was a friend, David Gould, the coach of my son's hockey team. He'd come by to pick up Michael and see if I wanted to ride with him to the game. "Dave? It's me, David Gould. Do you need some help getting up?"

I strained to stand, cold and stiff from a night on the lawn. I looked and felt like hell, and my son watched as his coach helped his father into the house. A tear fell from his eye as I passed him. Debbie came down the stairs in her nightgown.

"What happened? Is he all right?" She spoke about me as though I weren't there, as though I were an object and no longer her husband.

"I don't know," Gould said. "I think he spent the night on the front lawn."

"Oh, my God, David, what's happening to you? Can't you see you're destroying yourself?"

I stared at her with bloodshot, sunken eyes. "That's just the trouble, my dear. I can't see anything anymore."

I arrived at work around nine A.M., punched in my key code, and made my way to the office. For the first time in my career I could honestly say I had a jerk for a boss; his boss was a jerk, as well. But it was a small unit with a very flexible schedule; people pretty much came and went as they pleased, being trusted to do what they needed in order to keep their deception projects running. They were independent operators, some very capable and others hiding from the real army, the army outside their classified programs.

It cost $40,000 a month to house a small team of about eighteen deceivers. As at Sacred Cape, everyone was on a first-name basis. Rank, uniforms, and any semblance of military discipline disappeared the day you reported for duty. That seemed to be one of the big boasting points of this place, along with the free coffee supplied by the owner of the building.

By this point in my career I'd grown sick of intelligence prima donnas. They got promotions by the handful, winding up as lieutenant colonels and full colonels even when they'd joined the unit as nothing more than junior captains. And some of their private lives! A few staff members hardly bothered to conceal extramarital affairs. On one trip to Europe, my traveling companion hadn't been off the phone with his wife more than twenty minutes before he was slipping off into the hotel room of a fifty-two-year-old he'd been scoping out in the lobby. It was a real Peyton Place, and I hated it. And just in case I haven't made it clear that this place was a waste of money and time, let me top my description off with the colonel who sold Afghani rugs out of the trunk of his car in the parking lot. Oh, and we had a small fleet of leased cars available, so we could fool people and maintain our cover.

We all carried credentials indicating that the bearer was on official duty and acting on behalf of the intelligence services of the U.S. government. They were supposed to be treated as classified documents; you weren't even supposed to take them home with you between missions, but rather to store them in a safe at the unit. Yet I must have seen members of the unit display those things a hundred times to try and get upgrades on airlines or get out of a speeding ticket. I grew more and more cynical as I watched these hypocrites.

In fairness, I must admit that there were good men and women there as well, many of whom I looked up to and revered as professional soldiers. For instance, there was a noncommissioned officer in charge of security clearances, a thin man who smoked up a storm trying to calm his nerves. He used to sit in his office with nothing but a small fluorescent desk lamp casting a harsh light against his face. I'd walk by and glance in to see him there filling out yet another form of some sort; he was always there when I came in, and there when I left for the evening. He had a lousy, thankless job, trying to ride herd on the security practices of a bunch of guys who flashed their credentials to ticket agents and traffic cops. I liked him even though I probably never said more than twenty words to him a year. He had his nose to the grindstone every day, and all he ever got for it was the pleasure of having hypocrites and professional spooks put their hands on the back of his head and try to drive his nose deeper into the stone. He was a good man, conscientious, dedicated, and professional, and I felt very sorry for him having to exist in a place like this.

The executive officer, the unit's second in command, was a short firecracker who puffed his way through every day. He had boundless energy and was always full of good ideas and strangely concerned about the welfare of every soldier who reported to him, even though many of them didn't deserve to wear a uniform. He was protective and dedicated; he knew I hated the place and he did everything he could to protect me from zealots and headhunters.

And that was Team Five, or Allied Telecommunications, as it was known in intelligence circles.

My life was well past shitty by this point. Debbie and I were at odds, of course; I seldom saw the children, and when I walked into the parking lot at night I never knew whether I'd end up at home or slip into the ether and drive to Easton, Maryland. I was living like a hermit, sleeping in my car or with whoever would have me for the night. Every stitch of clothing I had was in my trunk or on the floor of the backseat. At this point, I'd lost all faith in the army, in my family, and most of all in myself. Someone once told me there was a kind of freedom that came from being so completely fucked that you knew things couldn't get any worse. I wrote that down and carried it with me everywhere I went. I thought I *had* hit bottom, until November 1990, when Debbie and I formally separated. My executive officer loaned me his legal separation papers, so I could copy them and save the expense of an attorney. I dropped them off at the house on my way to a bar, where I hoped to forget about what I'd just done.

For some time, the random, unpredictable shifts between the ether and reality had been making me sick. As I've mentioned, I couldn't fall asleep without the radio or TV blaring away to keep the noise in my head from driving me completely insane. Why I didn't put a gun in my mouth, I'll never know. Perhaps it was the angel's message, though that seemed faded now. Perhaps it was the love of my family, the kind of love that transcends time and space even better than viewers. Perhaps it was God having the decency and mercy to keep me from making that leap into the ether forever. I was like a junkie coming down from a two-year high. My mind and body craved the euphoria of the altered state, the rush of bilocating, the uniqueness of what I was in Sun Streak. At Team Five I was just another professional liar, sucking pay from the taxpayers and trying to bullshit my way through. Every time someone asked me what I did for a living I cringed. I felt like dung telling the lies our bosses expected us to spout. It was like pimping on Saturday night and getting up early on Sunday to preach to the congregation about morality.

It was a Tuesday; Desert Shield had become a Storm, and the hundred hours that followed were at an end. We'd won a clear victory, and there was no shortage of heroes. Like every other soldier who'd sat the war out, I felt cheated, as if I'd practiced for a football game every day for sixteen years, only to be asked, on the day of the only scheduled game in a decade, to go buy sodas for the team and have 'em iced down for the postgame party. I have to admit, though, that in the months after Desert Storm the leadership of the army did their best to put us bench-sitters at ease and make us feel a part of the team. Still, most of us felt as if we were hauling sodas to the party.

On this particular Tuesday, I was sitting in the office, staring out the small sliver of glass I had for a window and desultorily sketching the images that had come to me in the night. The phone rang, startling me back into reality.

"David? This is Robert Crocker. Do you remember me?"

"Sure, I remember you!" Crocker had been assigned to Sun Streak just before I left the unit.

"How have you been? How are the headaches, or whatever they were, coming along?"

"They're nightmares, not headaches. I'd take some aspirin if they were just headaches!"

"I'm sorry, I didn't mean to imply—"

"Look," I interrupted, "it's great hearing from you, and yes, I miss the unit; and yes, I'd get down on my knees to come back. So, given that that's not going to happen, what can I do for you?"

"Well, that's just it. Mr. Nofi would like you to come back."

"Mr. Nofi *what?*"

John Nofi had replaced Levy as the program director of Stargate, and had instituted his own brand of program management. To his credit, he had increased the level of unit activity in the drug wars; however, he had also placed, in my opinion, undue emphasis on unproven methods such as channeling and tarot cards.

"He wants you to come back—temporarily, that is—to help work a project in the Gulf."

"Are you pulling my chain? If you are, I'm gonna come over there right now and—"

"Look, Morehouse, he asked me to call you, and that's what I'm doing. You want to be an ass, be an ass to somebody else; I don't have the time."

There was a pause while my fuse burned. "You called me," I said furiously, "and I'm supposed to drop what I'm doing, which may not be much but I'm doing it nonetheless, and run over there to do some work for Nofi, just like that? Tell Nofi I said he could go fuck himself. I asked him to take me back *five months ago* and he told me no, he needed some fresh blood. What he *meant* was, he needed somebody who didn't have a head problem. Yeah, you tell him I said go fuck himself."

"Okay, I'll tell him." *Click.*

I took a deep breath and dialed. "Crocker, it's Morehouse. Don't tell him to go fuck himself. When do you want me there?"

"I wasn't going to tell him; I figured you'd come around."

"Oh. I appreciate it."

"Is tomorrow morning all right by you? Say about nine."

"Gee, that's a little early for me, but I can probably make it."

"Yeah, I heard you had rough duty there. . . . So, come to the main building and Mr. Nofi will brief you along with all the others. Okay?"

"Sure. Hey, who else are you bringing in? I mean, who else that's been gone?"

"Well, Mel Riley for sure, and one other person, a female. Remember Kathleen Miller?"

"Kathleen, huh? She's good, it'll be good to see her again."

"Should be one hell of a reunion. I'll see you tomorrow morning."

"You've got it." I set the receiver down and swallowed hard. I didn't know whether to scream, shout, or cry. I had a mission again, a real mission into the ether.

The next morning I arrived thirty minutes early. Jenny greeted me at the door and gave me a big squeeze and a hard kiss on the cheek. "I miss your sorry butt around here, you know that?"

"I'll tell you, Jenny, it's nice to be missed somewhere."

"How are things between you and Debbie? We heard you two were separated—you're not divorcing, are you?"

"I don't know, Jenny: things are so upside-down. I know I don't want a divorce, but I just can't seem to keep my head screwed on straight."

"I wish you well, you know that. You two are a great

couple, you can work it out somehow. Just don't ever stop trying." She smiled. "The coffee's on."

"When's Mel supposed to be here?"

"I already am. What the hell took you so long?" Mel was behind me, smiling and, naturally, taking a swig of coffee from his old cracked mug. "I found this thing while I was looking for a notepad in the closet. I thought I'd lost it forever."

"If you were any kind of a remote viewer at all, you'd've viewed it from Wisconsin and sent Jenny the instructions and money to mail it back to you."

Mel's face grew serious. "How's the family?"

"Not so good—like I was telling Jenny, we don't know what we're gonna do. I'm just hoping for the best right now."

The front door sprang open and in walked Robert Crocker, followed by a smiling and ever so pretty Kathleen Miller. She had a yard-wide smile across her face, and her arms were outstretched for Mel and me. She hadn't changed a bit in the months since I'd seen her, except that her belly was big enough to stuff a basketball in. She wrapped her arms around us.

Mel frowned at her. "Jesus Christ, don't tell me that sorry-ass husband of yours actually got you pregnant. Man, oh man, look at you!" He spun her in a pirouette.

"Come here, you," I said, hugging her again. "You look wonderful! Congratulations to both of you."

"Thanks. It finally happened, after all these years."

"Okay, I can see I'll have to be the one to ask," said Jenny. "When are you due?"

"In two months. And it won't be a minute too soon. I feel like an elephant."

"Well, you look beautiful!" Jenny said, smiling. "And if these lugs had any class they'd agree."

We shared a few more minutes of conversation before Nofi showed up. There was no emotion on his face; his pale eyes stared through his thick wire-rimmed glasses. He had let his hair grow out since any of us had last seen him, and he looked like a sixties professor from Berkeley. He walked straight past us and into his office without a word, and only when he was inside did he call, "Jenny! May I see you in here, please?"

She grabbed her pad and pen and headed for the office door. "This is the way it's been since he got here. Thinks he's a damned general." She disappeared into his office, only to emerge thirty seconds later. "His Highness would like to convene the briefing in five minutes in the conference room. Would you gentlemen and lady please make ready for his entrance?"

Carol and Judy were waiting at the conference table. There was no friendly reunion with them; it had always seemed to me that they despised the rest of us for liking each other so much. Their view, naturally, was that they were serious about the work, while the rest of us were mere dabblers.

Lyn Buchanan was there, in his stocking feet as usual. He was a good man and an excellent viewer; unfortunately, he was an even better trainer. That quality prompted the program managers to rely heavily on his teaching skills and limit his operational use—a mistake, in my opinion. Also, despite my strong opposition, Lyn had done what was asked of him and codified the research and protocols for remote influencing, creating a very dangerous offshoot of remote viewing. Somebody should have given him a medal for it, I guess, but that's not what they do for viewers.

People not even affiliated with the unit started laying claim to the technique, making wild claims about their exploits. Most of it was a crock; the only people to do that work were right here in the building.

I admired Lyn, especially under the present conditions. The office politics were thick enough to choke on, but he kept a sense of humor. Most of all, he was the one guy who believed in the unit and its potential when I and others had cast it off as hopeless and misguided. How could the unit refuse to share these life-saving, earth-shattering technologies? I was furious about the unit's direction and I was vocal about the fact. Lyn may well have been furious, but he was never vocal. There's something to be said about a man who will remain a patriot and loyal to his oath all the way to the end. I couldn't do what he had done, and in some way, I felt ashamed. Lyn suffered silently, waiting for the system to right itself and clear the way for the advancement of the technique, while I forsook my oath and called upon the people to challenge the system. A soldier would have done it Lyn's way. The question I struggled with then and struggle with now is: When did I stop being a soldier?

Nofi tossed his notebook onto the table, startling me, and looked around the table as if taking inventory. "I want to make one thing perfectly clear about this operation: I did not want to include those of you who are no longer active in this program, but I was instructed to do so by DIA—specifically, by Dr. Albert Krohn. He felt we needed your expertise to augment what we already have. Those of you who know me, know that I like to get things out in the open and let people know how I feel about them. So now you know how the coach feels about the playing field. Now let's discuss the game.

"I'm going to front-load you all. We don't have the time to spare with working blind just to get you on target. These are your assignments." He walked around the table, placing a single tasking sheet in front of each of us. "There will be no exchanges of assignments; as you can see, you will be required to work solo. If anyone feels a desperate need for a monitor"—he paused to glare at the returning team—"do come and see me in my office following this meeting and I'll discuss it with you personally."

I glanced at Judy and Carol, who were both smirking. Channelers don't use monitors; Nofi had obviously decided that what went for channelers would do for viewers as well.

"I'll place your time and room assignments on the board in ten minutes; your sketches and summaries are due back to me within one hour of the completion of your session.

As always—and as a reminder for those of you returning—you are not to discuss any of your findings with anyone but me. Is that clear?''

Everyone did the drinking bird routine, nodding in acknowledgment.

''Good. Then are there any questions?''

No one spoke a word.

''The meeting is adjourned. Good hunting to each of you.'' He picked up his files and left the room. Mel and I sat at the table looking at our assignments.

''I don't want to do this solo,'' I remarked. ''I'm going to go see the bastard right now. Will you monitor me, Mel?''

''You bet I will.''

I knocked on Nofi's half-open door but he didn't respond. I could see him sitting at his desk, making notes, so I knocked again, and again he didn't respond. I walked into the office, planted myself in front of his desk, and stood there waiting for him to look up at me. He didn't, so I started talking. ''I want Mel—''

Nofi raised his hand and slowly looked up at me. ''If I'm ready to carry on a conversation with you, I'll so indicate by making eye contact with you and inviting you to speak. This is not one of your battalion headquarters where chaos is supreme; we have the decency to wait our turn here, and if it's not our turn we are scolded.''

I felt my blood boil and my face heat. I had to tell myself to calm down, fast, or else I'd have grabbed that little puke from behind his desk and dusted the room with him. Nofi kept writing in his notebook. He was taking his time; he knew he'd pissed me off, but he figured I wouldn't kick his ass because I wasn't as much of a jerk as he was. People like him are right, most of the time.

I slammed my fist on his desk and made him drop his pen. Now I had his full attention. I leaned on his desk, stared straight into his face, and said: ''Now *you're* being scolded. I don't know you, but I do know you have a problem with me and maybe some of the others. Well, that's simply that, *your* problem. Let's get one thing very clear: you are not my boss, and I'm not in the habit of being treated like this by my peers. According to the card I carry in my pocket, majors and civilians of your grade are on an equal footing, so don't you dare treat me like a subordinate. In fact, don't you treat *any* of us who came back to bail out your sorry ass like subordinates. Somebody obviously thought you weren't up to this job, or they wouldn't have had you track us down and invite us to the party. Now I'm filling you in: Mel Riley is going to monitor me. If you have a problem with that, you can pick up your secure phone and call whoever shoved us up your ass and explain to them why you don't think I should work the mission with a monitor. If they want to tell me why a monitor isn't needed, I'll listen. But they won't do that, will they?" Then I walked out of the office, grabbed a cup of coffee, and yelled, "Hey, everybody, Mr. Nofi said he'd be a little late getting the board posted. It's my fault—I held him up talking to him so long." I winked at Jenny and took a swig from my mug.

Grinning, Mel poured himself a refill. "Next time you're counseling the boss, make sure the door is closed."

"He's not our boss, thank God. And you'll be monitoring me."

The board was posted fifteen minutes later, and excitement filled the office. None of us knew anything about what was going on in the Gulf except for what we saw on CNN. I didn't understand why remote viewers were being used now, when they could have been really useful during the planning and execution phases of Desert Storm. But why ask questions?

My target lay east of the area of operations, along the coast and inland. I'd been given a map, really just an outline sketch of the eastern border of Iraq, all of Kuwait, and the northeastern borders of Saudi Arabia. My mission was to advance to the encrypted coordinates and examine the surrounding terrain for anything of significance—in other words, to drop in and see if anything needed attention. I was certain that I'd be looking for Iraqi stay-behinds, small units lingering in the shadows, waiting for some unsuspecting coalition patrol to wander by. I might even run into some Scud missile units that had so far escaped detection. They could be hunkered down somewhere in the desert, waiting for the fighting to cool down before surfacing and blasting the shit out of Kuwait City or Dhahran. I had to stop getting ahead of myself. I checked the board and saw I had at least a half an hour to kill before hookup and prep, so I decided to get some fresh air.

Mel was sitting on the front porch. "Ten-thirty in Room Two."

"I know," he said, finishing his cigarette. "Something don't feel right about this." He got to his feet and motioned for me to follow him.

"It's been a long time since we had one of these walks," I said.

"Yeah, it has."

"I miss it, don't you?"

Mel snorted. "Hell, no! First off, I don't have to put up with this shit anymore. And second, I can walk out my back door and step into the canoe and head for the far side of the lake. If there's anything bothering me when I start, it ain't there by the time I get to the other side. It's a beautiful place, Scandinavia is. Edith and I love it there. You should drag Debbie and the kids up there and buy a house and we'd be neighbors."

We both laughed at the idea until I remembered that I didn't have a family anymore.

"Ahh, I'm sorry," Mel said. "I didn't mean to touch a nerve."

"Hell, I can't tiptoe around it forever." I felt my throat tightening and I fought back tears. "It's so hard to be alone now, after being a team for all those years. God, Mel, I really miss her and the kids."

Riley hugged me briefly and, holding me at arm's length, said: "Remember, we're like water—we travel to many different places in many different conditions, but eventually, we journey back to ourselves. The way is full of rocks and stones that make us tumble, and there are eddies that delay us and reduce us to a trickle, but our destiny is to return. That is an eternal law. You knew that God had a plan for you many years ago when you met Debbie. Let that plan unfold; all you have to do is believe in it. Debbie is not gone from you, nor you from her, as long as you continue to let her know that you love her. Put forth a little effort, like the water, and you'll work through everything else and be together again. I promise it.''

''You're a good friend, Mel Riley.'' I hugged him again. ''And a very wise man.''

''Hey!'' Posner shouted from the porch. ''If you two are done making each other feel good, you have a mission to run in five minutes.''

Mel said, ''Are you sure you're up to this?''

''Of course. It's the only peace I get these days. Let's do it!''

Nothing much had changed in the viewing rooms, except that there were some new microphones, and someone had placed black tape over the camera's red ''on'' light. Mel figured this was so nobody would know if they were being watched. But we had been watched during every session before Nofi arrived, and why would it be any different now?

I got hooked up and lay down to prepare myself, listening to Beethoven's ''Moonlight'' Sonata over and over. Five times before I started my countdown I listened to the anguished creation of a man who realized he didn't belong in the world he found himself in. Five times I listened before I found myself falling into a tunnel of light and passing into another world.

I landed crouching and lingered for a moment, gaining my equilibrium. When I rose to my feet I saw a black world of mist, and a hollow sun above me.

''Something's wrong! I'm not at the target, Mel!'' I cried. ''Mel! I'm off-planet somewhere!''

Riley was scrambling to figure out what to do. "Calm down, Morehouse, get a grip and tell me what you see."

"I'm off-planet and I—Wait, I hear something."

"What is it?"

"Quiet! Just wait." And then I saw it, a Bradley Fighting Vehicle roared past me out of the black haze. It was quickly followed by another, and yet another, and then three more. They disappeared into the smoke as quickly as they'd come. "Sorry, false alarm. I'm where I'm supposed to be." I don't think I'd ever grinned in the ether before. I thought for sure that Mel was cursing me under his breath.

"Give me a description of your surroundings, Dave. I need to try and pinpoint your location."

"Well, I can't see much from here . . . there's black smoke everywhere. I must be standing in the plume of a burning vehicle or something. Let me move to another vantage point." But no matter where I stopped I found myself completely immersed in choking black smoke.

"I can't seem to shake this stuff, it's everywhere. I need to get some real distance if I'm to get out of the smoke."

"Okay," Mel said, "whenever you're ready, I want you to move upward five hundred feet and to the north twenty miles. Go ahead any time."

I felt myself move upward rapidly, and the ground below me blurred as I sped across the terrain and settled in the new target area. Here, too, the air was thick with the black smoke, the ground littered with the rubble of the war. "I still can't see anything, Mel. I think the entire area is blanketed with this stuff."

"What's it made of?"

"It tastes and smells like petroleum, and it's sticky, it coats everything. It's got to be oil. I'm going to look around—keep listening, okay?"

"I'm here." Mel had to be impatient; he'd expected this to be easier, and so had I.

I started moving in large circles, surveying the ground beneath me and straining to see even fifty feet through the smoke. Periodically, I came upon wrecked vehicles, more often civilian than military ones. The tracks of hundreds of vehicles scarred the sand, almost all going north or northwest. I followed them. I knew the Iraqi army was in retreat, and I assumed they'd be heading away from the direction their destroyed weapons were facing in. I passed over the splayed bodies of many Iraqi soldiers; the smell of their flesh in the desert heat was masked by the equally sickening stench of the black smoke.

"I heard something roaring in the distance, Mel. I'm moving toward it, but the temperature is increasing rapidly."

"I know, I can see your temp rising here. Keep your distance and give me your perceptions."

"Don't worry, I'm getting too old to act stupid."

I traveled along the surface, where I could see more clearly. The roaring got louder and louder, and the heat became unbearable. I moved left and right until I found a spot where the heat was less intense and I could get close enough to glimpse the source.

"It's an oil well. It's burning like crazy; flames must be shooting fifty feet or more into the air. There's raw crude all over the ground, but most of it has already burned. Mel, I've never seen anything like this up close—it's like a blowtorch standing on end. I've got a hole in the smoke here, so I'm going straight up for a look."

My phantom body rose to a height of thirty meters or so above the well fire. I turned slowly in the air, surveying my surroundings. Everywhere, as far as I could see, blazing torches sprang out of the ground, belching flame and smoke. Plume mixed with plume until they all joined together in one massive black blanket. The heat beneath me reminded me that I had a job to do, and I returned to my lower vantage point.

"This is bad, Mel; every oil well for as far as I can see is on fire. This is real bad. I don't know what to do from here. Obviously they know about this—who could miss it? Do you think I should come back now?"

Riley thought for a moment. "No; keep looking around.

You're right, they surely know about the fires, so there must be something else. You've been on target for about fifty minutes now; can you give it another twenty or thirty minutes before you come back?''

"No problem. Even here, I like it better than back there. I'll keep snooping around."

As I turned away from the oil well, I spotted a small silver object in the sand. "Mel, I think I see something unusual—a small canister, looks like stainless steel. It's stuck in the sand downwind from the fire."

"What is it?" Riley asked.

"I don't know. It's empty, though—at least I think it's empty; nothing is coming out of it." I gazed at the object, which leaned like the Tower of Pisa. About twenty or so inches high and about three or four inches in diameter, it was a finished metal cylinder with perhaps four or six inches of its base wedged into the sand to hold it upright. It narrowed at the neck, where a valve was placed. A plastic seal had been torn away and a portion of it lay on the ground next to the cylinder. I circled it, trying to see something that might indicate what the cylinder was, but no luck. "There's something odd about this thing. It just doesn't belong here at all. I'm moving to another wellhead to see if I can find one that has some markings on it, or if there's a pattern here."

"Okay, but first can you get a fix on the location of this one?"

"Too late, I'm already moving. But I don't think I could give you a fix anyway; I can't see enough of the terrain to describe it."

"I understand. Let me know what you find at the next well."

I found similar canisters at every well I could get to in the next twenty minutes. They varied slightly in size and shape, but they were always downwind from the fire, as if to avoid burning their contents. Something about them troubled me deeply, but I couldn't tell what. "I'm breaking it off and coming home, Mel."

I completed my summary and sketches and was on my way to turn them in to Nofi when Kathleen returned from her session. She was white as a sheet.

"You all right, Kathleen?" Jenny asked as Mel ran to her.

"I'm fine, I think I just need to sit down for a while. It was hot in the room—" She slumped forward in Mel's arms; her session papers fell from her hand and scattered on the floor. I helped Mel carry her to the couch, where we laid her down. She was moaning as Jenny dialed 911. Paul Posner appeared with a cold washcloth to wipe her face, and Nofi scrambled out of his office in the commotion. I thought I saw him actually get nervous there for a minute; he thought he was in trouble.

Fortunately, the hospital was just across the street and down a block or so, and Kathleen was even coming to by the time the ambulance arrived. I noticed her papers still scattered on the floor, and I hurried to pick them up before the ambulance crew came in.

It turned out that Kathleen was dehydrated; the heat of the viewing room and the intensity of the session had taken their toll. She'd be fine, and so would the baby; she just wouldn't be doing any more viewing as long as she was pregnant.

After the ambulance left, I went back to my desk with a fresh cup of coffee. I'd set Kathleen's papers down there; now I started putting them in order. And my heart nearly stopped. There on page five was a sketch of the cylinder in the sand, a sketch identical to mine.

"Oh, my God," I said aloud.

Riley came to a stop in front of my desk.

I jumped up and looked around the cubicle doorway to see if anyone else was coming. The coast was clear, so I sat Mel down in the chair beside my desk and handed him my sketches and Kathleen's.

"Look at these." I showed him my results.

"So?"

"So? Are you kidding me? Look at them, they're the same as mine."

"Goddamn, Dave, they're *supposed* to be the same. You had nearly the same mission."

"No, I didn't. Look at Kathleen's tasking sheet, it's there at the bottom of the stack. *She* was supposed to look for evidence of chemical or biological agents. *I* was supposed to look for 'anything of military significance,' like a combat unit or a weapon, not to look for chemicals or bio-agents. What kind of fucking game are they playing here?"

Riley looked at me, confused. "I don't see what you're getting at, Dave."

Suddenly it all seemed clear to me. The DIA wanted to make sure that a chemical or biological agent had been released on U.S. troops, but they didn't want anyone else to know. So they made it appear to us remote viewers that we were targeting different areas, when in fact we were all targeted on the same area. They also tried to keep us from talking to one another.

If all of us remote viewers came up with the same results, the DIA would know that chemical or biological weapons had been used. However, none of *us* would know, because we would never be able to compare notes. Once the use of these unconventional weapons had been confirmed, the DIA could start their cover-up so the American public would never find out.

I took a deep breath and tried to calm down a bit. "Okay, look. We all got called in to help out. Nofi doesn't want us to help, but we're shoved into his lap from all across the United States. Second, we're all targeted into the same area, with just minor changes in the coordinates—something we wouldn't notice unless we sat down and compared notes, which is a violation of protocol. Third, each tasking is worded differently. They know we'll all stumble on the same thing, though—they know the signal line will lead us to the most significant aspect of the site. So we give them confirmation of the employment of biological or chemical weapons, and we never even realize what we've done, because the only one to put it together is Nofi.''

"And some closed intelligence cell at DIA,'' Mel said somberly.

"It's obvious that the Iraqis placed the canisters next to the fires to mask the plume from the canisters. So I think they released a slow-acting toxin to poison the coalition forces, and they covered it up with oil-well fires. Every soldier downwind of those fires must've inhaled the bug or whatever it was. The poor fuckers are walking around with time bombs inside themselves, and the rest of the world is distracted because the environment has been damaged. It's really slick. Un-fucking-believable.'' My face tingled, feeling as though it were a mask and not my own; my hands were numb. "They know it. Our fucking government knows it and they don't want anyone else to know it.''

"Yeah, can you imagine if this got out? The fucking war is over and the treaty is being worked on. If this got out, all hell would break loose!''

"I'm more cynical than that. I think some lawyer in the Pentagon put a bug in the secretary's ear about the ramifications of having to answer to fifty thousand legal or medical claims against the government. I don't think our illustrious leaders want to break the bank taking care of the thousands of military who are affected by this thing, especially since they don't know what the extent of the damage is. They'll just deny any knowledge of it, or spend the next seventy years faking research until everyone affected is in a box or in a VA hospital. This is a goddamned conspiracy, that's what it is.''

Riley grabbed me by the arm and shook me. "Just wait a fucking minute. It all sounds good sitting here at this desk, but think about what you're saying. Think for a minute, just think.'' He released me and sat down again, his head in his hands. "If this is true, it's far bigger than either of us. We need more evidence. We need some other sessions.''

"So pick one. Everybody in the place is going into the sand and smoke. When do you work the mission?''

Riley shook his head. "My session won't do any good: I've been shown the results of yours and Kathleen's, and anyone would say I duplicated your results to cause a ruckus. Goddammit, Dave, this is not good. We don't have anyone who will listen to us on this."

"We'll take it to the media!"

"Uh-huh. Who do you think will give you time to explain that you're a trained military psychic, who is part of this top-secret program at Fort Meade—and no, you don't really work there anymore, they just called you in to visit for this special project?" He paused to put his hand on my shoulder. "You getting the picture yet, buddy? We weren't supposed to find this out, and just in case we did, they brushed their tracks out of the sand. Nobody will ever believe you. Nobody."

I stared out the window, shaking my head in disbelief. "So what do we do, Mel? We've seen this; what do we do, ignore it? Then how are we any different from the guy they were fighting over there?"

"I don't know," Mel said quietly.

"I'm going to tell Nofi that I know. I'll leave you out of it, but I want the bastard to know that *I* know what the fuckers are up to." I grabbed the papers from the desk and started out, but Mel blocked my way. "Move, Mel. I'm doing this!"

"Over my dead body. If you go in there and let him know that you're on to him, you may walk out of here tonight. But are you going to make it home? Think about it, asshole, what are you to them? If they went to these lengths to keep this quiet, do you think they'll let a burnout like you spoil their secret for them? How long do you think it would take them to kill you—or just discredit you? Oh—how *are* those goddamned nightmares, anyway?"

"Fuck you, Mel!"

"No, fuck you! You want some more? Where's your wife and children? How come they don't live with you anymore? Is it because you see things in the night? Is it because you walk in your sleep and swing at phantoms?

What did you go home every night and tell your wife and kids about? Didn't you tell them that you could travel in time and see things remote in time and space? Didn't you do that, Major Morehouse? Isn't it true that you are simply delusional, perhaps psychotic?

"You want to take on the big intelligence machine. You want to stand up like some fucking hero and tell the world that you saw the sons and daughters of the world poisoned by a madman. Then you want to add that the U.S. government orchestrated a cover-up. Oh, yes, boys and girls, ladies and gentlemen of the court-martial jury, we have a prime lunatic on our hands. We strongly recommend that you find him guilty of treason and lock his fucking ass in Leavenworth until he dies. No, no—better yet, let's give him some good mind-altering drugs and keep him in a hospital somewhere so his mom and dad can watch their son eat baby food through a straw." Riley was shaking with anger and frustration. "You can't do this now." He dropped to the chair, exhausted. "You can't. It will serve no purpose, and you will die in the process, I promise you. You have a family to think about. Now, don't make me give you the fucking water parable again, okay? Just let it go for now. *Please* tell me you will let it go for now. Everything has its season; this will, too. But not now. Promise me."

I bit my lip in frustration, yet I knew he was right. Everything he said was true, and speaking up would solve nothing. The heroes had been poisoned and I could say nothing. Nobody would ever believe me.

"I promise." I wiped a tear from my eye. "I promise."

I saw what happened . . . and now, the babies of the heroes are dying.

SIX

THE DECISION

I rented a room off Chesapeake Street in Annapolis. It wasn't much to look at, a dark little upstairs corner in an ancient wooden house. I'd been keeping a journal for almost three years by now and it was filled with information I'd received from or about the ether—my training notes from Sun Streak, messages from the angel, records of my nightmares and visions, and sketches of entities and places found deep in the ether. I spent most nights roaming the halls of the old house, sketching and recording the visions.

The mental noise was becoming unbearable. I couldn't sleep or even stay in a quiet place; images and emotions from my surroundings would collect in my head. All I could do to control them was sketch them and make notes. Every two or three days I'd collapse from fatigue, and sleep without falling into the ether.

I didn't have a phone in my room, so I had to use my landlady's kitchen phone. I couldn't say the things I wanted to say to Debbie and the children. I spent all of my free time alone, because without my family, I found it difficult to be in public. Walking into a room full of people was like being a human antenna, bombarded incomprehensibly by every emotional and visual signal in the place.

In November 1990, I received a phone call at the office.

"Dave? It's Mel. How are you?"

"As well as can be expected."

"How are the nightmares?"

"Coming on like gangbusters. I have some interesting sketches, though. It'd be nice if we could get together and share a beer."

"We will, and soon. I have a proposition for you. I know a guy who wants me to do some remote viewing for him. A simple case, nothing too drastic, and I need a second set of eyes in the target area. Are you interested?"

"Sure, I guess so. Who's the customer, and what's the target?"

"Let's just say he works in the media business. He asked me to keep his name out of it."

"Really? How did you meet him?"

"Well, actually I never have; I've only talked to him on the phone. He knows I'm a remote viewer, and he's been trying to get information out of me for a few months. I referred him to some of the retired monitors and viewers, but none of them will talk to him because of the unit being classified. So he keeps coming back to me."

"What does he want?"

"He wants us to work Korean Air Lines Flight 007, the one the Soviets shot down in 1983 over the Sea of Japan."

"Wasn't it a surface-to-air missile that did it?"

"No, a pair of fighters, SU-7 Fencers." These were the Soviets' top fighters, with heavy armament. I recalled that the Soviets claimed the KAL jet violated their airspace and refused to respond to repeated warnings. Of course the South Koreans and the United States insisted it was an innocent mistake, but the Soviets obviously thought otherwise.

"And your media man wants us to find out whether the plane's location was a mistake or not?"

"Yes indeed. Are you up for it?"

"When do we report to the unit?"

"We don't. This is a nongovernment customer. You'll be working on your own."

"Here in my office?"

"No, do it wherever you're staying now. It probably

wouldn't be too wise to let anyone at work see you working a remote-viewing project. Can you view at home?''

"I have a room I'm renting; I'll do it there.''

"Don't worry too much about not being monitored—you've been around long enough to do this standing on your head. Just make sure you have a quiet place. I need a session as soon as possible. Can you get results to me tomorrow?''

"I can do the session tonight, but how am I supposed to get the results to you?''

"Fax them.''

"Do you have any coordinates for me?''

Mel gave them. "I'm going to view at the same time and place. We want to look at the entire scenario from start to finish—just see if anything doesn't look kosher, and get your results to me no later than, say, four tomorrow afternoon.''

"I'll do my best.''

I locked myself in the room at ten o'clock that evening. I'd never intentionally done a remote-viewing session outside the unit before, and I was apprehensive. I couldn't afford any accidents.

I paced, staring at the blank walls and sparse furnishings. I scribbled the coordinates and some brief instructions to myself and set the paper on the nightstand. Turning off the light, I lay there in the darkness and counted down. . . .

The veil of the ether parted and I found myself in the cockpit of the KAL jet. I stood for a moment watching the pilot, co-pilot, and engineer at their stations. I don't know what I expected to find, but I sensed nothing out of the ordinary. I touched the engineer with both hands; closing my phantom eyes, I read his thoughts. They were all to do with his responsibilities and with the progress of the craft. The co-pilot's mind was jumbled with thoughts of home, family, and finances. He didn't have a single thought about what was happening inside or outside the plane during the time I was in contact with him. I moved on to the pilot, sitting in the left seat.

He *was* thinking about something besides the plane, and it was troubling him. I sensed that he was up to something. It seemed to me that he was purposely letting the aircraft drift off course in very small increments. He was flying a heading of maybe 195 degrees west instead of the approved course of 189 or 192 degrees, and it looked like he was doing it without informing the co-pilot.

Off the starboard side of the aircraft I could see a faint streak of land on the horizon. I didn't see anything out of the port window. The pilot kept looking at the co-pilot. Although I could sense his tension, he appeared strangely cool about the flight.

I passed through the cabin door and walked down the aisle to the back of the plane, looking for anything out of the ordinary. I found nothing. I then dropped through the floor of the main cabin and into the frigid and noisy hold. I waded neck-deep through bags and cartons, toward the front of the plane, one cargo compartment after another.

On the starboard side of the hold was a metal object shaped like a pedestal or step. It was attached to the floor and the wall of the aircraft. On it stood an odd-looking device, a rectangular box about six inches high, eight to ten inches long, and perhaps six inches wide. It was painted dark gray and a nomenclature plate was attached to its top. There was a device protrusion on the end of the box closest to the skin of the aircraft. It looked like the flared portion of a bullhorn, except that the end was closed. I couldn't make out what with—metal or a composite or maybe a glass lens of some type—because the end was so close to the plane's inner wall. I'd have had to exit the aircraft to find out, and I wasn't willing to risk that working by myself. I tried to see what the function of the device might be, but it didn't move on its pedestal, nor did it have any visible moving parts. I sensed that it was a passive device, absorbing energy waves without emitting anything detectable. It wasn't scanning anything or photographing anything; it was feeling for or measuring energy emitting from the ground. But I didn't know what kind of energy, or why. All I knew was that it was a detector or sensor of some type, directed at energy sources below. I broke off the session and began my return to the physical dimension of the room.

As I drifted from the target, a projectile slammed into the starboard rear quarter of the airliner, striking it just behind the right wing. The jet erupted into a fantastic ball of flame, rolling violently to the right, nose down. The devastating image faded as I made my way forward in time and space to my room.

I lay there for a long time in the stillness, breathing deeply, savoring the euphoria of the altered state. It now took me longer and longer to recover from trips into the ether; I was losing the discipline I'd been taught at Sun Streak. The tether that held me to the physical dimension was stretching thin; I had begun to wonder what would happen if it broke.

I sketched well into the morning hours, producing images of the box and the aircraft. I then fleshed out the details of the journey in my summary. When I finished, it was four-thirty in the morning.

Mel called my office the next afternoon.

"I'll fax this stuff to you in the next hour or so, but one thing is clear to me," I said. "This wasn't a routine flight. I think one of the pilots knew what was happening, and I think he was a willing participant in the operation. I don't know exactly what he was supposed to be doing, but his aircraft was equipped with some sort of monitoring or detection device. I think he was flying into Soviet airspace, or near it, to measure something. I just don't know what."

"I do," Mel said somberly. "They were looking for holes in the radar coverage of the coastline. I saw a device, too. Did yours look like a box with a horn attached?"

"Exactly. Did you get anything on the pilot?"

"No, I didn't look in the cockpit. I guess I should have.

Send me your summary as soon as you can and I'll pass it along to our customer.''

''What is this guy going to do with the information, anyway? Is he going to the press with it?''

''He *is* the press! If he's brave enough, I imagine he'll make good use of it. If he thinks it's too hot, he'll probably just file it away. I haven't any idea, really.''

''I think we should give this to someone who'll use it. And I think *we* should use it to show the world what remote viewing can do. The Soviet Union's gone. Who are we hiding everything from?''

''Let's not talk about this any more on the phone, okay?''

''I've got a good deal of leave coming. I'd like to fly up and see you and Edith; maybe we can talk then. What do you say?''

''All right.''

I faxed my summary, and that was the last I heard from Mel for several weeks.

Eighteen days passed. I sat in my room sketching in the dark, the moonlight casting a dim wash across the small wooden table. I missed my family but I understood why Debbie felt the way she did. She had to protect the children from the frightening fallout from my remote viewing. In the years that had passed since I'd been shot, they'd forgotten what I was. They only knew what I'd become.

Danielle had made me a birthday card in September. My little seven-year-old—she drew every member of the family as a complete and whole person, and they all held hands in a loving chain. All except me. I was a colorless stick figure, transparent, hovering above the rest. Surrounding me were the solid dark figures of ghouls, clutching at me to drag me away from the family. On the card Danielle had written: ''Happy Birthday, Daddy! We love you more than them.'' I folded the card and returned it slowly to the drawer.

I walked quietly downstairs to the phone in the kitchen.

"David, it's two o'clock in the morning," said Debbie groggily.

"I know. I'm sorry, I just wanted to hear your voice."

"Well, it's late. I have to get up early."

"Debbie, please don't go just yet. Can we talk for a minute or two?"

"What do you want to talk about?"

I swallowed, fighting back tears. "I just wanted you to know that I love you, and that I'm thinking of you. And I really miss you."

"I love you too, David. I miss you."

"Can we give it another try? I think I've got a better grip on things now. Really I do."

"David, we've been through all this before."

I interrupted her. "I know, but—"

"David, that's just it—nothing *has* changed. You're out of control and you won't do anything about it. You can't live with us until you do. You know that. David, the children are scared to death of you. They think you're some kind of alien from the movies. What do you expect them to think? Why would you want to subject them to it again? I just can't let you do that to them—to us. Don't you understand?"

"Yeah, I do."

"All you have to do is get some help. It's your decision. I need a husband, and the children need a father. None of us needs a half-mad time traveler. Which is what you've become."

"The nightmares aren't that bad anymore, I promise!"

"David, that's simply not true. You're not normal! I want a husband I can talk to and sleep with without having to chase him down and bring him out of a trance or a nightmare or God knows what. You're getting worse, David, not better. One of these days you're going off the deep end, and you're not coming back. You're not like Mel! Mel's a natural; he was born with the ability. He's never known life without it. But that's *Mel.* You were shot in the head, David! Your ability was knocked into you, and your life was knocked out."

"I'm not that bad! I can control it!"

"Oh, David, when will you realize what you've gotten yourself into? I've got to go, I can't carry on like this, it hurts too much. Good night."

I sat in the kitchen listening to the silence on the phone, and I couldn't hold back the tears. I just couldn't give up the gift of my eyes. I was certain that I'd been given them for a reason. I folded my arms on the kitchen table and slept until the nightmares came. When they did, I walked the house until dawn.

As April came, I was feeling better about a lot of things in my life. I can't say anything had really changed; maybe I was getting used to being alone, or maybe I was just getting used to hiding from the world. When I was alone at night, my thoughts seemed to cut me like knives; but in the sunshine and warm breezes, things started to make sense and I didn't have to be afraid all the time.

It was Sunday, April 7, 1991. I was sketching and taking in the sun by the bay. I set my notebook aside to watch white sails on the horizon, and let my mind drift to another place and time.

"David!" the familiar voice of the angel called softly. "David!"

I turned to see him standing in the sun to my left. I'd seen him so many times over the years that although his visits never seemed ordinary, I was comfortable with him, not frightened and overwhelmed as I had been at first. I guess nothing good ever dies, and I'm thankful for that. The evil in my life and in the ether changed faces often, but the angel was an old and welcome friend.

"I'm here, just like I always am when you want me."

"I've come with a warning again."

"A warning? Why? Please don't, I beg you, please don't. I've done nothing wrong, I've worked hard to be what you want me to be. You want me to give something up; but I can't give up any more, I haven't got it to give."

"And so love is fleeting, dying, withdrawing from you."
He smiled. The beauty of this entity, I'd found, was his
ability to look straight to the heart of my apprehensions.
He invariably saw things the way they were supposed to
be seen. "You tremble at my warnings, but I offer you a
chance for a new life."

"No, you don't! You offer me nothing but a chance to
continue fighting. I've been fighting for over four years
now. All I've done is exist in the borderland, somewhere
between this world and others. What life is that?"

"Your life has been part adventure and part miracle, has
it not?"

"Those are your words, not mine. This existence has
been a struggle for power between good and evil, and I've
been caught up in that. And what power have *I* had? All
I've done—"

The angel interrupted me. "All you have done is learn
to be responsible for your life, and that is the only way to
change the world in which you live. The acceptance of that
responsibility will guide you through the next phase of your
learning." He gazed intently at me. "This phase will test
you beyond your limits. You will have to fight for your life
before it is over."

"I'm tired of fighting. I've *been* fighting for my life, and
I'm tired."

"A man is not what he says, but what he fights for; you
will be fighting for much more than yourself. You will be
fighting for your children, and your children's children. For
generations to come. You are but one link in a millennia-
long chain of warriors, but you are called, and much depends on you. Your fight rests on the gift you bear within
yourself. The gift is the power—not you, the gift. The test
of your strength will be in your ability to bring the gift to
others. Remember, the gift is the power! Give the power to
others when the time is right. You'll know when it is
right."

Without further protest I opened my eyes to see storm

clouds gathering over the bay as if to match the angel's prediction. I wept at the thought of what was to come. I had gathered strength, thinking I'd won a small victory; now I learned that what I thought was a victory was only a short interlude between great contests in the ether. I'd wanted only to be a soldier. Surely the majority was far more worthy and stronger than I. How was I to fight for my life, and the lives of others?

Four days later, I rented a single-engine Cessna 172 and headed for the small airport just outside Stevens Point, Wisconsin. I needed to see Mel and tell him what I was experiencing. The flight took me eight hours and two refueling stops. Mel greeted me at the airport and together we drove to his beautiful house, where Edith stood in the driveway, brimming with smiles.

We spent the rest of the day and a good chunk of the night catching up, laughing and drinking to new adventures and old memories. The next morning Mel and I woke early and hit the lake to fish and to talk about our future. At first, we said nothing, each of us waiting for the other to begin what we knew would be a long, hard conversation. Mel kept glancing at me, as if hoping that I would forget what I'd come for.

"I have to talk to somebody about what I'm feeling, Mel," I said, breaking the silence. "And except for Debbie you're the only one I trust."

"So, out with it. Stop worrying about it and let's talk."

"I'm not seeing things clearly anymore, and I don't believe in what I'm doing anymore. I hate the intelligence business. My family's life is a mess. When I close my eyes at night I don't know if I'll sleep or journey God only knows where. It's getting worse, and on top of everything else, the angel came to me again and told me that I'm in for a real bad ride. I think he wants me to tell the world about the gift."

Mel shook his head, never taking his eyes off the water. "I was afraid it would come to this."

"Come to what?"

"This—this division. That angel of yours isn't wrong, you know. I was always afraid that someday one or all of us would come to that conclusion. It was only a matter of time before someone decided to talk about remote viewing outside DIA. I always knew it was wrong to hide it."

I was dumbfounded and numb. "Do you realize how good that makes me feel? I thought I was turning traitor."

Mel laughed. "The fact that there are two of us doesn't make it any better. The government will still call it treason."

"But you agree that we need to bring this out?"

"Like I said, I've always believed it. I just thought I was alone. I guess I'm just as relieved as you to know I have some support."

I smiled and took a deep breath. "Even so, I feel terrible about this. It'll affect the lives of everyone close to us."

"Exactly."

I looked hard at Mel. "We love our country, and we love each other like brothers. And that's never going to change. Even when it was just a collection asset, we both knew remote viewing ought to be released to the people. But now they're turning it into a weapon. They've taken the gift and turned it into something vile, and I think that's why the angel is involved. He saw it coming."

"Your ability to turn the complex into simple analysis has always amazed me," Mel said. "Don't you realize what kind of behind-the-scenes manipulation has been going on around you? Call the source whatever you want— God, the Federation, an angel, the Virgin Mary—it doesn't matter. This plan was put into motion a long time ago. Think about it. You got shot in the head, and you've been fighting a private war ever since. Your entire life has changed; you've sacrificed everything you know to keep the gift, to keep your eyes. And that's just *your* sliver of the pie. I've had the gift since I was twelve, and all along I've known that its true worth rested in some higher calling. I just never had the guts to jump out there alone and make it happen.'' He shook his head. ''Now the chemistry is right. Didn't you ever wonder why *one* machine gun just happened to swing in the wrong direction and hit just you? I mean, it could have killed or wounded a dozen men. Figure out the odds.''

We didn't talk about our decision any more that morning. Going public with the gift frightened us, so Mel wisely changed the subject to fishing and local Indian lore.

Later, after dinner, he pulled me aside.

''There's something eating away at you, and you persist in holding on to it. I worry about you. I want you to know that up front. I'm elated that we agree the gift needs to be presented to the world, but I'm genuinely concerned about this personal war you're waging. Why don't you just let it go?''

''Because I can't! I used to believe in the government and the military as sacred institutions that I could believe in above and beyond all else. But everywhere I've turned, they've let me down. The remote-viewing unit is disintegrating. I'm afraid that the work being done there now will tarnish everything that we accomplished. Nothing seems to be going in the right direction, and there's nothing we can do about it. In fact, rumor has it that DIA leadership no longer sees the program as worthwhile and will cut back on funding. It's giving the whole gift a bad name.

''I'm not angry at any one person, Mel. I'm just worried about the future of remote viewing, and I'm worried about you and me. I'm worried about what lengths they might go to stop us, even if it means destroying viewing altogether.''

Mel said nothing but just listened, his eyes fixed on me.

''You know this better than I do. You taught me that of all paranormal disciplines, remote viewing is the only one that is proven. It's been given government funding, exhaustive research, and years of application. It's not a guess, it's not a circus act, it is a pure and simple gift to us from God. If it comes from God, then who's trying to control it for negative purposes? Remote viewing knows nothing but truth, and that won't change if it's used for the wrong purposes. Over time, it has evolved from something relatively crude into a precision technique, and, if we don't rescue it, I'm afraid it will either be taken away from us, or else something that has no business with it will become its master. Am I making any sense?''

"Of course you are, and I agree completely."

"Then why aren't we, the great, trained remote viewers, doing what we know we *should* be doing with this gift? Why aren't we helping mankind? We're approaching the millennium. That means many different things to many people, but it will be a significant event for all of us. There's a shift in human consciousness taking place out there, changing the way we see each other, changing the way we see the world."

"I still agree."

"Mel, I hurt inside. You know, over a hundred and seventy million people, innocent people, have perished in wars in this century alone. And the government I'm serving *right now* is sponsoring the continuation of that philosophy. They have a technology capable of altering human history, and they selfishly hide it away at Fort Meade. They're planning on using it to hurt, not help. So here I am, living a nightmare! I see what I shouldn't have to see, I know what most folks never know, and I've got something out there in the ether telling me I can make a difference, and folks back here telling me I can't, I have a screw loose."

Mel nodded.

"Mel, we both know that the future of remote viewing rests with the good it can do for everyone. We've been charged with the responsibility to use this gift to further, say, science—health, medicine, technology. I remember looking at human cells as if I were right there, microscopic. Remember that? You sent me."

"I remember. That was the time we looked at what killed those people in Afghanistan."

"And if we can do that, why can't we save lives, by telling doctors what's happening at the cellular level with cancer patients, or people with muscular dystrophy? We could take a roomful of viewers, and put them on a medical target, and find the answer. We should be doing that! But instead we're looking at military targets, cocaine ships, missile silos, double agents. Please tell me, how does that save the lives of the next generation of children?''

"I don't know. It probably doesn't, but I know it's not worthless, as you say. All of us have to follow what we feel is our calling.'' He sighed. "DIA believes it's doing the right thing by keeping remote viewing locked up. I don't think anyone's forgotten what we all set out to do for humankind. I don't think things are derailed—everything has to happen this way, or the plan gets turned on its head. Everyone has the right and freedom to choose their collective and individual destiny, to choose everything from simple rules, to laws, to governments, to religions, to their involvement in the direction of humankind. It's wrong for you to judge harshly the direction our government, and certain people in our government, have decided to go. All you can do is follow the counsel of whatever guides *you*, and put your piece of the puzzle into place. Then you walk away.''

Mel's eyes shone.

"Mankind is not lost, nor is it doing the wrong thing. Follow your heart and let everyone else follow his. I will most certainly follow mine. Working for the National Institutes of Health, trying to find a cure for AIDS—that's for you and those who choose to follow you. It's a valiant cause. But so are other viewers' causes. So is mine.''

I was humbled. "And what is your cause?'' I asked.

"I know it's here, in this land, with the Native American people. But exactly what my quest is, and how it will manifest itself, I'm not certain. The Creator will tell me in His own time.''

Mel's words comforted me. "So we're all just seeds. We're planted here with this gift to see what only God can see. And each of us has a mission of his own, to find a calling, to teach and to pursue it for the greater good, no matter what that good might be.''

''Exactly. That's exactly what we're here for. And that's exactly what's in store for remote viewing—many roads, and many places, but all for the good of mankind, and by the grace of the Creator, as long as good people with pure hearts choose to exercise their free agency and fight for what they believe is right. Don't condemn your nation or the world or individuals; that's what the evil inside yourself wants, and that's why you see your face in it. It wants you to be angry, to judge and cast doubt. Let it go! The energy inside you, evil will turn against you; it reflects it back. To win this war, *you* have to be the reflector. And to do that you must empty your heart of anger and self-doubt. Trust in goodness and purity; you can see evil as well as good much more clearly than those without the gift. It's a tool. Use it! Okay?''

The next morning, I lifted the nose of my Cessna and climbed into the Wisconsin sky on a southeasterly heading, bound for home. I felt as though a millstone had been lifted from my neck. I didn't have to fear what DIA or the CIA or anyone else might do next with remote viewing, nor did I have to worry that the intended work of remote viewing wasn't being carried out. The responsibility rested with me, not anyone else. I had to do what I had been set apart to do; I would have to follow my path, alone. The battle I'd been fighting for years would rage on until I learned what Mel already knew.

In August 1991, I drove to Fort Leavenworth, Kansas, and signed in to my next assignment—the U.S. Army's Command and General Staff College. The first few weeks were hectic with guest speakers, Gulf War heroes, and an endless stream of rules and regulations. I had to buy uniforms, which I hadn't worn in five years. It was amazing how much had changed in five years.

The college had a designated place for virtually everything at every time. Each officer had a spot for mail and messages, a box for books, a seat in class, a seat in the library, a card to carry to get into the library, a seat in the main lecture hall, a class leader, a section leader, and about five leaders in-between; designated breaks, designated lunch, roll call, attendance, quizzes, tests, study hall, electives.

I was assigned to Section 22A, and what an eclectic group it was. We were from every walk of life and every branch of the army. We had one of the finest naval officers I'd ever met, Lieutenant Commander Jim Waters; an army surgeon and former Ranger battalion member, Major Michael "Doc" Schaub; and even a Greek lieutenant colonel, Nicholas Gialiris II. They were wonderful, bright and energetic; I envied them all. We shared a great deal during the year we were together; I wish I'd confided in them more; instead, I kept to myself as much as possible. I continued living as reclusive an existence as I could; only Mike Omura and Jim Waters coaxed me out once in a while.

I lived in a rented room. My landlady was a kind and gentle woman named Carolyn Finney. She took care of me as if I were one of her own sons; if not for her, I would not have survived another year alone. She cooked for me often; otherwise I would not have eaten regularly. She'd bang on the door of the room and convince me to venture out to drink a beer or two with family and friends. She was wonderful.

It was another year of personal transformation. I'd had a faint hope that maybe all I'd gone through was just a dream and that I was now going to wake up and go on with my life, grow back into the army. But it wasn't, of course. I could not escape the calling, the gift, or the nightmares. I had changed too much; no matter how much I needed to be a soldier again, the magic was gone from me. I listened to army leaders speak to my classmates, young men and women who were the future generals and great battle commanders of the nation; but the leaders often spoke to them in deceptive and condescending terms. They had little tolerance for their subordinates' passionate questions, and they often minimized the officers' worries about their families, their careers, and the future of our armed forces. In changing times, people were frightened. They wanted and deserved honest answers to questions that would affect the rest of their lives. What they got was rhetoric and political pabulum.

At one briefing, a four-star general's responses to poignant questions could be summed up in one repeated answer: "I have a dialogue ongoing about that; you don't need to worry about it. Keep your dauber out of the dirt and don't get snot on your chin strap." Brilliant.

With each passing week I became more convinced that the corruption, secrecy, and political agendas of the undercover intelligence community were not unique. We were heading for a catastrophe, stripping the military of leaders and filling it with politicians and managers. I waxed bitter, losing my focus only months into the school year. I tried to share my feelings with my section mates, but through no fault of their own they didn't understand. How could they? They were all career military officers, and I—Well, I was something else entirely.

After I completed Staff College, I reported to the headquarters of the second battalion of the 505th Parachute Infantry Regiment of the 82nd Airborne Division. Brigadier General Jack P. Nix, an old friend from the Ranger battalion, had recruited me while I was at CGSOC. It was a typical example of who you know and not what you know. I was lucky Nix knew me; otherwise I'd have ended up right back in intelligence. Colonel Dan K. McNeil was the 3rd Brigade commander, and Lieutenant Colonel Timothy Scully was one of three battalion commanders under him. I was to be Lieutenant Colonel Scully's second in command, his battalion executive officer. Both men were an inspiration to me, the last of a breed, I came to believe. I learned a great deal from both of them; and I will be forever grateful.

Seven months into my assignment, the battalion jumped

into Sicily drop zone, a favorite of the 82nd, for a training exercise. Six hundred and eighty-six men cascaded from C-141 Starlifters in the darkness. For several days we moved, fortified, fought an opposing force, then moved and did it all over again. Both sides in this mock war were being evaluated and both wanted desperately to do well, so the nights were long and the days filled with endless activity. On the sixth day, we bivouacked along a defensive line extending several kilometers along a small creek. At 0200 hours my driver and I stopped inside the battalion head-quarters perimeter for some much-needed rest. I gave Lieutenant Colonel Scully a final update on some logistics issues and headed to my vehicle for some sleep.

The trail leading to the vehicle was narrow and black as pitch on the moonless night, and it was there that the ether began overtaking my everyday life. I followed the small lights that led down into the low ground to my position. Pushing a large branch out of the way, I closed my eyes to protect them. I opened them to sunlight and a beautiful tropical garden filled with waterfalls and enormous pools.

"Welcome! My colleagues and I have been waiting for you."

For a moment I just stood there overwhelmed, staring into the garden, listening to the rush of the waterfalls. A few yards from me sat a man impeccably dressed in a dark suit, white shirt, and tie. He sat at a glass table in an enormous white chair with a flared back that extended well above his head. Accompanying him at the table were six identical men identically dressed.

I looked up to see a surreal sky, crimson with wisps of black streaking across it. "Where am I?"

"You are where you belong." The first man swept his arm in a welcoming gesture. "This is your home, if you are worthy."

"Really? And what constitutes worthiness?"

"The acceptance of things as they are and were meant to be. The wisdom and willingness to use your new gifts correctly, for the right purpose." He pointed toward the seat directly opposite him. "Please sit with us."

I sat cautiously, keeping an eye on the men with him. They didn't budge or look around or even blink, not once. "Who are you?"

The man gave a thin smile. "We are your brothers, your friends . . . we are whatever you need, and we will always be there for you when you need us. We are everything you could want. Just ask and your wants shall be fulfilled; we have been directed to care for you."

"By whom? The angel?"

"Yes, of course, the angel. He asked that we watch over you and counsel you on the use of your gift. It is quite remarkable, is it not? The gift, I mean. Its potential is quite limitless, and the beauty of it is that all your brothers and sisters possess it. You are simply one of the few to have harnessed it. Congratulations."

"Why am I here? What do you want from me? Why did the angel send you now?"

"Merely to inform you. He wanted you to know who I am, to feel comfortable with me." His eyes bored into mine. "You *are* comfortable with me, aren't you?"

"No, I'm not at all comfortable. As a matter of fact I think something's foul. A lot of what has happened to me doesn't make much sense, but this makes even less. You have no message, no lesson. I don't know who or what you are, but I'm not afraid of you! Leave me alone!"

The man continued smiling, his eyes still boring into mine. I felt as though he were turning me inside out with his eyes, revealing the contents of my soul. Something stank, something I knew but couldn't recognize. His smile turned to cruel and wicked laughter. I backed away, stumbling, and looked up to see my face on the man who was the haunting, evil being of my nightmares. All around me a voice called my name laced with evil laughter. I spun in every direction, trying to break the connection, trying desperately to get back to the physical world. The garden morphed, and the stench of the water grew thicker and thicker, the water running a sluggish dark red like the sky.

An amber glow was cast across the garden, mixing with the hot wind and the laughter. I tried to get away. Concentrating, I raised myself above the beings and crossed the water, tracking the waterfall up and over its source, desperately trying to escape this baneful place. As my spectral body crested the falls, I saw the most terrible sight: there, on the banks of the narrow river, stood a great assembly of people gathered like cattle, spread before me as far as my eyes could see. And there, on the banks of the river, faceless beings systematically beckoned each man, woman, and child to step forward and come to them. Apathetically, they obeyed. As they did, the beings slit their throats, snatched them up, and held them aloft by the ankles. It was their blood that turned the river, the falls, and the pools dark red. The drained bodies were piled in great heaps. Now I recognized the stench: it was blood, the blood of a people, the blood of a world.

"Oh, my God, why am I seeing this?" I cried aloud, dropping to my knees to cover my eyes and head as a beaten child would.

"Halt! Who goes there?" demanded a voice out of the darkness. "I said, who goes there?"

"It's Major Morehouse."

"Advance and be recognized."

I walked toward the voice, stopping when a red flashlight beam struck my face.

"Sir, what the hell was going on out there? What were you yelling about—you want to give our position away?"

"Sorry—I got a branch in my eye."

"I've pulled that stunt a time or two myself, sir. You want me to get a medic over here to take a look at it?"

"No, thanks anyway. Who are you? I can't see your name tag."

"Private First Class Collins, sir!"

"Collins, I appreciate your asking. Keep up the good work. And, say, do you happen to know where my vehicle is parked? I seem to be a bit disoriented."

"Yes, sir. It's right over there"—he pointed with the

flashlight beam—"about thirty or forty meters. You sure you're all right, Major?"

I touched his shoulder in the darkness. "I'll be fine. I just need some sleep. Thanks again, Collins."

"Airborne! Sir."

I stumbled away, found my vehicle, and lay on the ground next to it, staring into the night sky until sleep came to me. The time the angel had spoken of must be growing near. The battle inside me raged on.

Six weeks passed. Mel and I had many phone conversations about how and when to go public, discussing over and over every possible way to take the information safely to the people. We agreed and then disagreed on how best to do it; our families, the unit, and whether or not to try and involve other viewers became paramount issues. We finally concluded that we couldn't do it on our own; some outside third party would have to help us. But who would help and how remained a mystery.

It's a difficult decision to violate a security oath. The penalties are stiff, but they don't hurt nearly as much as the attitudes of your comrades when they learn of your decision. I was about to break an oath that I had honored since the day I first saluted and swore my allegiance to the United States, promising to support and defend it against all enemies, foreign and domestic. I was about to become a domestic enemy.

I had to define clearly what I was about to do. First I considered whether telling my story would endanger the national security of the United States, the country I love dearly and had sacrificed for. I concluded that it would not. The Cold War was over. A year ago our Soviet counterparts had told the entire world what they had been doing for the past forty years in the paranormal arena. I wasn't giving away launch codes or the names of top-secret operatives. I was telling a story about psychic spies, whose existence was already an established fact.

Second, would telling my story endanger anyone's life?

During the Cold War, when the two major superpowers were still at each other's throats, the answer might have been yes. But not today. Today it was I who would face the greatest risk. In my opinion, this was a story that had to be told for mankind's sake; if I was going to take heat for doing so, so be it. Too much had been learned to continue to allow remote viewing to be bottled up in some secret dungeon, never to be shared with the people who paid for it.

On October 1, 1992, I mustered the courage to call Debbie. It had been nearly six months since I'd talked with her and the children. They needed to know what I was planning to do.

"Hello, Deb."

"Well, it's been a long time."

"Too long."

"How are you feeling these days?"

"I'm doing better, I think."

"Maybe someday you'll share it with me."

"I'm going to go public with the remote-viewing story. I've decided it's too important to keep under wraps any longer."

There was silence on the phone. "Do you realize what you're saying?" Deb's voice quivered. "Do you really think they'll let you do that?"

"There's got to be a way, and that's what I want you to help me with. Help me decide how best to do this. All I know is that it needs to be done, for all mankind."

"David, I know how important it is; I've always known that. I'm proud of you, but think of the price! Is it worth your career? Your life?"

"C'mon, Debbie, you're exaggerating. Once people see what marvelous potential remote viewing has, don't you think they'll support my decision?"

"No, they won't. First of all, they won't believe you. Second, the people in charge will discredit you. Or they may even go to greater extremes. You just don't know."

"You're right—but this is something I need to do. It's my destiny."

"Destiny isn't a matter of fact, David. It's a matter of choice."

"I can't change what I've become."

"Yes, you can! You haven't become what you're supposed to be."

"What am I supposed to be? I love you, Debbie, but I can't go on like this. I need someone to stand beside me." I waited, but she said nothing. "Okay, I understand."

Hours later the phone rang.

"David? It's Debbie. I love you. Why don't you come home for Christmas?"

My father and mother came to be with us that year. For the first time in a long while we were all together. Michael, growing like a weed, was already taller than me. Mariah and Danielle were discovering boys, and makeup, and clothes, and music . . . God, I'd missed a lot. We decorated the tree together, wrapped presents, shopped, and wrapped more presents. Grandma and Grandpa loved shopping for the kids, who hadn't enjoyed such a bountiful Christmas in years. As for me, it was a wonderful Christmas, a time to touch the place where I truly belonged and wanted to be. I was constantly full of emotion, almost enlightened with it. The goodness of everyone around me seemed to flow into me; I was in love with life again, brimming with enthusiasm. For a few days I put aside the difficult issue confronting me and enjoyed my family.

One evening after dinner, Dad and I walked to a small park a few blocks from the house and sat on a cold bench, with only the oak trees as company.

"So things are working out for you and Debbie again, are they?"

I crossed my fingers. "If she were as mixed up as I am, we'd be divorced already. It's really her spirit that keeps us together. I'm always so far out in left field these days.

It's tough to keep the important physical aspects of your life together.''

"Well, Debbie and the children are far more than *physical* aspects of your life; they're the most spiritual things you have or ever will have. Believe me, you mustn't sacrifice that kind of love for anything, and I mean anything.'' He looked at me intently. "Do you understand me?''

"I think I do. But I also know that I have to do what I've been set apart to do. You know about that, don't you, Dad? You know I've been selected to be a part of something special—don't you?''

Dad didn't look at me, but into the trees, as if he were searching for memories he'd put away long ago. Slowly, he rose to his feet and headed deeper into the park.

As we walked he began speaking, the timbre and cadence of his voice unlike anything I'd heard from him. "I want you to know, before I tell you this, that I don't consider myself unique in any way. I'm just a man who loved his family and did what was asked of him—no more than any of your relatives did, no more than millions of other Americans and Allied soldiers did. In two wars I never fought above battalion level, so I was always close to the enemy. I had a lot of close calls in World War II and Korea, but I had an inner feeling that something was watching over me.'' He stopped, his modesty overtaking him. "It's difficult to talk about this; I put it behind me decades ago.''

"It's okay, Dad, I understand. You don't have to tell me about it.''

"You need to know!'' He composed himself and continued. "As I was saying, I had this inner sense that I was being watched over. I wish everyone had the advantage of feeling that way. When I was aboard ship, transiting the Atlantic, we were warned about the wolf packs that would track the convoys and sink whatever came into their sights. More than once we were locked up in our holds, below the waterline, listening to depth charges trying to keep the subs from getting a shot at us. Those were weird episodes . . . time seemed to stand still. A lot of guys nearly went crazy anticipating a torpedo; others prayed; still others cried.''

"Don't you think we all have an angel looking out for us at times?''

"Yes. I also think that whether you're aware of its presence is entirely up to the angel.''

"Why wouldn't the angel want you to know it was there?''

"Maybe only some people need to know. Maybe knowing is what steers them in a certain direction in life, causes them to make certain choices. I don't know. Maybe I was given the knowledge that I had an angel because without it I wouldn't have been as brave as others.'' He smiled. "But I want to say that I think there was a reason some were spared in the war and some were called away from this life, and it has nothing to do with deserving to live or not. It has everything to do with the purpose of some larger plan that I can't even begin to comprehend. There are angels out there. I know mine.''

"You, too?''

"I was in Korea, assigned to the 224th Infantry Regiment. One night I lay down and it came to me. My angel.''

"Why didn't you ever tell me this?''

He laughed. "It's not something you bring up for high school graduation, now is it? It was hard enough for me to accept, let alone try and tell someone else about it.''

"Did you tell Mom?''

"She was the first person I told. You're the second, and you'll be the last in this lifetime.''

"Did your angel speak to you?''

"What he said confused the hell out of me, so I just let it go. It never made any sense until now.''

"What was it?''

"He said that a part of me would one day struggle to deliver a message.''

"And?''

"That he would leave me, to protect the part of me in peril. . . . It made no sense to me for nearly—what? Fifty years? But it makes sense now.''

"What do you mean?"

"You're the part of me he spoke of, and you're getting ready to talk about this thing you call the gift. Aren't you?"

I hung my head, realizing how transparent I was to this man. "Yeah, I am. Mel and I think it needs to be done. What do you think?"

"It doesn't matter what I think. The angel's yours now, you know. I've given him to you, just as he said I would. He took good care of me; I know he'll do the same for you." He paused briefly, troubled by his thoughts. "You're going to have a difficult time with this, son. The keepers of the secret won't take it lightly."

"I know."

"Keep your wits about you and stay perfectly clean, because they will look for any weakness they can exploit. That's how they work—you know that, you've been among them for five years now."

"It should be harder for them to get to me in the 82nd."

"No, it won't. You won't have as much chance of knowing what they're up to. Just remember, you can be better than your reputation, but never better than your principles."

In retrospect, I thank God for that brief interlude before the storm. I wasn't reminded of my decision until January 3, 1993. I was playing a game with my son when the phone rang.

After a short pause an unfamiliar voice broke the silence. "Is this Major David Morehouse?"

"It is; who's this?"

"We know what you're trying to do. My advice to you is that you change your plans. People who tell secrets pay a big price in the long run."

"Wait a minute! Who the hell are you? What the—"

"Are you willing to pay that price?"

The phone went dead.

SEVEN

THE FALL

I had been at Fort Bragg as the battalion executive officer for about nine months. Life there was no different for the enlisted men than at any other army post. If they weren't training for war, there were always leaves to rake, weeds to pull, and barracks to paint. I did everything I could to improve the men's quality of life, and it was a good time for me; I felt worth something again. I still had trouble with the remote-viewing fallout, nightmares and altered states, and because of that I still lived alone, unable to return to the family. Also, unbeknownst to my fellow soldiers, I planned to reveal classified information. But for a year I was back where I belonged, making a difference in the lives of soldiers. It was a blessing.

Ingo Swann, a highly respected paranormal researcher and expert, suggested to Mel that we consider telling the story of remote viewing in a book. This, he believed, was the only way to get a clear, complete statement out to the public. We suspected that the news media would cover the story briefly and superficially, chasing after any bone the government threw their way and taking official government statements about Sun Streak at face value. The story would die quickly—if it aired at all. Eventually we did put out some feelers to the news media, but were met with considerable skepticism. I told Mel we just had to find a long-term, detailed way of telling our story.

We spent many nights pondering the question of what risk we were taking; what might the government do, or try to do, to us? Since that anonymous phone call, we'd had no indication that the government was trying to squelch our effort. In fact, though, they were gathering information to discredit our story.

Both at Sun Streak and at the Defense Intelligence Agency, it was well known that someone intended to expose the unit and its secret weapon. Sun Streak members had been warned not to talk to Mel and me; threats were made, investigations were under way, and meetings were hurriedly taking place in the Pentagon and at DIA. The higher-ups' only question was how to crush us.

Because he was retired, Mel was not in much official danger: to take any action against him, the army would have to approach Congress for permission to bring him back on active duty. Only if Congress agreed to this could the army prepare to court-martial him or otherwise punish him. And Congress would demand to know why Mel should be reactivated; to explain, DIA would have to describe a top-secret psychic-warfare program two decades old, the existence of which was known to just five members of Congress. From an intelligence perspective, that was not the best option. Most "exotic" programs stay alive by limiting the number of people who know anything about them. No way was DIA going to approach Congress.

That left them to target me: I was on active duty, so I could be court-martialed quietly.

But at first Mel and I were convinced that nothing much would be done. Some administrative action might be taken against me; maybe there would be a letter of reprimand, maybe a warning to stop immediately. These repercussions I would welcome, because they offered the chance to force DIA to admit that Sun Streak existed. Once the agency did so, I could tell my general officer friends about my past and they'd probably stand by me, given my record and the potential of remote viewing. I was confident that they would protect me, or at least buy me time to pursue another route.

So we took Ingo Swann's recommendation. He put us in touch with his literary agent, Sandra Martin—he told her, "If they aren't killed for telling this story, then I'll tell mine"—and she introduced us to an investigative journalist, Jim Marrs. Jim was the author of *Crossfire: The Plot That Killed Kennedy,* to which Oliver Stone bought the film rights for his 1991 movie *JFK.* Jim is a conscientious and modest man, who shared our fascination with remote viewing and with its potential to help mankind; he worked hard to pull our story together. We began with short visits and interviews, phone conversations, and fax exchanges. (I should mention that, to date, Jim's book has not been published. This book, in case there's any confusion, is entirely my own and was written after this time.)

Mel and I meanwhile remained oblivious to what was going on at DIA. I had no idea how quickly a soldier is cut from the fold when he breaks ranks.

It wasn't long before our phones were tapped. Cassette tapes of my conversations with Marrs, Mel, Sandra, and anyone else I called from my home or office started showing up in the mail. For several weeks little cardboard packages or envelopes with no return address arrived at my parents' house and at Debbie's. (Thinking she might need them at some future date, Debbie saved the ones sent to her and put them in a safe place.) I couldn't see the point of this harassment, and my first thought was that it was a prank, but it worried everyone sick. I've since heard that such mail campaigns are used to frighten an undesirable off a project—his terrified family members convince him to drop it and go away. My harassers, though, failed to understand that *my* family had seen me through a bullet to the head and knew me to talk with angels and be pursued by my personal demons. Having spent years coping with my travels in the ether, they didn't back down.

* * *

My plans to go public with the remote-viewing story never interfered with my duties as an Army officer. When my time as an executive officer at Fort Bragg was up, I was named the division training officer—chief of G3 training was the official title. Being a training officer is extremely difficult, but I was blessed with the help of two of the best majors in the army: Bren Flannigan and Tony Tata. I had what army people call a suck job, but theirs were even more difficult. All of us put in long hard hours, trying to do in a week what most people do in a month, but Tony and Bren managed to shove two months' work into their weekly rucksacks.

Just as I was getting a handle on my new responsibilities, Debbie called me at the office.

"I told you they would try to hurt us." She was crying.

"What happened? Are the kids okay?"

"Someone broke in last night while we were home."

"Is everyone all right?"

"Yes, but they ransacked your office—opened all of the cabinets, drawers, and files. The police are here now, taking a report. I called David Gould." David, the friend who'd found me after my night on the lawn, was a police officer. "He's here helping them. They've found a piece of a latex glove and some imprints in the dust on the shelves, where whoever it was pulled books out. Probably to look behind them for something."

"Deb, let me talk to him."

Dave was calm. "You had some visitors last night," he said mildly. "Everybody's okay. It looks like they were searching for something. Real pros, too—hardly left a scratch on the front door. Came in while everyone was sleeping, did their thing, and exited by the front door again. Bastards left it open, too. Just to let you know they were here."

"I never thought they'd take it this far."

"Do you want me to tell the investigating officer what you think this is all about?"

"I think we should, don't you?"

"I guess it couldn't hurt. Look, I'm going to tell him that we believe someone from the federal government is doing this without authorization. The officers should probably just fill out a normal report, though. If he writes certain things, it will prompt a certain response at headquarters, and I don't think we want a federal investigation just yet. Let's just make it a matter of record: he can put some subtle entry in the report about who the owner thinks may have done this. That okay?"

"Yeah. Thanks for being there, Dave."

Debbie came back on the line. "What were they looking for?"

"Probably the documents Mel and I have, about the unit. I think they want to catch us with them, for the court-martial if there is one. They also want to scare us, to make us feel unsafe and violated."

"It's working. It's working really well, David."

"I'll come up this weekend, if it's okay with you."

"I know the children would love to see you, and so would I."

My commanding officer frowned on my leaving for the weekend, but my family had been violated and I was going to see them whether he liked it or not. I dropped off a leave form and drove away from headquarters after the weekly staff meeting in the commanding general's office.

Just off the installation, I spotted a dark blue sedan several cars behind mine. Normally I would never have noticed, but I happened to see the car just before I pulled in to the shop on post. It must have registered subconsciously, or maybe the angel was sending me a message. And when I came out of the store I saw the blue car again, parked alone several rows away. As I was leaving the parking lot of the mini mart my eyes met the driver's; he quickly turned his head.

It was getting dark, and I lost the blue car in the headlights of everything behind me. It could have been following me when I hit Interstate 95 and headed north, but I wouldn't have known. At first I was amused at the idea that

DIA had nothing better to do than follow me, but just past the turnoff to Raleigh, North Carolina, my right rear tire exploded and I swerved out of control at seventy-five miles an hour. I was in the far left lane and the blowout sent me onto the grass median. I swerved in the soft soil and climbed back onto the highway, trying to hold the car steady while I slowed to a stop on the left shoulder. I was in a sweat and my heart was pounding. The car shook violently every time a truck or car blew past me in the left lane; I needed to get across to the right shoulder. When the road finally cleared, I wobbled across the asphalt and stopped.

While I was fumbling with the jack a freelance tow truck pulled up behind me and honked. I was still shaky from all the stunt driving, and I must have jumped a foot.

"Let me give ya a hand," said the driver. He moved me out of the way and began twisting the nuts off the wheel. When he'd gotten the tire off he turned it around to inspect in his headlights. "This ain't a blowout. This here tire's been cut to blow." He pointed.

"What do you mean, 'cut to blow'?"

"What I mean is, somebody cut this here tire so it would blow when you got to driving fast. Look, see this?" He pointed to a rectangular cut on the inside wall of the tire. "They make a cut here, not all the way through, but just enough that when you get going, say, fifty or sixty miles an hour, that spinning tire throws this piece here outward— tears it—and your tire does this." He tugged at the ragged edges of the tire. "She explodes!"

When he'd finished changing the tire I paid him, threw the blown tire into the back of the Jeep, and crawled under the car with a flashlight. The other tires were intact. I spent the rest of the six-hour drive trying to figure out who'd cut my tire and planning what I'd do if I ever caught them.

It had been four months since my last visit to my family; the long stays at Fort Bragg were taking their toll. I took Michael to one of his hockey games in Baltimore, where I stood alone watching him play and mulling over events. There wasn't a second of my life that wasn't preoccupied with remote viewing, or our book, or the attacks.

Two men in suits stood in the warming room, peering at me from behind the glass doors. I looked at them briefly out of the corner of my eye, trying not to let them know that I'd spotted them. They were definitely watching me; they never took their eyes off me. Still not looking at them, I walked toward the warming room, thinking I might be able to grab a cup of coffee and scope them out, maybe even ask them what the hell they were up to. But as I opened the door, the two men retreated, slipping out the front door. After a few seconds I followed. They were strolling toward their car, looking back over their shoulders every few seconds. One of them was wearing a pair of military low quarter shoes. He fumbled with the keys, trying to open the car door, while his partner looked everywhere but at me. They climbed into their gray late-model Chrysler and sped off.

Things were certainly heating up. I knew I had to go on the record about remote viewing before whoever was behind the surveillance and sabotage escalated things any further.

Soon after my weekend with the family, Mel, Jim Marrs, and I met with Sandra Martin in New York City to work on the book. Over dinner I described some of the events that had taken place. I'd kept Mel briefed, but otherwise I'd mentioned them only in passing before now.

Mel was looking worn. "I think they're after us with the influencing," he announced.

Jim and Sandra didn't know what he was talking about, but I did. "What makes you think that?"

"I can feel them working away at me. You know how it is—you get that itchy, jumpy feeling inside, as if someone's dragging their fingernails across your blackboard."

Sandra shivered in her seat. "Really? They can do that, and you can tell when?"

Jim started taking notes.

"It's something you learn in the program," I said. "You know how it feels when someone stands way too close to you at a party? You know that uneasy and oppressive sensation you get? That's how it feels when someone is in your space from a distance as well. It's no different. You get the same sensation, and it drives you crazy until you figure out what it is."

"How can you protect yourself from it?" Sandra asked. "Or can you?"

Mel replied. "You can. You create an energy ball and surround yourself with it. You give it a reflective surface, and that bounces the probes back out into the ether. The only problem is, I forget to do it sometimes and they get in. Then it's like trying to rid your basement of mice—it's a lot harder once they get in."

"Do they stay forever?" Jim asked.

"No, they have to break it off just like we do. It's just another viewer doing it, probably working at the unit."

Sandra and Jim told us they'd been followed by mysterious figures who had photographed them and slipped into crowds. "Well," I said softly, "it looks as if we're all under attack in some way. You should obviously assume your phone is tapped. You shouldn't be alone anywhere, either. Try to stay with other people as much as you can, at least until the book comes out and this all blows over."

"I don't think it's going to blow over," Mel said. "I think they're going to try and ride us into the ground." He looked at me. "You much more than us. There's not much they can legally do to the rest of us, but you're dog meat."

"I'm beginning to sense that," I said.

In order to fight back and to protect my family, I needed to know what my opponents were capable of. At my request, Sandra set up a meeting for me with one of her clients who had expert knowledge of the CIA and its surveillance techniques.

"You're a target," the expert told me, "and because of

your active-duty status, you're a sitting duck; that's all there is to it.''

"What are they trying to do, just scare me? Just scare my family?''

"That's exactly what they want to do for now: scare the hell out of you. And force you into doing things you or your family wouldn't ordinarily do. You're going to have to keep your wits about you and watch your back.''

"But why my family?''

"Because your family's the only thing that matters to you. If they can undermine your family, they've got you. You need to understand, this is only the beginning. If scare tactics don't work, they'll start taking more drastic measures. And you're an easy target—a recluse, living apart from your family, traveling alone. My advice to you is, get a vest and wear it. You need to be alert, my friend, every minute of every day. Don't get drunk. Don't be anywhere alone for long.''

All I could do was swallow.

A few weeks later, I was called in to see my commanding officer at Fort Bragg.

The chief was standing in his doorway, his lips pressed together and his demeanor like an undertaker's. "Would you come in here, please?''

I walked into his office to find an army prosecutor.

"Major Morehouse, I have brought you here to inform you that certain serious allegations have been made against you: adultery, communicating a threat, larceny of government property, and multiple counts of conduct unbecoming an officer. You are to report to the Criminal Investigation Division tomorrow morning at 0800 hours for questioning. Do you have any questions?''

"Sir? What's this all about?''

"Do you have any questions, Major Morehouse?''

"Yes, sir. What is the meaning of this? I haven't done anything of that nature. Who is making these allegations?''

"That's none of your business!" snapped the prosecutor, brittle-faced.

As soon as I was dismissed I found myself a representative—an army defense lawyer.

"I called the prosecutor's office to see what was going on," he said. He took a deep breath and exhaled slowly, looking at his notes. "Are you aware of what's happening, Major Morehouse?"

I shook my head. I found it difficult even to focus on him.

"Well, you were told what the allegations are. It appears that someone"—he named a civilian woman I knew from around the base—"has sworn a complaint against you. Do you know her?"

"Yes. What is her complaint against me, and why would she be doing this?"

"Well, I certainly don't know why, but her complaint is that you verbally threatened her with physical violence. She also claims that you were sexually involved with her for three months."

"I knew her. In fact, you could say we had a relationship of sorts. I've spent the last four years of my life alone. Sometimes you just want to talk to another person, you know, someone who doesn't have to shave his face."

He laughed.

"I poured my heart out to this woman. She was a good listener, too—kind and caring." I shook my head disbelievingly. "I told her everything about what was going on with me, everything—Debbie, the kids, the nightmares. I thought I knew her. I thought I could trust her. I guess you never really know anybody, do you?"

"Okay. Do you know of any reason why she might be making these allegations?"

My eyes shot with anger. "I believe I just asked you that question."

"What about the larceny charge? The prosecutor has alleged that you stole an army computer and gave it to this woman."

"I gave her a computer for her work. It was an old Commodore, worthless; my wife and I decided that we didn't need it anymore, and we agreed to help her out. She's even talked to Deb on the phone. After all, we were both separated. I don't understand this at all."

He glanced at his notes again. "Well, the computer cited in the charges is a Zenith laptop, and it has a military serial number."

"That laptop is hand-receipted to me; I own it. I have the documentation. I did give it to her, but only so she could take it in for repair."

"They're claiming that you gave it to her."

"I did give her a computer—the Commodore. Her brother is a computer repairman; she agreed to take the Zenith to him for repair and then return it to me with his bill. The video card in it was burned out."

"Well, isn't that something the Army should take care of?"

"The technicians in the training shop tried, but they didn't have the parts, and the army didn't feel it was worth the trouble of repairing. We documented all this at the shop. The soldiers under my command were told to turn it in for salvage. I figured if I could get it repaired I'd have another computer for the shop to work with. She had it for three days to make the repairs. Who's behind all this? It's ridiculous."

"I'm trying to figure that out. Here's what's going to happen from here. Tomorrow morning you are to see CID. They will read you your rights and try to get you to make a statement. I would prefer that you not say anything to them; all you have to do is tell them that on the advice of counsel you choose to make no statement at this time. They'll fingerprint you, and then I'd like you to come back here and tell me what went on. Okay?"

I tried to speak but nothing came out of my mouth.

"Look, sir. Try to relax. If what you're telling me is true, and if I can substantiate it, then we'll hammer 'em.

Go home and get some rest and try not to think about it too much.''

I thanked him and walked out of the office into the icy November air. Then I called the office and told them I was going home for the day. I sat in my room on the foot of the bed, staring at a blank wall; like a broken record, I kept replaying my life and career. All night I sat there, never sleeping, never moving. At seven in the morning I drove to CID.

The investigators did just as the representative had said they would, and I said just what he'd told me to say. It was over in an hour.

''Jesus, sir, didn't you shave before you went over there?'' my attorney said when I walked into his office.

''I guess I forgot; I didn't sleep last night. I just stood up and walked out of the house this morning.''

''You need to get a grip on yourself, sir. You can't walk around like this; don't let them know how you're feeling. Just go up there to that headquarters and play good soldier. There are people on your side in this.''

''It doesn't matter who's on my side. If they are now, they won't be soon enough. And if they stay with me, they'll go down with me, and I don't want that to happen.''

''What are you saying, sir?''

''This is bigger than you'll ever know; it's part of a plan being put together by some people who want to destroy me.''

''You're not making any sense, sir.''

''The point of this is to discredit me, to destroy me before I do what I know I have to do. When's the last time you saw an officer who was legally separated from his wife being charged with adultery?''

''Well . . . I haven't ever seen it.''

''The military doesn't have to worry about precedents, does it? The prosecutors can just resurrect whatever arcane law is on the books and nail anyone they need to with it. They can't prove any of this, and they don't care; what matters is the allegation. The smear!'' I got myself under control. "I'm sorry I raised my voice—you're not the enemy."

"Sir? What are you talking about?"

"It's a long story. I'll explain when I get back. Right now I'm going home to see my family and tell them what new magic trick the intelligence community has pulled out of its hat." I left the lawyer trying to figure out what the hell I'd just said.

In the weeks that followed, the government prepared a four-page list of charges against me. In my view the most serious and damaging—and insulting—was, of course, the charge of larceny. The rest were things like "dereliction of duty, for failing to sign in a visitor to the headquarters building" and "conduct unbecoming an officer, for use of threatening language."

Every step of the way, protocols for the proper handling of an officer of my rank were violated. And every violation was a twist of the knife in my back by people I'd once trusted. I have to say that by now the pressure was getting to me. I was looking at the tarnished and absurd end of a very bright and promising military career. And as word of the charges spread, few of my former comrades would even speak to me. Some friends suggested to me that nobody really cared about the charges: "You're a marked man, and that makes people nervous. They don't want to get on them any of whatever's on you."

CID investigators hauled in and interrogated my friends; my room was searched; my old units were contacted in an effort to dig up anything that could be used against me. They even questioned the salesman who'd sold me my car. And never mind if fifty people said I was a good guy; the fifty-first, who didn't like me, captured the spotlight.

I had to borrow $10,000 to pay for my own investigation. If I was to be court-martialed, which had not yet been determined, I needed to have evidence to counter the allegations. I didn't know what to do; my lawyer's opinion was that either this would all go away, or we would win in court. In my next meeting with him, though, the army's position became clear:

"I am required to inform you," he told me, "that the government is offering you a chance to resign. If you choose that option, you will have certain rights, and you will assume certain risks. This is what happens: you tender your resignation for the good of the service. All charges pending against you are dropped, and the Eighty-second recommends that the resignation be approved. It will also make a recommendation concerning the type of discharge you should receive. Those recommendations pass through the commander of PERSCOM in Alexandria, who in turn can recommend approval or disapproval of the resignation and the type of discharge. From there, the paperwork goes to the under secretary of the army; he makes the final decision." The lawyer paused to look at me very seriously. "I have no doubt that the resignation will be approved. What I'm concerned about is what type of discharge you'll receive."

"What's your guess?"

"There is nothing in the charges that warrants a dishonorable discharge; that would require a trial, and I don't think the government wants to try this case. I think you have some friends you didn't know you had; also, there is a new prosecutor now and he doesn't see the issue. That's good for us if we have to go to trial, but it does nothing for us if you resign. If you resign, I think you will be recommended for an 'other than honorable' discharge. It's clear that the government wants you discredited and gone."

"I have an impeccable record and sixteen years of service. Has the government conducted any investigation in support of me, and has that evidence been brought before the commanding general so as to inform him of the merit—or lack thereof—of the allegations? Has any of that been done?"

"Well . . . no. I'm working on a capital murder case; I was going to start investigating as soon as I finished with that. In the meantime I was planning to request that a CID investigator be assigned to the case permanently, to work for us.''

''You haven't done that yet? I mean, no offense, but all you've done so far is give me bad news. They have nothing—you said so yourself. Why would I throw sixteen years of my life away without a fight?''

''For some reason, Major, you're deep in the soup and they aren't going to let you out of it unless you resign.''

''I don't expect anyone to *let* me out of it. I know why I'm in it. All I'm asking for is a little support. I don't want to resign. I know that the decision I made, to divulge classified information, is not a popular one, but given the nature of my real infraction, I'd think that I could at least get a hearing where I could tell someone with a brain what I'm doing and why this is all happening.''

''Major Morehouse, you're not charged with disclosure of classified information, and I can't get anyone to confirm that you're so much as being investigated for wrongful disclosure.''

''That's because it's happening deep in the intelligence community; they don't want anyone to know about it, or what they're doing now wouldn't work. I can't deal with this alone. I don't have the resources. And every time I tell a civilian attorney or investigator the truth about all this I chalk up another count of wrongful disclosure. There's nowhere to turn. All I can do is face these charges and hope to God that someone with some common sense can unravel the thing.''

''Or you can resign and take your chances on the discharge.''

''What happens to me if I get an 'other than honorable'? I mean what do I lose?''

''Do you have a VA home loan?''

''Yes.''

''Well, you'll lose it. You'll lose the right to draw unemployment; you'll lose the right to military interment; you'll lose your pension; and you'll most likely never work for the government again in any capacity.''

"Boy, what a prize. And I get to wear this badge of dishonor for the rest of my life."

"That's true. But on the other hand, the government has to drop the charges, which makes it clear that they're unfounded. Otherwise the army would take you to court.

"Think about it. They'll drop the charges; you'll have no conviction and no trial, and you walk out of uniform and back into your life."

"The army *is* my life. I'll be walking into a world I know nothing of and that knows nothing of me. I'm nobody out there. In here I'm Major Morehouse. I have a life. A career. I used to have a future. Two months ago I was picked for an assignment to the Chief of Staff for the army's study group as a nonlethal weapons expert; now, I'm weighing whether to face trial or resign in disgrace."

"I do find it hard to believe," my lawyer agreed softly. "But whatever decision you made about whatever it is you were involved with makes you a liability to the army."

I stared out his window as a formation of troops marched by. "I won't resign under those conditions. I've done nothing dishonorable, and I'll not sully my father's name by stepping out of the fray. I've broken ranks by telling a secret; I will accept the penalty for doing that, and that only. I'll admit to disclosure and I'll resign, if that's what they want me to do. But I won't walk away from this. It's shameful and wrong." I started out of the room. "You call them and tell them that Major Morehouse said they can come to court and prove to a jury of my peers that I'm guilty of the charges they've filed against me."

I went home for Christmas, setting my problems aside as much as I could and doing everything I could to make the time special for my family. The charges hurt us all, but Debbie and the children stood by me and held me together.

While I was at home I spoke to Mel a few times about the book and the charges. He tried his best to put my mind at ease, but I could feel that this was the beginning of the end, just as the angel had said. It was tearing me apart. I fought back by working on the book with Jim Marrs. He'd ask me how certain scenes and places looked, and I'd build them up for him, helping him to understand how things worked in the ether and at the unit. These exchanges often took several hours on the phone; afterward Jim would excitedly sign off and pound the keyboard for hours on end reconstructing our conversations. I used to smile as I closed my eyes at night; I swore I could hear him typing away, creating images in words.

As the New Year came and the time for me to return to Fort Bragg drew near, I drank in the warmth and love of the family. God, I missed being with them. Debbie and I sat quietly one evening discussing the charges. We were both immeasurably distressed by them, first because they were ludicrous, and second because of the impact they would have on our lives. We chose to remain separated, but I was still the father of my children, and I honored my financial obligations to them.

Early one afternoon, our power went out. Almost everyone up and down the street had a small generator to power essential appliances. Debbie and I pulled ours out into the driveway and fired it up, running an extension cord back to the house through the garage so we could power up the television for the kids, the refrigerator, and the freezer. I let down the garage door but couldn't lock it because of the extension cord at the bottom.

The children went to bed around nine o'clock, and Debbie soon followed. Because we were both emotionally drained and because of our separation, I was sleeping on the sofa in the family room. I watched television for a few hours; as I dozed off, out of the corner of my eye I saw the cat get up, stagger a few feet across the floor, and fall flat on his side. He lay motionless, struggling for breath. I stood quickly and tried to walk to him, but I fell to the floor and began retching and gagging for air. My head felt as if a wedge had been driven into it. It pumped and throbbed until I thought it would burst like a melon. I squeezed my head in my hands, to no effect. My eyes felt as if they were popping out of their sockets. *Air!* I crawled to the back door and opened it, letting the icy air rush in. Each frigid lungful stung its way into my body.

"Debbie! Get up! You have to get up, something's wrong!" I screamed as loud as I could into the blackness at the top of the stairs. "Debbie, Mike! Wake up!" Silence.

I got to my feet and staggered upstairs, clinging to the hand rail. Danielle's bedroom was the first one at the top of the stairs. It was dark and cold, the air tomblike: no power meant no heat, and no circulating air. I shook Danielle, but she didn't respond. I screamed and shook her again and again until her eyes opened to narrow slits. She began crying, dazed and frightened.

"My head hurts!" she whimpered. "What's happening?"

"Danielle, you have to try and get downstairs! Do you understand me? You have to get downstairs. Come on, honey, try to get up. Take your blanket with you—come on." I dragged her out of the bed and tried to make her stand. Her little legs kept crumbling under her weight, so I grabbed her with one arm and shuffled to the door of her room, screaming for everyone else to wake up. At last Michael staggered out of his room, holding his head.

"What's happening, Dad? My head feels like it's going to explode."

"I don't know, son. Help me get your sister downstairs and into some fresh air. Can you do that?"

Without hesitation, the fifteen-year-old snatched his sister from me and carried her downstairs, his legs wobbling beneath him. I rushed into the master bedroom, where Debbie was sitting on the side of the bed trying to get her bearings. Even in the darkness I could see the confusion on her face.

"I don't know what's wrong, but there's no air in the house. We need to get everyone downstairs, quick!"

Debbie stood and fell against me, then steadied herself. She held on to me as we moved quickly to Mariah's room. Our breath hung in the chilled air of the house like icy smoke, illuminated by a beam of light coming from the stairway. Michael had grabbed a flashlight and was coming back upstairs to help. Debbie ran to Mariah and tried to wake her, slapping her wrists and face lightly, shaking her and calling her name repeatedly in the blackness of the room. Mariah's dark eyes opened briefly, then closed, squinting in the flashlight beam. She mumbled something unintelligible and tried to fight off her attackers. Debbie persisted. "Mariah! Something's wrong—you need to wake up. Come on, Mariah! Get up! Get up now!"

Debbie and I each took an arm and dragged Mariah from the bed and to the door.

"Grab some blankets, Mike," I directed. "Stay right here with us! Just grab a handful of whatever's on the bed and bring it."

We slowly descended the stairs, none of us in full control of our limbs. Danielle had passed out again on the floor. Her body was turning blue from the cold and from lack of oxygen.

"Mike!" I said. "Keep Danielle awake, don't let her go to sleep!"

Debbie and I sat Mariah down next to her sister, and Debbie ran for the phone. I knelt in front of my children as the knowledge of what was happening sank into me. "The generator!" I said aloud. I could still hear its rumbling outside the house. The sound had been going so long that I'd stopped being aware of it. I stood to make my way outside, but Michael cried out to me. "Dad! Danielle's not waking up! I can't make her keep her eyes open!"

Now Mariah began retching. Her vomit misted and froze to her and to the blankets she'd wrapped herself in. Michael pulled another blanket from the pile and wrapped it around his sister, trying to comfort her. I looked at Danielle's face in the beam of the flashlight; she was pale as death. Her lips were blue; the tissue around her eyes was dark and sunken, and she was listless and unresponsive.

"God, baby! You have to fight this. Danielle, you have to help Daddy take care of you—you have to fight. Breathe for Daddy! Take deep breaths, come on, baby, you can do it!''

Danielle sagged in my arms, still not responding to my voice. Michael began calling her name, yelling at her, trying to make her hear him. It was as if her spirit had already left her body behind, as if she were standing apart, watching us scream and shake her. I held her close to me and screamed as loud as I could, ''Don't die, baby, don't die!''

Someone grabbed my shoulder and turned me away from my baby. I swung wildly, striking him in the arm. A bright light pierced the darkness and stopped me cold.

''Take it easy, buddy! We're here to help!'' I shielded my eyes as someone passed me and began talking to my daughter.

''What happened here?''

I was still confused; what was happening? Bright light spilled in from the street and yard, casting a supernatural glow over the house. At last the gleam of helmets and a sudden burst of radio traffic made sense.

''It's the fire department, Dad!'' Michael tugged on my pant leg.

I sat down on the bottom step of the staircase. ''Oh, thank God! Thank you for coming!''

''This one's pretty bad, Captain!'' announced the man attending to Danielle. ''We need to get her to the hyperbaric chamber stat!'' He carried Danielle toward the door. Debbie appeared next to me and put an icy hand on my shoulder. One of the firemen picked up a blanket and wrapped it around the two of us as we sat there on the stairs.

''What happened?'' Debbie asked.

''Carbon monoxide poisoning, ma'am,'' the captain answered. ''At least, that's what it looks like.''

Debbie looked curiously at me. ''How could that happen?''

''I don't have any idea,'' I said. ''Unless the wind blew the gas back into the house.''

"Where's my baby?" Debbie's voice quivered. "Is she going to be all right?"

"Ma'am, the paramedics are looking at her. She was pretty sick, nearly comatose, when we got here. She should be okay if we can get some oxygen in her. The problem is getting the carbon off her red blood cells."

Debbie, being a critical care nurse, understood what he was talking about. I knew carbon monoxide was deadly, but I had no idea exactly how. "What do you mean, get it off her blood?"

"The carbon molecules stick to the blood cells and don't let any oxygen molecules attach themselves, so you slowly die from lack of oxygen. She was nearly comatose, and that's the last step before death. We were real close."

The radio in his hand crackled. "Captain? The paramedics think she needs to be medevaced right away. They want to take her to Children's in D.C. and run some tests. . . . If she's as bad as it appears then they'll get her to Georgetown to the hyperbaric chamber. Right now, though, she's starting to respond to the oxygen."

"I'll ride with her," Debbie said. "I work at Children's, in the neonatal intensive care unit."

Two firemen took Debbie's arms to escort her across the frozen lawn to the ambulance. At the doorway she turned to me. "Find out what happened. I'll give you a call from the hospital as soon as I can."

"Okay." But I felt helpless. I couldn't imagine what had happened.

Some firemen attended to Michael and Mariah, while others brought huge fans into the house to blow out the poisonous gas. They also combed the house from top to bottom, taking no chances of leaving someone behind; they knew we weren't completely coherent yet. I began to shake, from the cold or from nerves, I don't know which. I tugged at the blanket, pulling it tighter around me.

Two young firemen approached the captain, flashlights in hand. They mumbled something to him I couldn't hear. The captain turned to me, shining his light in my face.

"What the hell is your generator doing running in the garage?"

"What do you mean?"

"Come here and we'll show you," one of the other men said.

I gathered my blanket around me and walked to the front door with the men, the captain leading the way. We stopped in front of the door, which was raised completely. The generator was sitting in the middle of the garage.

"The door was closed, too."

"No!" I said. "I know better than that. I put it right here." I pointed to the spot on the driveway where I had set the generator several hours earlier. "That's why there's no car in the driveway, because the generator was sitting right here. Look, the grounding rod is still there." I pointed to the copper rod I'd pounded into the ice when I set up the generator. "I wouldn't have put it in the garage. I'm not stupid!"

"Well, somebody picked it up and moved it for you," said the captain. "You got any pissed-off neighbors?"

There in the snow and ice were two sets of footprints. Whoever made them had picked up the generator and put it in the garage, quietly closing the door behind them. A shiver ran down my spine.

"I've seen something like this before," the captain said. "Somebody gets tired of hearing your generator run and they try to retaliate in some way. But whoever did this could have killed you all. Fucking idiots."

Anger began to swell inside me. "They weren't idiots."

"What?"

"It's a long story. But whoever did this knew exactly what they were doing. All we had to do was go to bed, and their troubles would be over."

"You mean *you'd* all be over! If you'd gone to bed, nobody in that house would have gotten up tomorrow morning. Your youngest almost died as it was." The captain's voice was chilling.

Another fireman put in: "And you know what the headlines would have read, don't you? 'Family of Five Dies in Generator Mishap.' Dozens of people die that way every winter.''

I ran my fingers through my hair.

"We can call the police if you want," the captain said. "You may want to make an official report about this, although I don't know what would come of it." He turned his gaze skyward. "It's starting to snow right now; in fifteen or twenty minutes all this will be covered." He pointed to the markings in the snow. "I don't think this gives them much to go on, anyway. These footprints have been out here in the wind for hours.''

I was learning fast. Whoever was trying to shut me up had just given it his best shot, and nearly succeeded. I decided that after I heard from Debbie I'd call our policeman friend, David Gould, and see what he thought I should do.

I went back into the house with Michael and Mariah while the firemen cleared away their fans and power cords. The entire street was afire with red lights and crackling with radio talk. Finally they were all gone, and the house was dark and quiet again.

Almost six hours had passed when Debbie called me to ask me to come and pick her and Danielle up. When I pulled up to the front door of Children's in D.C., Debbie looked like a ghost, tired and frightened. I decided not to tell her what I'd learned until she'd had some rest and hot food.

It turned out that Debbie had a story of her own. The ambulance she and Danielle rode in had mysteriously died just past the District of Columbia border, and they'd waited by the side of the road for nearly an hour and a half before another one showed up. Debbie's hands shook as she relived the details for me. "I was sure she was going to die while we waited. I was just sure of it.''

I tucked her into bed, combed her hair, and pulled the cover up over her. Danielle slept next to her; neither would let the other out of her sight. Debbie's arm rested over Danielle, keeping track of her while she slept.

Michael brought our fully recovered cat, Ranger, into the room. He gently tucked him into bed next to Danielle. After the initial scare, Ranger seemed to have fared considerably better than the rest of us. I think he used up at least one of his lives; but his warning, intentional or not, saved all of ours.

Later that afternoon, as my wife relived the event in her nightmares, I called David Gould.

"What can I do?" I asked.

"I have to be honest with you," David said, "not a whole hell of a lot. If the government is behind this, who would the police go after? I wouldn't even know where to begin. Suppose the Prince Georges County Police Department calls the FBI, what are they going to say? 'A guy in our jurisdiction decided to tell the world about a classified program, and he thinks the government just tried to kill his family to stop him from doing it. Will you begin an investigation?' I don't think we can count on them to be of any help."

"So I've basically got no options?"

"Well, you can decide not to tell the secret, and maybe they'll go away and leave you alone. I wish there was something else I could do or say."

"I know. And thank you for looking out for the family while I've been gone all these years. I really would appreciate it if you'd keep an extra close watch these days."

"You can count on it!"

A few days later I had to get back to Fort Bragg. Before I left, I made sure that Dave was looking in on Debbie and the kids every day and that everyone knew how to reach me at all times. I will never forget that night, or the pain I felt in having to leave my family to face further indignity from the army. I turned off the capital Beltway and began the journey south to Richmond. It was eleven-thirty at night and traffic was light. I was happy to be making good time through the most congested area. But the weather reports were forecasting heavy fog along the coastal waterways. And sure enough, I hit the fog.

The last worldly object I remember is the sign for Fairfax, Virginia, but I must have pulled off the highway for a brief rest to let the fog lift. As I waited, I fell into the ether.

I stood alone in darkness, in a place so black I could not see the ground. I was afraid to take a step, afraid that I might step into an abyss. In the distance of this place I saw a glow, so faint that I had to look at it sideways to see it. When I looked at it directly, it seemed to fade into the darkness. I moved cautiously toward it. A wind began to blow—softly at first, then with increasing ferocity until I had to lean into it to make my way toward the dim glow on the horizon.

The darkness subsided as I came closer to the glow, and I could see a horizon very clearly now. Leaving the darkness behind me, I passed into a vast open space, perfectly flat and completely empty. I turned to look behind me and saw the darkness swirling there. Before me was a dimly lit landscape. I stood on the border of light and dark, able to see both with equal clarity. I was at a crossroads of sorts. The light appealed to me. The darkness behind was frightening.

I turned toward the lighter world and walked deeper into it. Then a portal opened in front of me, and I looked into a foul and horrible wasteland. Frightened, I spun away and ran toward the darkness. I ran deep into it, looking back at the portal several times to see if it remained. At last I slowed and caught my breath. In the blackness another portal opened, revealing a beautiful garden filled with flowers and shrubs of all kinds. Their scents wafted out of the portal and into the darkness where I stood. I inhaled the sweet smells of the garden deeply and felt its warmth on my skin. But as I moved to step into the opening, it quickly closed, leaving me in darkness once again.

"David," a familiar voice called from somewhere around me. I turned, but didn't see the angel anywhere. "What have you learned from this visit, David?"

"Where are you? Why can't I see you this time?"

"Answer my question and you'll know the answer to yours. What did you learn here?"

"I learned that there is darkness and light and neutrality in the world."

"There is no neutrality. Everything is a choice; you cannot stand in the world without choice."

"Then I learned that there is darkness and light, and that each represents some aspect of the world . . . I think, of my world."

"You knew that even before you came here. Search deeper—what did you learn?"

"I learned that darkness is not always evil and that light does not always represent goodness. I learned that perceptions can mask the truth."

"Very well. Then how do you know the truth of your world?"

"I don't know."

"You do! How do you know the truth of your world?"

"In the words of the holy, in law, in Scripture . . . in physical laws . . . I don't know."

"When you know the truth of something, where does it touch you? Where do you feel it?"

"Here!" I touched my chest. "Inside me."

"You feel it and know it in your heart."

"Yes, that's where I feel it! Why is that lesson important to me now? I haven't any problem feeling love."

"It is truth you seek, not love; it is truth that evades you now. All that you believed, all that you wanted, all that you once were is now lost in a haze of deception. You must battle it, just as I foretold. How will you know the truth? How will you guide your family to the truth? How will you bring the truth forward? How will you know it *is* the truth? How will you gauge it and know it among the deceivers?"

"I don't know."

"You must follow your heart; it will not deceive you; it will not let you be deceived. But you must learn to listen. You will soon find blackness where you once thought there was only light, and light where you once saw only darkness.''

"Is the light God?"

"It is, for some; for others it represents life, purity, power, and spirituality, among other things.''

"And the darkness within the light, what is that? How can it exist there if the light represents those good things?''

"Light and darkness exist within you on many levels, and the veil separating them is often thin. The truth lies beyond the veil, but you haven't the time to search beyond, living each existence in each level one after the other until the truth confronts you. The spirit and voice of your heart reach through the many levels to the truth. Those who refuse to listen experience each level, each veil, with all of its tricks and false light; however, those who listen find answers in light and in darkness. They can exist in the presence of pure evil because their heart has touched the truth, and evil has no power over those who know truth. Its power dominates only the confounded, the complacent, those who live in the light but do not know truth.''

"I understand . . . I think. But why did you call me here to learn this? Why do I need it?''

"All humanity needs it; it is a part of the gift. There are those around you who possess this knowledge; one sought you out long ago. He is your friend, and you will need him in your life.''

"Who is he?"

"You know him well. One day you will call on him to strengthen you with his wisdom in this world. You will be weak and broken. You will not listen to what you have learned here until your past life is over; only then will you humble yourself and ask for what is needed. I warned you long ago of this ending.''

"You never told me why I must endure this torture, this failure.''

"Consider it a cleansing. You are not yet what you are supposed to be; you are only walking the path. You have much to experience.''

"But what if I don't want to do this? I want to go back to what I was; I'm tired of this, I want to just be me again, like I was before the bullet."

"It was all decided long before the bullet."

In an instant the voice and the world in which I stood were gone; my eyes focused on a small building in front of me. A man walked toward me, turning left before he got to my car; he headed down the path, got into a car, and slammed the door shut. I opened my door to the brisk night air and walked to the building. A large man was attached to the wall inside. The "You Are Here" arrow pointed to a small rest area just south of the West Virginia border. I was on I-77 heading north out of Virginia and into West Virginia. I had no idea how I'd gotten here or why I had stopped. I returned to the car, poured myself a cup of hot coffee from the Thermos, and quickly scribbled some notes before I forgot the details of what had just happened. Then I slammed the notebook shut and checked the time.

I'd been at the rest stop for three and a half hours. As morning slowly crept across the horizon I called the office on the car phone to let them know that I would be late.

In March 1994 the government convened what is referred to as an Article 32b hearing. This is a gathering of prosecutors and witnesses for the prosecution, and of defenders and witnesses for the defense. An appointed officer from the division hears both sides of the story and makes a recommendation to the court-martial convening authority as to whether the case ought to be tried. I arrived at my lawyer's office about an hour before the hearing was scheduled to begin.

"I've decided not to present anything in your behalf today," he said as he shuffled through some papers and crammed them into his briefcase.

"Why not? Wouldn't it be to my advantage to shoot down their case in front of the hearing officer instead of at trial? You have enough to kill at least three quarters of what they're suggesting."

"I don't want to tip our hand just yet. I think it's wiser to hit them with everything in court, when they don't have any idea what our case will be. I think it will make a bigger impact if we do it that way. Okay?"

"So what do we do, just sit there and let them peel my skin off in front of the investigating officer?"

"I'll have a chance to cross-examine their witnesses. They're calling the woman who claims you had a sexual relationship with her. And the division's systems automation officer, to have him testify that the computer in question was indeed a military computer. By the way, they extracted all the information from the hard drive, even stuff that had been deleted."

"And?"

"And it's just as you said. Everything was military-related, nothing personal or civilian." He grinned. "Let's go to court!"

He did a wonderful job on cross-examination and, in my opinion, cast considerable doubt on the prosecution's case. After the meeting, I called Mel. "They're going to court-martial me."

"Dave, we can quit any time. We don't have to do this."

"No. We're doing it no matter what! It's destiny, Mel, remember?"

"Be careful, Dave. Sooner or later it will be all right."

"I think later rather than sooner."

Three hours later I was on the road to Washington to see Debbie. But the pressure had taken a toll; I fell back into the ether. When I awoke it was to Debbie's comforting voice. She held my hand, her face creased with stress, her eyes wet.

"Where am I?"

"You're home. You're in the front yard, but you're home."

She tried to help me to my feet, but I staggered and fell to my knees. Finally, together, we walked into the house.

"What time is it?" I asked.

"It's five-thirty."

"I must have made good time; I think I left at one o'clock."

"David, everyone has been looking for you for *three days*. This is Tuesday morning; you left Fort Bragg on Friday afternoon. Where have you been?"

I rubbed my throbbing head. "I don't know. I remember leaving, that's all."

"David," she said softly, "this has gone on for too long. You're sick, David. You need medical attention. Please let me get it for you. You can't do this alone anymore. You aren't under the care of the unit, you don't have Levy, or Mel. You're dying, David."

I looked across the room and saw my image in the mirror. An old man looked back at me. "Okay."

The next thing I remember is the smiling face of the orderly who was pulling a blood-pressure cuff from around my arm.

"Major Morehouse? Do you know where you are?"

"Am I in the hospital?" I asked.

"Yes, sir, but do you know which hospital?"

"No I don't." I felt a hand touch my shoulder, and when I turned toward it Debbie's face came into view.

"You're in Walter Reed, David. You're safe now, and these people will help you. They're not like the others; they care about you."

"That's right, Major. You look a little rough, and your wife says it's been a while since you ate anything or bathed. How about a shower and some lunch before you see the doctor?"

I nodded.

"Great! That's the spirit."

I did everything they wanted me to do, and Debbie sat with me while I talked with a young air force medical student. He listened to me and then to Debbie and then to me again. He was taking notes almost faster than we were talking. Debbie chronicled my entire history for him, from Ranger battalion to the present.

"This is a very interesting case," said the medical student when the attending physician came in. "I'll let them tell it to you themselves—but *trust me,* you're in for a wild ride."

The attending physician, whom I'll call Dr. Damioli, was a petite, intense woman, with diverse psychiatric experience in the government. Debbie began with the story of the bullet and the very first visions and nightmares, then described Sun Streak and the conversations with Dr. Barker and with Levy. She spent two hours detailing every event she could recall, and had dug up phone numbers for everyone she had on file. Some were friends. Some were not. But they would all have to confirm what had happened to her husband.

Dr. Damioli called the psychologist associated with the remote-viewing unit while Debbie and I sat in the lounge, then called us back into her office. The medical student was present as well.

"I spoke to the remote-viewing psychologist on the phone. Did you know he's assigned to Fort Bragg now?"

I looked at Debbie, furious. He must have told all of them—the prosecutors, my superiors, everyone else involved—everything: what would set me off, how to get to me, how to get me to shut up.

"Well," Dr. Damioli continued, "he confirmed the existence of Sun Streak. He also told me that he hospitalized another officer back in 1985 or '86 for symptoms similar to yours. But then he suggested that your problem stemmed from a pending court-martial. He feels that you are probably malingering."

"That's ridiculous!" Debbie shouted. "He's the man who got David involved with this in the first place. Now he wants to bail out on him." She looked at me, her eyes aflame. "What kind of people did you call your friends? You used to call this man your friend, and he just politely stuck a knife in your back!"

The doctor leaned over and took Debbie's hand. "Mrs. Morehouse, please! Just relax." Her voice calmed Debbie. "I don't care what he suggests. He's only a psychologist, not a medical doctor. It was clear to me that he was anxious about something, and his comment about malingering only served to settle that thought for me. If what you're saying is true—and I believe it is—then we have a unique situation on our hands.'' She paused to look at me. ''Why are you crying, David?''

I reached for my face, as surprised as I could be. ''I don't know. I didn't realize I was.'' My face was wet with tears.

''You've obviously been through a great deal. I want to keep you here indefinitely for now, to explore this issue further. Mrs. Morehouse, do you understand that?''

''I do. I've been trying to get David in here for nearly seven years.''

Days turned into weeks, and weeks into months. And Dr. Damioli not only understood what *had* happened, she knew what was happening within me now. Despite the counsel of her colleagues, she refused to medicate me, insisting that what I saw was explainable apart from biological problems. She was a hero. I paid little if any attention to what was going on at Fort Bragg—it didn't matter to me anymore; what mattered was understanding the meaning of the angel and of the importance of the gift. For the first time in seven years I could speak freely and openly about what I saw and felt and heard. I didn't have to worry about frightening family members, or making my peers shrink from me, or losing the respect of my superiors. Even at Sun Streak, I hadn't been able to share everything, except with Mel. Here there was help, and partial answers. I was encouraged to sketch and to discuss what I saw in the ether. I became the subject of much controversy over whether drugs or even shock therapy was more in order than the counseling and reading assignments Dr. Damioli prescribed.

I was brought before the directors of Walter Reed's psychiatry department. Eventually it was decided that I would be medically retired, as no longer being fit to do what I had been trained to do. They told me that I was too emotionally unstable to go on wearing a uniform.

The retirement process began. I filled out papers and endured more tests, but also enjoyed time with Debbie and the children, who came by every day. We were sitting in the hall one day in early June, when a familiar face appeared. It was a major from Sun Streak.

"Hello, David, Debbie. I was wondering if we could talk alone for a minute."

I looked around at the children and Debbie. "I don't think that's such a good idea. I'll send the kids to get a soda, but Debbie is going to stay right here with me."

"I wanted to talk to you about why you're in here."

"Are you still with Sun Streak?"

"No, I'm in a section of DIA headquarters that has limited oversight responsibility for it."

"In other words, you've been moved up to the head shed to oversee some of the operations. Is that it?"

"Yes, and I've been asked to find out exactly what you're telling them here in the hospital."

"I see." I was getting upset but didn't want to show it. "I'm in here because something happened to me a long time ago that I should have taken care of. Instead, I played good soldier and did what I was asked to do. I tried to protect my career and be the best remote viewer I could; and now I'm here." I smiled at him. "And yes, I'm telling them everything I can about the unit."

He cleared his throat and crossed his legs, folding his hands in front of his knees. His thick glasses dwarfed his face and magnified his eyes. "I, uh, see. Then, I want you to know that I will do whatever is necessary to protect the unit. We can't let you destroy it."

Debbie jumped up from her chair and stood between Pratt and me. "What kind of human being are you? David's not trying to do anything to your precious unit; he's not here because of that. He's here because the unit made what was already wrong with him worse."

"Frankly, Debbie, I just don't see how that could happen."

"Don't you? Did you and the rest of your cronies become medical doctors since I last saw you? Where do you get off coming to a conclusion like that—because you didn't have any problems? You and the handful of psychics you're here to protect didn't have any problems, so nobody else can, is that it?''

"I can see you're upset." He stood. "I'll do what I can; but my original statement stands; we won't let you destroy the unit with any claims, regardless of what they are." He nodded to Debbie. "Good day."

"You can tell your friends at DIA that I won't stand for any more shenanigans with my family," I called as he walked away.

He stopped dead in his tracks and looked back over his shoulder. "What are you talking about?"

"Just what I said. First your boys broke into my house and ransacked my office; then they tried to kill me and my family. I won't let that happen again, I might just have to put some of my old Ranger training to use. You know what I mean . . . old buddy?"

"I have no idea what you're talking about; that sounds like something you and Mel would cook up."

"You get the hell out of here and don't come back. I thought you were a friend, but you're nothing but a weasel with an opinion. I thought I was part of a profession, but apparently I joined a fraternity, full of secret little clubs with special handshakes. Step out of line and your brothers pull a bag over your head and beat you to death. Well, you go ahead and swing away, but remember this: the bag is off and I can see who's swinging the clubs."

He looked at Debbie and me from over the tops of his glasses and smiled. "Oh, you have no idea who's swinging, my friend. You really don't have any idea at all. And you remember this: in this world, even when you *can* see who's swinging, you'll never see the one that gets you." He winked, turned, and walked away.

A few days after that encounter, I had a relapse, falling back into the ether. The ceiling above me dissolved away in a blue-and-white swirl until a large oddly shaped hole appeared. In it I saw the darkness of the evil place I feared so much. I trembled violently and cried out for help. The darkness widened above me, and the phantoms of that dimension slithered out of the hole and across the ceiling to the walls; several dropped into the bed where I lay. I kicked and screamed to get them off me, yelling at the top of my lungs; I struck out at them, but my hands passed through their vaporous forms. They scratched at me, calling me by name and screeching to me that I was nothing in this form. They slashed at me over and over until I closed my eyes from the pain; at last the room grew quiet once again. I lay there quivering, waiting for the next blow.

"Oh, my God! I need some help in here! Somebody! I need some help!"

I opened my eyes to see the medical student screaming over his shoulder, his face pale, his eyes wide.

"Oh, my God, Dave—what happened? What happened?"

"I don't know," I said, still groggy from the nightmare. "What's wrong?"

"Your face—it's covered in blood. What happened? What happened?"

In seconds the room was filled with attendants. My body was covered with blood; legs, face, bedsheets, everything was covered with blood. Pages had been torn from my notebook, and sketches had been made on them in my blood. I felt my head to find blood was matted and caked in my hair. I nearly fainted. I dropped my hands to the sheets and I began weeping uncontrollably as they whisked me out of the room.

Two days later Debbie and I sat in Dr. Damioli's office. My legs and head were bandaged, and I was now under constant observation. I didn't go anywhere or do anything without an attendant present.

"I have to start you on medications now, David. I have no choice, and now you have no choice, either."

I sat there with my hands folded in my lap and my head down, completely confused. "I don't know what happened.

They've never touched me before; I didn't believe that they could.''

"You're speaking of the dark ones?"

"Yes! I didn't know they could touch me. How could they do it? How could they do it?"

Debbie wept softly. "He's seen them for years," she said to Dr. Damioli. "But they never did anything like this."

The doctor's eyebrows rose. "I'm certain they didn't do it this time, either. I believe that what you see in the ether is very real to you, and I believe that there is a great deal more to the human mind's capabilities than we have even begun to discover. But I don't believe that something from another dimension lacerated your flesh." She pulled out a plastic specimen cup, twisted the lid off, and poured a single razor blade onto her desk, then held it up for us to see. "Do you know where this came from, David?"

"No."

She frowned. "Well, it was stuck in the table next to your bed; I believe it's what cut you."

The blade shimmered. "I still don't know where it came from, Doctor. Why would I cut myself?"

"That's what I can't figure out, what worries me most. Something triggered a dissociative episode that ended—or began—with you carving your body. Perhaps—and I repeat, *perhaps*—at the suggestion of what you call the dark ones."

"Are you suggesting that what he sees in the ether has that kind of power over him?" Debbie asked.

"I don't know the answer to that yet. The problem is that I wanted to continue to examine and treat David without giving him antipsychotic and antidepressant medications. Now my hands are tied."

"Doctor," I said, "can you please try and tie all of this together for me? I'm missing a few pieces here; I think you have some idea of what's going on, but I still don't."

"I'm not sure I do, either," said Debbie.

"It's both simple and very complex. You mustn't let yourself believe that something came out of the darkness and lacerated you; that just can't happen. However, what you see in the visions can affect you once you're drawn into a dissociative state—what you call an altered state.''

''You mean, while I'm out of it, I can actually play a role in the nightmares? I can actually do something to myself because something in the vision tells me to?''

''That's a little more simplistic than I'd like to make it, but it is pretty much my theory. I'm convinced that what you are experiencing is not chemical. My colleagues believe that the bullet made your brain stop producing some chemical it needs to function properly. What *I* believe is that the impact of the bullet, and the subsequent trauma, opened something you were not prepared for, and that there is a logical or philosophical explanation for everything going on inside your head. Everywhere I look there are indicators leading me to this conclusion; your sketches carry some very important messages about what is happening to you. You think they are images of what you see in the ether, and I won't dispute that. However, I also believe that the images that come freely to you—the ones that pierce your consciousness at will and without provocation—are messages or symbols from deep in your limbic system.''

''But you believe that he cut himself with the razor blade?''

''I'm certain of it.''

''But where did I get the blade?''

''God knows. It could very well have been during an outing around the hospital grounds. If you were in a dissociative state you might have picked it up and hidden it without ever consciously knowing you'd done so. It appears that your altered states are linked in some way—you pick up where you left off each time. It's quite fascinating, actually. The biggest problem people have with this, David, is that you appear quite normal; you're sensible, intelligent, and articulate, which is not typical of people who are having experiences like yours. Consequently many people dismiss you as a malingerer. But you are indeed having real difficulties. And although you are not psychotic or delusional, what you describe fits the classic definition of someone who is. You see? You are a new type of patient, and you will require some modified treatment.''

Debbie took my hand. ''Well, at least we're getting somewhere positive. We really appreciate your efforts to unravel this, Doctor.''

''Well, it's my job to help, not to pass judgment on David without exploring all the possibilities. Unfortunately, I fear that antipsychotics and antidepressants will hamper our progress.'' Dr. Damioli pulled a book from the shelf behind her and handed it to me. ''I want you to read this book; I'll have several others for you later. I think it imperative that you grasp the full meaning of what I'm talking about, and I think you'll find Jung's account of his visions very interesting. Perhaps you'll find that touching the darkness is not so unusual after all.'' She smiled warmly. ''You possess a unique quality—a gift, if you will. You can see what most of us will never see and, frankly, don't want to see. The task is to be able to control it.''

''What about the remote viewing—is it affecting this, or will it be affected by controlling the dissociative states?'' Debbie asked.

''For now, I believe they're unrelated. I think that perhaps the remote viewing exacerbates the dissociative disorder, but I don't believe they're otherwise connected. If we can learn to harness and control the dissociative disorder, then I think remote viewing can occur without incident; but we'll have to see.'' She picked up the file on her desk and opened it. ''There's one more thing that concerns me. David will be medically retired within a few days, so I need to arrange follow-up care at a veterans' hospital here in the D.C. area. I want your promise that you will continue with his care, and work with me and whoever is assigned to you until you get control of this situation.''

''You have my word. And thank you from the bottom of my heart.''

''Yes, Doctor, thank you,'' Debbie added.

*　　*　　*

I was given Halcion and Prozac, as well as a number of other medications, to stop what the "biological" psychiatrists believed were hallucinations. Their effect was devastating. I wandered about in a cloud, as if my mind were wrapped in a blanket that kept out the light. I had no visions, no nightmares, nothing but the haze of the drugs.

I met daily with Dr. Damioli and often with her more trusted colleagues; sometimes more hostile physicians would attend. Often, while I was alone sketching or writing, someone I didn't know would sit and talk with me. These doctors would ask me questions about what I saw and what I did. They seemed more interested in information than in treatment, and I think a number of these visits took place behind Dr. Damioli's back.

In late June, she called Debbie and me in to see her and dropped a bombshell. "I'm afraid I have some bad news." Her hands were trembling. "You're not going to be medically discharged."

"What's going to happen to him, then? This is terrible. What about your treatment plan?" Debbie asked.

"David's going to be transferred to the psychiatric ward at Womack Army Hospital in Fort Bragg, where they can proceed with the court-martial as planned. I'm sorry. I've done everything I can."

My heart fell to my feet.

Debbie cried, "How can they do that? How can they be so cruel?"

"Why won't they let me get well?" I asked through the haze of the drugs.

"It appears the commanding general of the Eighty-second won't drop the charges so that you can be medically discharged; he is forcing you to stand trial. Apparently he's gone so far as to call the hospital commander to demand that you be moved back under his control. I'm really very sorry. I've been told in no uncertain terms to step aside."

Debbie was shaking with rage. "I feel so violated and helpless. He'll drop the charges to let David resign so he can give him an 'other than honorable' discharge, but he won't let him be discharged so that he can get medical attention. What kind of animal is this man?''

During the next two days Debbie wrote letters to congressmen, phoned officer friends all over the world, even wrote the general's superior officer. But nothing worked. The decision was now etched in stone: I had to return to Fort Bragg. Instead of being thirty minutes away from my family, instead of getting supportive care, I would be alone in the darkness again. It was just how they wanted it.

On a Wednesday morning, I bade farewell to the hospital staff who had become my friends, who had cared and helped me to understand the many levels on which I was fighting. I lay on a gurney as instructed and was strapped in; a nurse who had been with me held my hand, tenderly stroking it and looking into my eyes.

"You remember one thing, Major Morehouse." Her eyes misted with emotion. "Trust in God! He knows what you're going through; you trust in Him and everything will be all right."

Dr. Damioli approached me just as they wheeled me to the door of the van that would transport me to Andrews Air Force Base. She, too, held my hand. "You get well, my friend; you fight and get well."

The hollow doors to the van slammed shut with the finality of a death sentence. I tried to weep, but nothing came; the drugs held their ground.

EIGHT

THE REBIRTH

A thousand times I have been visited by the memory of the night; and I know that I shall be visited a thousand times again. The earth shall forget the pain of furrows plowed, ere I shall forget the lessons of the night.

The medevac plane touched down at Pope Air Force Base; I was transported to Womack Army Hospital and processed into the psychiatric ward. Within hours I was ordered into a uniform and driven to the courtroom, where for the first time in nearly three months I saw my legal counsel.

He filled me in on the proceedings. "They will read the charges against you, and then you will be asked to enter a plea. At that time you must stand and face the judge and say, 'Not guilty, Your Honor.' I'll take it from there, and we should be out in fifteen to twenty minutes. I should tell you that I'm trying to make this a classified trial so that I can bring in the issue of Sun Streak. If they're going to railroad you for your disclosure, I think they should have to face it openly."

"What will that do for us?"

"Well, they will have to read everyone on to the program—the judge, court officers, jury, defense, prosecution, maybe even all of the witnesses. I don't know for sure. It'll make them think twice about how far they want to take this charade.''

''Thank you.''

''How are you feeling? I understand they have you on some pretty powerful medications. In fact, the skin around your eyes looks green.''

The hearing—the first of many over the next ten weeks—was called to order. It proceeded just as my lawyer had said. Enduring the humiliation of court-martial was certainly one of the most difficult things I've ever had to do. Worst of all was the realization that everything I'd done in my life up to that point meant nothing. If it had been only me being abandoned after sixteen years, I could probably have understood, but the Army turned its back on an entire family. One good thing that came out of this experience was that I learned who would stand by me, who believed in me.

During the trial, Debbie, my parents, my friends, and my brother and sister rallied to my side. They wrote letters extolling my virtues and my sacrifices; my record was described, and all of my friends pleaded for mercy. They explained that since becoming a part of Sun Streak I had become reclusive, had cut myself off from everything I once knew and trusted. But it was no use. I had broken ranks, and I came to realize that no mercy would be shown to me or to my family.

In late August, with Debbie and my parents by my side, I asked to be released from the hospital. My days consisted of taking drugs and sitting through classes designed for substance abusers preparing to go to one of the military rehabilitation centers.* Group therapy was performed by

---

*The drugs I was given were overwhelming—a cupful every day by the time I left the hospital. I was on forty milligrams of Loxitane (a powerful antipsychotic), sixty milligrams of Prozac (an antidepressant), six milligrams of Cogentin (to offset the tremors caused by the Loxitane), and thirty milligrams of Restoril (a tranquilizer). Most mornings these drugs knocked me to the floor. Although I didn't have any dissociative episodes or trips into the ether, I spent day after day in a fog.

orderlies in a makeshift weight room; for exercise I was allowed several minutes on a caged rooftop with the other patients twice a day. It took Debbie six hours to drive to Fayetteville for a brief visit—when she could get time off from work. One physician had told us frankly that he was too close to retirement to get involved in this case, with its connection to Sun Streak. Another just avoided me as much as possible. I just played the game, proving myself a compliant patient.

In the first week of September, Debbie signed her husband, the father of her children, out of the Fort Bragg hospital. The months we both had endured while I was there had been for nothing. Debbie was understandably bitter. All these years, she had believed that the army would take care of its own, would care about a soldier and his family, would help him get well again. Now, she realized she had been betrayed, and she hated the army, hated it more than she had ever thought she was capable of hating anything. I had taken her away from her family and friends and introduced her to life in the army, to a profession that I believed would protect me from false accusations and unjust treatment. Instead, the army became the tool the intelligence community used to destroy me and my family. Far from standing by me, the commander of my division vowed to take away everything I had.

After my release from the hospital I was assigned to write a ''Leader's Guide to Caring for Families'' for the 82nd Airborne Division—an assignment that added insult to injury.

Debbie, as well as other family members and friends, wrote to the division commander countless times, pleading with him to reconsider his plan to proceed with the court-martial. They asked for appointments with him, and he refused. He refused my wife and my father. He refused the father of a soldier, a father who had fought the enemies of his nation in two wars. He refused the wife of a soldier, a wife who had spent thousands of hours in the service of his nation, counseling the wives of her husband's subordinates, balancing their checkbooks, shopping for them, cooking for their children and caring for them when they were ill just as she would have cared for her own family; a wife who had cared for the men serving with her husband and made them a part of our family. Worst of all, he abandoned a woman who believed in the cause and taught her children to believe in the cause although every night they lay in their beds with their father gone. He abandoned our family.

God must have known that I could go no lower, that I could not drag my family deeper into the pit that was being dug for me. In the third week of November 1994, the phone rang at our house in Bowie.

"David, you won't remember me and I don't want you to. There are several of us who worked with you many years ago when you were a lieutenant and young captain, and we know what's been happening. I just want to tell you something about what is happening to you and then I'm going to hang up and let you make your decision. You cannot go through with the court-martial. It's a setup. You're going to court to defend yourself and your name, correct?"

"Of course."

"When you can't back out of a trial, they will try to charge you with wrongful disclosure of classified information." If the military judge allowed this brutal strategy, it would force a continuance on the army prosecutors so my attorneys could prepare for the new charge. But by then my tormentors would have me where they wanted me—committed to a defense I couldn't win. The caller agreed. "You won't beat that charge, David. They know what you've done and they'll give the prosecutors the necessary evidence to convict you and put you in prison."

"I see."

"You thought the charges were foolish. They were, though maybe not to the Eighty-second. But they were perfect—foolish enough to encourage your lawyer to try and fight them in court, which is exactly where they wanted you. You'd be focusing all your energy on charges you thought you could beat easily, while they prepared a case that would send you to Leavenworth for years. You'd never see it coming until too late."

"What can I do?"

"They still have to let you resign; the charges pending aren't serious enough for them to do otherwise. It may piss them off, but they'll have to comply. If the convening authority drags his feet, others will get involved. You still have some friends left, David; it hasn't all been for nothing."

"So I should tell my counsel that I want to resign?"

"Yes, and as soon as possible. If they get word that you plan to resign they'll up the ante—that means bringing more charges if they have to. Remember, they don't have to have definite proof; all they need is an allegation, and the entire process begins again. Resign as soon as possible—and good luck, David."

The phone went dead before I could say good-bye.

I returned to Fort Bragg the next day. My parents were with me, as they had been since my release from the hospital. I needed constant supervision because of the medications and my unstable emotional condition. I was deeply embarrassed by that—I was a thirty-nine-year-old man who had to be baby-sat by his seventy-year-old parents—but I couldn't function without them. While my father waited in the hall, tears in his eyes, I stepped into my lawyer's office for the final time and agreed to resign my commission in the United States Army for the good of the service. Then I notified my supervisor, who said sadly, "I wish it had gone another way for you, but I understand your decision." Then I drove home, took off the uniform I had so proudly donned sixteen years ago, and walked out of the life I had sacrificed everything for.

Thirty days later the charges against me were dropped, and after yet another barrage of supportive letters from friends and family the undersecretary of the army approved my resignation and bestowed upon me an "other than honorable'' discharge, ensuring that all our devotion to the army was wiped away. It was as if the last nineteen years of our lives had never existed.

And every decision by the division leadership and even the undersecretary of the army was made without any evidence being presented in my behalf. Not once in over a year did the government ever perform any investigations on my behalf. My attorney never deposed anyone, never petitioned the court for an investigator; and never was any evidence supporting me presented to either my commanding general, the judge, the commander of PERSCOM, or the undersecretary of the army. The only depositions made on my behalf were those I personally paid a private investigator $5,000 to obtain, and they were never used, although they would have destroyed the government's case. During the hearings I was never allowed to tell my side of the story. I think that was the most frustrating part of the whole experience—I couldn't stand up in my own defense, explain that the charges were false and were meant only to discredit me. And my mental state aided and abetted my opponents all the way. In many ways I had played right into their hands—but of course, they did have my psychological profile, and I suppose they knew me better than I knew myself.

There were so many people who could have helped but didn't for fear of destroying their own careers. So now Debbie and I were starting over with nothing but each other. I'd lost our retirement benefits, the VA loan on our home, the right to unemployment benefits, the right to be buried in a military cemetery. I was even denied access to the American Legion. Once I'd been an officer ''destined to wear stars''; now I was a worthless outcast, still suffering from visions and nightmares unless I drugged myself with poisons.

My beautiful wife took these blows like the trooper she was. ''It wasn't worth losing you to prison,'' she said. ''We've been through enough. Now let's get you well, and get on with our lives." But I felt hopeless, and I didn't want to suffer any longer.

As soon as the medications ran out, I did without; we couldn't afford a civilian doctor, to renew the prescription; nor could we afford the medications. Because I had a pre-existing condition we couldn't begin to afford insurance, either.

I routinely contemplated my death, wondering what it would be like to join Mike Foley and the others I'd seen in the ether over the years. One moment of pain and shock and it would all be over, for eternity. I wouldn't embarrass anyone again. I wouldn't have to endure one more vision, one more nightmare. I could experience peace.

I decided several times to take my life, but each time something stopped me. First, the faces of Michael, Mariah, and Danielle came to me magically each time I went too far. And then there was Debbie's angelic face, her kind eyes leading me away from what would harm me and back to safety. She always told me that my most valued possession had never been lost: the love of my family.

"We will always be here for you, David," she said to comfort me. But who gave her comfort? I was a cripple, incapable of life on my own. Debbie struggled to hold the family together, pay the bills, and care for a husband who was sinking deeper and deeper into despair by the hour. It wasn't long before she, too, began to disintegrate emotionally. She'd married a strong, promising young infantry officer; sixteen years later, she had a devastated, empty shell of a man who could no more be a father and husband than he could care for himself, who was a melancholy testimonial to what he could have been. Each day was a struggle to keep her own sanity, her own sense of worth, and to somehow instill in our children a belief in themselves and a renewed love and understanding for what was once their father.

In April 1995, Debbie loaded me in a car and drove nineteen hours to Russellville, Wisconsin.

"How is he?" Mel asked quietly.

"See for yourself," Debbie said, and broke down sobbing in his arms. He gently passed her to Edith, who helped her into the house.

Mel looked at me. "How you doing, brother?"

"Not so good."

Mel recognized that only half a man stood before him, and he knew what had to be done to free me from whatever held me in darkness. While I rested in the house, he prepared a very sacred ceremony to save his brother. He made four small cloth bundles of bits of bone, claw, and hide scrapings from a black bear; these he set in the four corners of his property. That night he brought me to his tepee; we sat inside with a small fire fueled by the purifying green sage and the flat leaves of the white cedar. He tied a large black-and-white eagle feather to the top of the entrance, where it hung to ward off unwanted spirits.

The fire heated the interior of the tepee until sweat poured from me, soaking my shirt and pants. I watched as Mel pulled a pipe from a hand-sewn bag. Its long stem was adorned with horsehair, feathers, and intricate beadwork; he reverently packed the bowl with a mixture of sacred tobacco, the inner bark of the red willow, and dried sumac leaves. He lit the pipe and took a long draw, then exhaled the smoke as a pious offering to the Great Spirit. Holding the burning pipe, he respectfully offered smoke to the four corners of the world and to Mother Earth. He passed the pipe to me and I repeated his offering; the aromatic smoke swirled about my head, intoxicating and freeing my dead spirit. I sat there feeling it begin to turn and shift within me. My walled-up emotions gently came to life as I watched Mel slowly and deliberately empty the ashes of the pipe into the burning embers of the fire.

Around my neck, he placed the rock medicine he'd given me years ago, and with a paint he'd made from clay he drew two horizontal lines across my forehead, the top one black and the lower one red. He then painted my chin red and placed a small pouch of tobacco in my left hand. This was a symbolic offering in a ceremony of death and in preparation for the rebirth of my spirit. As he did so a strange rush of wind rattled the walls of the tepee, and the grunts and rootings of a large animal circled outside. As if all that was as he had expected, Mel calmly packed away his pipe and stowed the sacred tobacco. Next to me he placed a small war bundle containing weapons to be used by the spirit to combat evil in the ether; his final preparatory act was to unveil the skull of "George," an ancient Indian medicine man who had been with him for decades; this he placed opposite me, the fire between us.

I remained as reverent as I could; though I didn't fully understand what my friend was doing, I did know that he was trying to help me, and that his methods were sacred and powerful.

"Go into the ether, Wank'hok'isak'a [Half Man]," he said in a tribal tongue. "There you must look for Rezi-wak'antcank'a [the Holy Tongue]. I will be outside praying for you on the rock near the water."

Mel left me alone in the lodge, taking his medicine and pipe with him for use during his prayers. I sat staring into the flame, inhaling the scent of the smoke and entering the ether.

I plunged into the tunnel of light, falling toward something I didn't know, some place and time I'd never been. I tumbled in the rush and flurry of sounds and images that filled the signal line. I fell until I pierced the veil and found myself in a strange world laced with a mixture of darkness and color.

"A-Ho(! Wank'hok'isak'a, I have been waiting for you."

I stood in the presence of the elderly medicine man whom Mel affectionately called George. George had been watching over Mel ever since the early sixties, when he had rescued the skull from a pair of traders who were planning to defile it by driving an arrowhead into it. Their aim was to increase its value to unsuspecting tourists or novice collectors. Mel gave a week's pay to liberate George from his captors, and ever since the Indian's spirit had been with him, guiding and comforting Mel and his family in times of crisis. Every Riley had a story of how George had manifested himself to them. And countless remote-viewing sessions had been run at Sun Streak to learn George's history and fate. Many years ago, as a greenhorn remote viewer, I, too, had searched his past; now I stood before him in all his glory. A red and blue blanket covered him from shoulders to thighs; a single eagle feather crested his head. His powerful hands were exposed only at the fingertips; his legs and feet were covered in finely sewn deerhide. A brightly colored and meticulously beaded bag hung from his shoulder; I assume it held his spirit medicine.

"I am honored to be in your presence."

"You have been led to me by a man of great wisdom and spirit, a man with eyes for this and other worlds."

"I am grateful, but I am frightened."

"You carry bear medicine; the one who brought you considers you a bear warrior, of the Bear Clan. You must be as brave here as he believes you to be."

"I will try."

"You are here to die. Did you know that?"

"I am already dead in the spirit."

"You were told it would be so, were you not?"

"I was told by the angel who watched over my father that I would give up a great deal to reveal the gift."

"And now you must die completely and be reborn in spirit to carry on the work of your world."

"I'm ashamed that I fell so terribly; I'm ashamed."

The medicine man laughed. "All spirits fall; it's nothing to be ashamed of. There is nothing in the world more true than the death and rebirth of the spirit. All things in the world possess the spirit. All things in the world die and live again. I am speaking not of physical death, but of spiritual death, of the death brought on by the living of life in the pursuit of wisdom and understanding. It is as you were taught in the beginning: you will become something other than what you were. As you were told, the wisdom brought by the gift of eyes extracts a toll. Your spirit is dying because it must be reborn to soar to a higher plane; that is what makes some more than others. The fear of seeking the wisdom that brings about transformation is also what makes some less than others. You made the journey; you lay down upon the altar and gave willingly to become more than you were before the gift. So many have been offered it and refused it for fear of change.''

"I'm grateful for your explanation."

"Then it is time for you to die."

I followed the medicine man to a gathering of elders; all were clad in sacred priestly robes. My eyes saw them as elderly Indian holy men; but I was wise enough to understand that they could take on whatever form my heart accepted. These beings, like everything else I saw on this journey, were symbolic representations of the unseen power that governs not only what is in our hearts, but also our world and everything in it. The interconnectiveness of lives and spirits; of knowledge, of life, and of death was becoming clear. For just an instant, I was blessed to see clearly the meaning of my life and the lives of all humanity. In the presence of these great men I looked into eternity to see the flow of time, and I knew my place within it.

As I stood looking into eternity, the men encircled me, each carrying his medicine. When the circle was complete, a brilliant flash of light passed before my eyes and I fell to the beings' feet. Spiritually dead, I gazed into the heavens of this world and watched as the beings symbolically breathed life into me, their breath becoming mine until I stood before them, reborn of spirit.

The circle parted and the medicine man who had brought me took my arm and led me away to a place just before the veil. Here he turned to me and said:

"I will tell you a story which you must always carry in your heart from this time forward. A war party came to the camp of their enemies; they watched from a distance to learn the ways of their enemies; and once they believed that they could learn no more, they crossed the river separating them from the enemy camp.

"A small girl saw them crossing and alerted the warriors of her camp, who rose in defense, killing many of the war party as they crossed the river. One warrior, however, fought so fiercely that he crossed the river and made his way into the thick brush separating the camp from the river.

"In the brush, he fought so mightily that the warriors protecting the camp backed away, afraid to enter the brush and fight the warrior face to face. Throughout the long night they cast stones and flaming torches into the brush to wound and torment the brave warrior. As the night deepened, the sounds coming from the brush, which had been war cries and whoops, became the growls and snarls of the bear, further confounding and frightening the warriors who surrounded the brush.

"As dawn broke, the camp's warriors rushed into the brush to overwhelm the enemy warrior, but they did not find him there. His spirit had died as he realized his calling; reborn, he was transformed in spirit and form into a fierce bear. The bear warrior killed many of those who surrounded him, and they fled the village, taking the women and children with them.

"The spirit of the bear warrior and of what was done there has never left the banks of the river. From that day forward, whenever a people tried to settle there, the bear warrior came from the darkness in power and glory and frightened them away. From the day of his transformation his spirit and life increased through the power of his legend. Despite what he gave up, the mark he made because of his rebirth will never be forgotten."

Saying nothing else, the medicine man brought me into the veil. When I opened my eyes I saw the interior of the tepee; Mel, smiling, sat across the embers from me.

"Welcome back, my brother." His eyes misted with tears. "I prayed for you!"

I wiped the tears from my eyes. "Thank you for knowing how to give me my life again. I'll never forget you, in this life or any other."

Mel sprinkled another handful of sage over the embers,

sending a cloud of purifying smoke into the air around us. "It's over now. All the poison of the past is gone. More will come, it always does; but you'll see it differently now. I made some things for you a few years ago; now is the right time for you to have them."

He reached for a blanket made of red trader's cloth and threw it open. "This is your shield. It's willow with deer-hide stretched over it; the markings, like those on your rock medicine, represent the bear and his power to turn aside the weapons of his enemies. These five feathers across the bottom are called barred turkey feathers; the white fluff decorating them is eagle fluff; the white skin is otter, and this cloth draped to the side is trader's cloth.

"This is your war ax." Mel picked it up. "The handle is wrapped in deerhide and beadwork in the black and red of the Bear Clan. The feathers are crow and red-tailed hawk. This is your lance; there are twenty-eight barred turkey feathers with eagle fluff, with bearskin and otterskin on either end of the shaft. The head is hammered metal from a wagon wheel, and the Bear Clan symbol is notched in it as well as in your war ax. I want you to have these; I made them for you to be reminders of your rebirth and of your warrior lineage." He wrapped them in the blanket and passed them over the fire to me.

"I don't know what to say, Mel. You have been with me and cared for me for so long now. I'm humbled by you, and forever grateful for your love and friendship. Thank you for that, and for these wonderful gifts."

He smiled. "Well, it's probably appropriate for you to say *megwitch*, which means 'thank you' in a local tongue. Maybe it just sounds better when you're exchanging Indian gifts."

"Okay, *megwitch*. . . . George told me a story about an Indian warrior who became a bear and never left those that killed him alone again. Have you ever heard that story?"

Mel stirred the embers with a stick and poured water from a clay jug onto them. "Yup. That's a true story, by the way."

"Well, he told me to remember it always. Do you know why? And is it written down somewhere?"

"It's not written anywhere I know of, but I'm sure he gave it to you as a parable for your life. Take each part of the story and compare it to what you've experienced over the last seven years; I think you'll find some parallels . . . Hey! You ready for a beer?"

"Actually, I'm ready for a truckload; but one will be more than enough. I think I sweated out half my body weight." We climbed to our feet and left the tepee. Just before I entered the house I paused to look back at the place where I had died. I smiled warmly, hoping George was there watching.

Debbie and I got ready to leave the next morning. We hadn't arrived with much, but we sure as hell were leaving with plenty. I kissed and hugged Edith, thanking her for taking such good care of Mel. Debbie embraced Mel and Edith, thanking them for taking such good care of her husband.

"Oh! I almost forgot!" Mel ran upstairs. When he reappeared he had a blanket under his arm. Unrolled, it revealed a large deerskin. He flipped it fur side down to show me a pictograph of the story George had told me. "This should be on your wall, where you'll never forget it. I should have known that I'd have to write the story down for an infantryman."

"Yeah, and it's even in pictures—no big words to try and pronounce," Debbie said, smirking. We left Russellville and drove back to Bowie to begin life anew.

Among those who anchored me in this world again was Mike Foley, my dear friend who was shot down in the Panama chopper crash. He came to see me in one of those moments of despair, and his words were prophetic and clear. What he and the angel said helped me to understand the insignificance of what happens here, in contrast to what we do here.

The key to my rebirth was inside myself. Aside from the

symbolic death of my spirit, the only ingredient I required, I already had: the pure love of my family. And of course, I'd almost forgotten the reason for all my troubles: to get the message out that we are more than just the body; we are spirits loosely tethered to earth, and there are dimensions and worlds far beyond what we know here. There is more than we have dreamed of—but none of that matters if we cannot grasp the significance of this life.

You can spend a lifetime tapping into the ether to explore other realms, but you have to come home sooner or later. You can mingle with gods and other peoples and other species—and you can think yourself unique for it—but they will not be there to help you make your way in this life. What we do here in support of others is where true happiness lies. I found that out the hard way.

There were many tearful, angry nights and days in between where I was and where I am today. At this point in my life all I want to do is tell the story of remote viewing to anyone who will listen, not because it is amazing or controversial but because it carries a message for all mankind. There are other worlds out there, other dimensions, with civilizations, intelligences, love, hatred, success, and failure, everything we experience here in our world. There are also benevolent as well as evil energies out there. Some have the express purpose of destroying or hindering our progress here, and they have spent millennia practicing their craft.

It became clear to me that remote viewing is both a blessing and a curse. It also became clear, through the message of the angel, that truth is in the hearts of men, not in the worlds of others. It became clear in the ceremony that there is no shame in failing because you've stretched yourself to new boundaries, or because you've followed your heart and done what you believed was right. To reach beyond your limits intellectually, spiritually, morally, and ethically sometimes requires you to take on a new and fresh spirit. I learned many things over my years in the ether; now I learned that the cycle of birth, growth, death, and rebirth of the spirit is eternal.

EPILOGUE

In December 1995, I got on my knees and humbly asked Debbie to marry me again. After more than five years of separation, she said yes, and for a second time in my life she made me the happiest man on the planet. We plan to be married in the mountains of Wyoming, at Paint Rock Lodge. There we can stand on a rock and look out over a world we'd forgotten existed. There we can put aside all the loneliness and empty nights, and live as husband and wife. Ours has been a long and terrible ordeal, and it's time to rest and love again.

Debbie and I decided to discuss with the children everything that happened to me. Many of my decisions affected them in ways that they would have to deal with for the rest of their lives. Answering their questions would be the first step in the healing process. I'm not ashamed of what happened to me, but I had been out of their lives for over five years and they didn't know me anymore. When they did see me, I was in the hospital or just coming out of the ether. They had grown up without me.

I'd spent their childhood years in the pursuit of intangibles—ideas, beliefs, and ideals. I'd sacrificed being part of their growth so that I could continue in my work as a remote viewer, so that I could bring the gift out of hiding. I'll spend the rest of my life wondering whether I did the right thing. Did I have a choice? Why did I choose the path that I did, and what were the lessons? And, most important: after the troubled life I gave my children, can they ever forgive me and love me again?

I used to proselytize to my children, trying to convince them that what I was suffering and making them suffer was for the good of humanity. I tried, in the early years, to make them understand that I was engaged in an assault on the bedrock of contemporary thought. While I cannot say that I'm sorry for the path I walked, I do regret the petty way in which I held their feelings and emotions at bay. I rationalized that children get over things quickly. But what I found is that children are profoundly affected by their parents' actions. My decisions, and the amount of time Debbie has had to spend keeping me together, indelibly marked the personalities of each of my children. I know they will replay these events again and again in their own nightmares.

I wish that as this phase of my life comes to a close I could look back and say that I did what destiny dictated, that I did what the angel—and, I think, God—asked of me, that I followed through with a plan that was established long before I came into this world. Despite what I wish, this is what I believe: I have stolen something from my children; I have challenged them in areas no child should have to compete in; I have created scars where wounds should never have been inflicted. When I pass from this life, I will leave my children a complex and troubled legacy. Where and how they deal with those complexities is up to them, but I lament the fact that they will have to make choices about the memory of their father. I will always remember my parents as kind, wise, and loving; but I could only guess how my children would speak of and relive life with me. It was time to talk about everything.

Debbie and I brought the children together late one evening. I could see in their faces that the pain of the past had conditioned them to quickly throw up walls to protect themselves.

"Your mother and I wanted you to know that we intend

to work very hard at being a family again, and I have asked your mother to marry me again.''

"You were never divorced!'' Mariah said flatly. "How can you get married again?''

"Well, we are going to renew our vows, which means there will be a small wedding, where we will commit to one another again in ceremony and in the presence of witnesses.'' I glanced down, afraid to look into their eyes. "I guess what I mean is, I love your mom, I always have, and being apart from her and from you has been very painful for me. I want to be her husband again. I want to be your father again.''

Danielle's eyes began to water, but she wiped the tears away, refusing to let them fall and be noticed. Mariah swallowed hard; she, too, was fighting back the painful memories. Michael sat bent forward, his elbows on his knees, his fingers interlaced, his gaze fixed on the ground.

"We want to be married again,'' I continued. "We want you to be there with us, to see us recommit to each other and to you.''

"Mom doesn't need to recommit to us!'' Michael said. "She's always been here for us.'' A tear dropped from his eye. "You're the only one who left. You're the one who thought remote viewing and all that other crap was more important than us. You're the one who tried to leave us forever. What do you want from us now?''

His pain and the truth of his words stung. Mariah's body shook with sobs. Danielle ran to her mother and embraced her as if to say, "Protect me.'' Debbie hugged her little daughter, combing her hair with her fingers and whispering comforting words. She rocked her gently to calm her, and wept quietly as I tried to find words to bridge the gap I'd made between myself and my family.

I wiped tears from my face and struggled to speak with some degree of composure. "I know that I've caused a great deal of pain in our family.'' I took a deep breath and tried to focus on my words. "I cannot recreate time and relive the decisions of the past. If I had known what damage

I would do by making the decisions I did, I would not have made them. But even so, I should have known what I was doing to all of us. I did what I thought I was supposed to be doing. I looked deep inside myself and thought I was doing what God wanted me to do. I have to believe that I was. I brought a very valuable thing out of hiding, and I thought I was the only one paying a price for doing that. I was foolish and selfish to think so. I should have let you all know what was happening. I should have done then what I'm doing now, and let you all decide whether to support me or not. As it turned out, I made all the decisions without you. I was wrong.''

"You were very wrong!" Mariah sobbed. "When we were little we knew you were a soldier. We understood why you were gone, and we always knew you'd come back to us unless you died. We knew you loved us, but we didn't know that when you left us five years ago. Sure you came home once in a while, for a Christmas visit, or you called us now and then—but you weren't our dad anymore, you were somebody else!"

"You were a stranger in our lives," Michael agreed, still not looking at me. "You came and went, you tried to be our friend or you tried to tell us what to do; but"—he laughed sarcastically—"the way we looked at it was like, Who the hell is this guy to walk in here for five days a year and try to make a difference? I mean, you were our dad, but you were no different than some guy who lived down the street. I got more out of my coaches than I ever got out of you!" He sobbed, looking at me now, his eyes filled with love and pain and sorrow. "You abandoned us for something we couldn't even see! If you'd left Mom for another woman, we might have been able to cope with that, but what you left us for was invisible. We couldn't see your angel! We didn't know what went on in the nightmares! We didn't share your interest in the ether or whatever you call it. We were hurt! And we had nothing in front of us to be angry at, only a memory of what our dad used to be like.'' He wiped the tears from his cheeks, shaking his head in disbelief. "Do you know what it·was like for me to come to Fort Bragg and see you starving yourself? Or how about being told by the doctor that my father tried to kill himself? Did your father ever do that to you?" He looked painfully into my eyes. "Well, did he?"

"No, my father never put me through anything like what I put you guys through. My father would have made the right choices. I hope that you won't make the wrong choices with your families because of me."

"Believe me," Mariah said, "I won't *ever* do to my children and husband what you did to us. I know how much it hurts to see your dad fall apart. I'll never forget that. I never want my children to feel like the world has come to an end, like they want to die because their father wants to die."

Debbie kissed Danielle on the cheek and turned her around to face me as she spoke. "This is the children's time to speak, so I'll make one point here and then I'll bow out. You and your father have to talk about what has happened. All of you need to settle this and come to some closure." She stopped to gather her thoughts. "I want to try and explain why I think your dad tried to take his life. You have to understand that the army was giving Dad drugs that changed the way he thought. They were supposed to make the angel go away so that your father wouldn't talk about him anymore. The drugs were very powerful and poisonous; they distorted how he saw things and how he processed what he saw. The doctors tried to take his mind way, and the army tried to take his career away. Under the influence of the drugs, he thought that his life was over."

"I felt that I had been condemned to death already," I said. "In my mind, there was nothing left for me here. Everything I loved had been stripped away from me; my family, my life in the army, my pride, my reputation, my future, my ability to provide for all of you. I felt I had nothing left to give anyone. Everywhere I turned, more horrors awaited. Friends turned on me; people lied about me; people who should have defended me and my family turned their backs to protect their own careers. It was as if someone had opened the floodgates to a dam, and I was chained in the spillway. I was overwhelmed, and overcome, and I wanted to end it! Thank God for you and your mother; you all gave me strength and hope and courage.

"I remember your mother coming to me in the hospital and saying, 'They can take everything away from you except your integrity and your family. If it is all gone tomorrow, everything you believed in, we'll still be here, and we'll still love you and you will still have your integrity and the principles you based your decision on.' When she said that, it turned a light on in my cold and dark mind. I started to see through the fog of the drugs and the pain of the events, and I realized that it didn't matter what the army did or what the doctors tried to do. All that mattered was us, our family.

"I did what I believe the angel wanted me to do. I acted on principle and in the name of all humanity to bring remote viewing out of hiding, because I believe it can do wonderful things for all of us if it's used properly. I did so alone, and that's where I made the mistake. I didn't believe that you and your mother were capable of standing by me; I didn't believe that you shared my dream and my hopes, and I sacrificed you to them. I was wrong, and I know it." I began weeping openly, unable to control the anguish and remorse. "All I can do now is ask for your forgiveness, for a second chance at being a father, and for your blessing on what your mother and I are proposing to do, to renew our vows. I make no excuses anymore; you're part of me and I will never forsake you again. I can't bear the thought that we won't be a family again. I can't complete my contribution to this life without you by my side, testifying with me about what we endured. I am strong only when I am with all of you. I am weak without you. I am lost without you. I am nothing without you."

Mariah stood slowly and walked to me. She held my head, caressing it as if I were a child. Michael and Danielle embraced me and each other, and Debbie joyfully joined in.

"We are a part of you," Michael said, finding words an eighteen-year-old should never have to say. "We will all heal in time. We know that you did what you thought was right. And, just like Grandpa Bosch says, 'When you believe in something enough, you just have to reach through the flames and get it.' You reached through more than flames to do what you believed in, and I know we all respect that. In a way we're proud of what you did. What happened to you was cheap and heartless, and we'll all remember it. I'm not ashamed of your actions!"

"Me either," Mariah said.

"I'm not ashamed of you, Dad," Danielle said, kissing me on the cheek and wiping tears from her face and mine.

"Thank you," I said, choking. "Thank you for believing in me and what I meant to do. So you'll all be eating cake at the wedding?"

"Do I get to be the best man?" Michael asked, grinning tearfully.

A few months before Debbie accepted my marriage proposal, I had the unique opportunity to begin working on one of my new careers: I participated in the Mikhail Gorbachev Foundation's first annual State of the World Forum. I sat in the presence of men like George Bush, Mr. Gorbachev, Zbigniew Brzezinski, Senator Alan Cranston, and the prime ministers of Japan and of Canada. An eclectic group of world leaders, spiritualists, scientists, authors, and peacemakers gathered for five days to produce some answers that would give hope and direction to the "new world order." At one of the many round-table discussions on the future of humanity, I discussed nonlethal weapons—which as I mentioned earlier, had become one of my passions in the waning years of my military service. I was humbled to be in the presence of these great men and women, and I pray that I will one day have the benefit of their company again.

After the conference ended I began writing. Reliving my experiences was traumatic but cleansing. For every ten horrible and negative things, I always came upon some small sliver of hope—for instance, a note someone had passed to me when things were most painful. It was good to reread the encouraging words of my colleagues. One colonel apologized for the way in which I was treated by the military and by certain individuals. To know that he was professionally and personally embarrassed offered me new strength and encouraged me to keep writing when depression began to take root once again. And one colonel, who is now a brigadier general, wrote, "This too shall pass!" Only now do I realize how those words helped me get through my troubles.

As I was in the midst of writing, in October 1995, the Central Intelligence Agency, in cooperation with the Defense Intelligence Agency, began a carefully planned and well-executed media blitz regarding the government's psychic research and former psychic-warfare program, Stargate, formerly Sun Streak. In newspapers, radio, and television shows across the country, research experts and people supposedly affiliated with the program came out of the woodwork to tell the American people about the program.

I laughed with Mel and others on the phone about it. None of us had ever heard of the people who appeared on television claiming to have been affiliated with the program and citing a mere 15 percent accuracy rate based upon their "long-term" research and analysis. They certainly didn't check my or Mel's statistics.

It is not my intent to second-guess the CIA's motives or data. I can only offer my experience. When I was a young captain I learned an invaluable lesson during a conversation with the army's deputy Chief of Staff for intelligence, the highest-ranking intelligence officer in the army. He told me and the two others present: "The CIA does nothing, says nothing, allows nothing unless its own interests are served. They are the biggest assembly of liars and thieves this country ever put under one roof and they are an abomination.'' Now those are his words, not mine, but they stuck with me. If what he said is true, then in serving its interests the CIA presents only what it thinks the average American citizen needs to hear, or what it believes will steer the public to the CIA's desired conclusions.

The CIA is in the business of manipulating the belief systems of entire nations. I doubt that they're above working in their own backyard if it suits them. The most important thing about secret programs is that they prevent not only the bad guys but also the good guys from finding out what's going on. This system gives the holder of the secrets enormous power. I don't believe that the director of the CIA or any of the top leaders at DIA or the National Security Agency or the Pentagon is behind this disinformation campaign. They have much bigger fish to fry. However, their lieutenants tell their bosses what they want those bosses to hear, and then get permission to execute whatever program they think necessary to achieve their objectives. You might ask why the boss doesn't know when he's being led into a decision. Well, most bosses in the intelligence community don't know what their subordinates are doing. If you were the director of the CIA, would you want to know the specifics of every single program under your command? No: there are just too many programs for one person to oversee. The same applies to DIA and NSA. Again, that's the result of compartmentalization in intelligence circles. Only a select few know the real story, and even they don't know when they know it.

Not only did the fall of 1995 see a classic disinformation campaign, but most of the information circulating on the Internet was also misleading. In fact, Lyn Buchanan set up a Web page to respond to all the untruths. What made this page unique was the fact that most if not all of the former Stargate/Sun Streak crowd and a host of actual remote viewers who had worked in the ether for years regularly logged on and shared their experiences. The page was gaining in popularity, with people from around the world assessing it routinely. But one day someone hacked into the mainframe where the Web page was kept. This wasn't Lyn's computer, but that belonging to a company that posted and managed many Web pages, including Lyn's. Oddly, the hacker erased only Lyn Buchanan's files. In my opinion, someone or some group of people didn't like the fact that actual government remote viewers were on the Net countering point by point the claims of the CIA and others.

Lyn and the company providing the service worked feverishly for three days to reinstall the files and get the page back online. They succeeded—and within seventy-two hours someone hacked into the system again, only this time they destroyed the entire system and everything on it. I don't know what Lyn will do from here. I hope he rebuilds the page and gets it online again. We need some truth out there.

There are hundreds of people who claim that they're remote viewers and can train you to become one. They hold the keys to the kingdom—they say. When you see or hear one of these "experts," ask yourself: "Where does this expert (and his or her foundation) get their research funds— privately, or from the government? Are they in line for another grant or contract?" If you want to know the truth, you can dig it out with a little work. I believe the government is continuing to fund psychic and paranormal research, whatever the CIA would have you believe. And those looking for a meal ticket will say anything the pursestring holder tells them to say in order to secure that next contract. As in any field, there are legitimate researchers and there are fly-by-nights. Some people are trying to make money, others to make a name for themselves or rescue their reputations. Some are really trying to help. Those interested in learning more about remote viewing should look very carefully at those offering training and judge carefully anything they see or hear. Until the absolute truth comes out—until the people force it to come out so that it can be used to society's benefit—the miraculous potential of the science will remain obscured somewhere in the archives of the intelligence community.

I have one last comment on this issue: I believe that remote viewing for intelligence purposes remains now very fully funded, very hidden, and very protected—and is now very deadly. I don't think the government intends to make the same mistake it did with Stargate/Sun Streak. I know three remote viewers who are still affiliated with a government-backed remote-viewing program. Mel, Lyn, and I believe that they are now working for the CIA as part of another program that paralleled the old Sun Streak. We'd always suspected that there was another program, more secret and even more powerful than ours; I learned of it from a very reliable source who spoke of training a stoic and secretive group many years ago. He wouldn't elaborate, and I understand why he shouldn't. The word on the street is that remote influencing is all the rage in intelligence. I believe that the CIA is heavily involved in this insidious technique. If they could influence someone to kill from a distance of thousands of miles—and remote influencing has this potential—they would hold an extremely valuable weapon.

Remote viewing is not a dead issue; it hasn't gone away.

Just after the CIA broke its version of the remote-viewing story, I received a call from Dr. Damioli, the psychiatrist who'd first treated me at Walter Reed.

"Have you seen the papers?" she asked.

"Yes," I said.

"Isn't it exciting? I can talk about everything now. I'd like to see you as soon as possible, if I may."

"I can see you tomorrow, but I'd like to bring Debbie along."

"Certainly!"

At five the next day Debbie and I knocked on the door to the doctor's office.

"Please sit down, I'd like to talk to you about all of this." Dr. Damioli held up a copy of *The Washington Post* with the article about the CIA's involvement in psychic warfare.

Debbie and I nodded. "It exists just as we said it did, doesn't it?"

"I never doubted you for a minute. When your Stargate psychologist admitted to me that the program existed and that I should proceed carefully, I knew there was something to it all. I just couldn't do anything for you while you were with me; my hands were tied."

"Who tied your hands? What do you mean?"

"The government, my supervisors . . . They ordered me to give you the drugs and they ordered me to change my diagnosis of you. They wanted me to describe you as psychotic and delusional, but I refused." The doctor reflected for a moment. "It cost me my position with the hospital."

"But you were the ward attending physician; you were a senior psychiatrist. How could they do anything to you? And you're a civilian, at that; you should have been Teflon-coated!" Debbie said.

"That's what makes this so unbelievable. When I refused to alter the diagnosis, they took away the position I'd worked so many years to earn. I was isolated from my colleagues and professionally destroyed. I had to hire an attorney to protect my professional record, but I was forced to resign after twelve years of government service. I lost everything—my pension, everything. I wanted you to know that I didn't abandon you. They took you away from me and sent you to Fort Bragg, where they could have absolute control over you."

We were stunned. "I'm sorry, Doctor," I said. "I lost only sixteen years, but you lost a lifetime. Thank you for telling us. Do you mind if we have an attorney take your deposition—for the record, I mean?"

"Not at all! I just want you to know that if you want to fight for an honorable discharge, I will be there for you every step of the way. You should have been given the medical discharge I asked for, and I would support that even more strongly today! I was even ordered to alter your records. And remember that I gave you the smallest possible dose of antipsychotics?"

"It didn't matter," Debbie said angrily. "Once they got him to Fort Bragg they kicked the dosage up as much as they could. David was practically a zombie."

"It's all over, and thank God we have our lives to live," I said. "I'm sorry you wound up as one of the casualties of my quest. But from the bottom of our hearts, we thank you for being there."

The doctor paused. "What I want you to know, David, is this. You beat them by doing two things. You didn't kill yourself, which I think is what they really wanted you to do. And you never gave up the fight. You never stopped telling the story. You forced them to come out with this."

I can't answer for how Debbie felt, but to hear this was a relief to me. Dr. Damioli's story confirmed that my trial had been about much more than anyone knew. But I didn't die and my family is safe. They didn't win; I did.

Lyn Buchanan, Mel Riley, and I arrived in Baltimore for an extraordinary reunion in the ether. Lyn drove from Mechanicsville in southern Maryland to my home in Bowie. He and I greeted each other like schoolboys, gorging ourselves on Debbie's sweet rolls and my coffee before heading to the rendezvous with Mel, who'd flown in from Wisconsin. It was the first time I'd seen them together in years. We'd gathered together to journey back in time on behalf of the Baltimore County Police Department.

Our first meeting was with Detective Lieutenant Sam Bowerman, head of the department's criminal profiling unit. Mel and I spoke of Sun Streak; because the program remained classified, Lyn would only discuss remote viewing in general terms. However, we described our capabilities as remote viewers. And we were careful to state our limits, too; we knew of several people offering "guaranteed 100 percent accurate results"—for a price—and we didn't want to align ourselves with such claims, raising false hopes to make a buck. That's not what the gift is for. On the other hand, we knew what we could do to help the department; and we were willing to prove it.

"We want you to know what we can do, and what we can't," I said. "This isn't magic!"

Lyn chimed in. "No, it's not. It's a discipline devoid of guesswork or speculation."

I carefully watched the lieutenant's face for signs of skepticism, but he didn't raise an eyebrow as Lyn continued talking; he was like a sponge, taking it all in, waiting to see the evidence before passing judgment. While Lyn talked, I looked around at the bookshelves and documents. Bowerman was no slouch; he held a master's degree in psychology, and around that diploma hung a myriad of awards and decorations, department citations and unit memorabilia. He proudly displayed photographs of his children on his desk and credenza; the labels on his files indicated that he taught criminal profiling and criminology at a local university. Immaculately dressed and groomed, he had a gentle intensity about him that made you feel at ease yet completely aware that he was a serious professional law officer. I sensed very clearly that if we did what we said we could do, Bowerman would acknowledge it appropriately. However, if we failed to measure up to our claims, he would politely excuse himself and dismiss us from the project.

I wrapped up the meeting. "You see, we can't sit down and in one or two sessions give you directions to a body, for example. The information the viewers provided would supplement what you got by conventional means, and the more remote-viewing effort was made, the shorter investigations could be. The difficulty is that you need a dedicated remote-viewing team, with controlled feedback and some administrative support. Ideally, you would train and utilize a team of remote viewers right here in the department; they'd belong to you, take their assignments from you, and turn in their product to you for analysis. If you could organize something like that and keep it alive, you'd make law enforcement and investigative history."

Lieutenant Bowerman leaned back in his chair. "Thank you for the briefing. I hope you can do all you say you can do; if so, it'll be a tremendous breakthrough for those of us in this business. I'll admit to you that this seems far-out, but I have an open mind, so let's give this a try. Do you need anything to steer you by, like a photograph or an article of clothing?"

"No, not for this first session," Mel said. "We'd like to see how quickly we can get on target, and after we do an analysis, we can decide from there. Does everyone agree?"

Lyn and I nodded.

"Okay, what's next?" asked the lieutenant.

"We need to discuss the target question," Mel said.

Lyn agreed. "We need to make sure that we don't inadvertently get any front-loading. We need to get the parameters of the target without a description. That would spin us off target, theoretically onto some other place or thing, or maybe even some obscure aspect of the original target."

"What's front-loading?" Bowerman asked.

I answered. "Essentially, we don't want to know things such as whether the target is male or female, dead or alive, missing or found, the suspected perpetrator or the victim. We only want a question that we can use to access the target with minimal psychic noise. For example, if the target was the location of stolen goods, we wouldn't want you to ask us to describe the location of the money stolen in Wednesday's robbery of the Wells Fargo Bank. That's front-loading; it drives us psychically in six different directions at once. A better target statement would be 'Describe the current location of an object'—that's it!"

Bowerman's mouth dropped open. "That's *it?* That's all you want?"

Mel laughed out loud.

The three of us decided that we would work simultaneous solo CRV rather than ERV missions, each entering the ether without a monitor. For me, this was a risky endeavor; but necessary to prove the accuracy and validity of the

viewing product. Of us three, I was the only extended remote viewer; Mel and Lyn consistently used coordinate remote viewing, so the impact was minimal. Also, we wanted
to conduct solo missions in part to rule out any suggestion
that we'd collaborated or shared our results. If we worked
in separate rooms and only compared sketches and data in
the presence of third parties, we might still be accused of
collaboration—skeptics will be skeptics no matter what—
but a fair reviewer could see that we were not tampering
with the data.

At nine-thirty A.M. Mel, Lyn, and I went into separate
interrogation rooms and prepared for our mission. The
rooms were crude by remote-viewing standards: the lighting wasn't adjustable, and we had to work from small metal
desks and metal folding chairs. In each room was a large
two-way mirror, from behind which Lieutenant Bowerman
and anyone else he chose could watch us while we worked.
I'm certain they watched out of curiosity more than anything else; it didn't hurt our credibility any to have oversight. (Perhaps if we'd had more oversight in Sun Streak
the program would have done a little more.) The sessions
were captured on video as well—America's first look at
trained military remote viewers entering the ether and coming home again.

I took one last look at my tasking sheet and waved to
Mel and Lyn as we disappeared into our respective rooms.
I positioned myself at the table so that I was facing the
mirror; then I closed my eyes and stepped into the ether. It
felt great.

POINTS OF DEPARTURE

This work is not a quest for faith in the unseen. It is not a plea for spiritual tokens or selfless offerings; it is a testimony to the reality of other worlds, of benevolent leaders, of creators—and, more important, of life beyond this physical existence and dimension. I could write volumes more on what I've seen in the ether, as could countless other military-trained remote viewers. It was commonplace for us to have spiritual experiences. We knew and accepted the reality of those things just as easily as we did the existence of missile silos, or Soviet submarines, or cocaine shipments hidden in the bowels of freighters. Our sacrifices were made so that you could know, as surely as we do, that there is much more around us than our physical eyes can see.

I can say with absolute confidence that the gift spoken of in this chronicle is a precious and wonderful tool that we have been fortunate enough to see in our lifetime. I can also say, with equal conviction, that, like anything placed in mortal hands, the gift can be transformed into a curse that will plague mankind rather than serve, protect, and advance it. This will be my fear so long as remote viewing remains a secret weapon of the Defense Department. The choice is ours. The secret is out: remote viewing exists, it works, it has been tested, proven, and used in intelligence for over two decades. The recent government admissions concerning the use of psychic warfare are crucial, irrefutable testimony that what I have said here is the truth. The government of the most powerful nation on the face of the earth has admitted that it knows humans can transcend time and space to view distant persons, places, things, and events, and that information thus gathered can be brought back. I hope you comprehend the significance of that information.

Great sacrifices were made to bring the reality and knowledge of this gift to the world. It's up to you, the people, not to let it slip back into secrecy for another twenty years. This old soldier is going to swell with pride as I watch my children give all they can to human progress and the understanding of spirituality. They go into this life armed with the ability to see what others don't. They have an insatiable appetite for the answers that will illuminate our deepest anxieties, frailties, and hopes. The quest for knowledge is not over, and in the ether, nothing is ever still. They are the new warriors . . . watch for them.

They go where no one else will go.
They do what no one else will do.
And they're proud to be called . . .

TWILIGHT WARRIORS

INSIDE THE WORLD'S SPECIAL FORCES

MARTIN C. AROSTEGUI

From deadly Scud hunts in the Gulf War to daring hostage rescue missions at London's Iranian Embassy, Special Forces go where no other army would dare—fighting for their countries and their lives on the world's most dangerous missions. Now, journalist and counter-terrorism expert Martin C. Arostegui tells their story—a fascinating true account of bravery, daring, and the ultimate risk.

ISBN: 0-312-96493-5

**AVAILABLE WHEREVER BOOKS ARE SOLD
FROM ST. MARTIN'S PAPERBACKS**

UNARMED, UNDERWATER, UNDER FIRE— THEY WENT TO WAR, AND BEGUN THE LEGEND OF THE NAVY SEALS.

Facing a fanatical, dug-in enemy in Europe and in the Pacific, U.S. planners turned to a new kind of warrior: daring swimmers who could knock out mines, map out enemy beaches, and pave the way for Allied naval assaults. With a few extraordinary and brave men, the U.S. Navy's Underwater Demolition Teams went to war.

Now, a founder and legendary commander of UDT-1 takes you into the world of underwater soldiers. This is the inside story of a unique breed of warrior— and the bloody battles they helped win.

NAKED WARRIORS

Cdr. Francis Douglas Fane, USNR (Ret.)
and Don Moore

ISBN: 0-312-95985-0

AVAILABLE WHEREVER BOOKS ARE SOLD FROM ST. MARTIN'S PAPERBACKS

NW 1/97